KNOWLEDGE,
REASON,
AND TASTE

KNOWLEDGE, REASON, AND TASTE

Kant's Response to Hume

Paul Guyer

PRINCETON UNIVERSITY PRESS

PRINCETON AND OXFORD

Copyright © 2008 by Princeton University Press

Published by Princeton University Press, 41 William Street,
Princeton, New Jersey 08540
In the United Kingdom: Princeton University Press, 3 Market Place,
Woodstock, Oxfordshire OX20 1SY

All Rights Reserved

Library of Congress Cataloging-in-Publication Data

Guyer, Paul, 1948–
Knowledge, reason, and taste : Kant's response to Hume / Paul Guyer.
p.   cm.
Includes bibliographical references and index.
ISBN 978-0-691-13439-0 (hardcover : alk. paper)
1. Kant, Immanuel, 1724–1804. 2. Hume, David, 1711–1776. I. Title.
B2798.G895 2008
193—dc22   2007019554

British Library Cataloging-in-Publication Data is available
This book has been composed in Adobe Caslon Typeface
Printed on acid-free paper. ∞
press.princeton.edu
Printed in the United States of America

1 3 5 7 9 10 8 6 4 2

Contents

Credits

CHAPTER 1: Originally published as "Kant on Common Sense and Skepticism," *Kantian Review* 7 (2003): 1–37. Reprinted with the permission of the *Kantian Review*.

CHAPTER 2: Originally published as "Kant's Answer to Hume?" *Philosophical Topics* 31, nos. 1–2 (2003): 127–64. Reprinted with the permission of the University of Arkansas Press.

CHAPTER 3: Originally published as "Object, Self, and Cause: Kant's Answers to Hume," in *Early Modern Metaphysics: Essays in Honor of Vere Chappell*, ed. Paul Hoffman, David Owen, and Gideon Yaffee (Peterborough, ON: Broadview Press, 2007). Reprinted with the permission of Broadview Press.

CHAPTER 4: Originally presented as "Hume and Kant on Reason, Desire, and Action," not previously published.

CHAPTER 5: Originally published as "Kant's Ambitions in the Third *Critique*," in *The Cambridge Companion to Kant and Modern Philosophy*, ed. Paul Guyer (Cambridge: Cambridge University Press, 2006), 538–87. Reprinted with the permission of Cambridge University Press.

I would like to thank Brian Chance for discussing much of this material with me; Patrick Frierson for very helpful comments on chapter 4; Rob Tempio of Princeton University Press for his invitation to put these papers together to make this volume; Eric Watkins and another, anonymous, referee for their support and useful suggestions.

Sources and Abbreviations

Hume

Treatise	*A Treatise of Human Nature.* Edited by David Fate and Mary J. Norton. Oxford: Oxford University Press, 2000.
Enquiry I	*An Enquiry concerning Human Understanding.* Edited by Tom L. Beauchamp. Oxford: Clarendon Press, 2000.
Enquiry II	*An Enquiry concerning the Principles of Morals.* Edited by Tom L. Beauchamp. Oxford: Clarendon Press, 1998.
Essays	*Essays Moral, Political, and Literary.* Edited by Eugene F. Miller, revised edition. Indianapolis: Liberty Fund, 1987.
Dialogues	*Dialogues concerning Natural Religion,* in *The Natural History of Religion* and *Dialogues concerning Natural Religion,* edited by A. Wayne Colver and John Valdimir Price. Oxford: Clarendon Press, 1976.

Kant

Pure Reason	*Critique of Pure Reason.* Edited and translated by Paul Guyer and Allen W. Wood. Cambridge: Cambridge University Press, 1998.
Prolegomena	*Prolegomena to Any Future Metaphysics.* Translated by Gary Hatfield, from *Theoretical Philosophy after* 1781, edited by Henry Allison and Peter

Heath, translated by Gary Hatfield, Michael
Friedman, Henry Allison, and Peter Heath.
Cambridge: Cambridge University Press, 2001.

Groundwork   *Groundwork of the Metaphysics of Morals*, from
Practical Philosophy. Edited and translated by
Mary J. Gregor. Cambridge: Cambridge University Press, 1996.

Practical   *Critique of Practical Reason*, from *Practical*
Reason   *Philosophy*

Judgment   *Critique of the Power of Judgment.* Edited by
Paul Guyer, translated by Paul Guyer and Eric
Matthews. Cambridge: Cambridge University
Press, 2000.

MM   *Metaphysics of Morals*, from *Practical Philosophy*

LE   *Lectures on Ethics.* Edited by Peter Heath and
J. B. Schneewind, translated by Peter Heath.
Cambridge: Cambridge University Press, 1997.

LL   *Lectures on Logic.* Edited by J. Michael Young.
Cambridge: Cambridge University Press, 1992.

LM   *Lectures on Metaphysics.* Edited by Karl Ameriks
and Steven Naragon. Cambridge: Cambridge
University Press, 1997.

Notes and   *Notes and Fragments.* Edited by Paul Guyer,
Fragments   translated by Curtis Bowman, Paul Guyer, and
Frederick Rauscher. Cambridge: Cambridge
University Press, 2005.

Passages from the *Critique of Pure Reason* are cited by the
pagination of the first (1781) and/or second (1787) editions, "A"
and "B" respectively; the citation of both "A" and "B" means
that the passage occurred in both editions. Other works by Kant
are cited by the volume and page number of the "Academy
edition," *Kant's gesammelte Schriften*, edited by the Royal Prussian (subsequently German and then Berlin-Brandenburg)

Academy of Sciences (Berlin: Georg Reimer, subsequently Walter de Gruyter and Co., 1900–). Boldface type within quotations indicates Kant's original emphasis in *Fettdruck*. Kant's use of Roman type for non-German words is indicated with italics.

KNOWLEDGE,

REASON,

AND TASTE

INTRODUCTION

In the *Prolegomena to Any Future Metaphysics that could come forth as Science* that he published in 1783 in the hope of both defending and popularizing the *Critique of Pure Reason* that he had published two years earlier, Immanuel Kant famously wrote "I freely admit that the *Erinnerung* of **David Hume** was the very thing that many years ago first interrupted my dogmatic slumber and gave my investigations in the field of speculative philosophy a completely different direction" (*Prolegomena*, Preface, 4: 260). I have left *Erinnerung*, which typically means "recollection" or "remembrance," but could also mean "reminder" in the sense of "admonition," untranslated in order to sidestep a scholarly debate about chronology—did Kant mean that it was only the recollection of Hume some years after he had first read the early German translations that interrupted his dogmatic slumbers, or did he mean that the admonition of Hume had interrupted his dogmatic slumbers as soon as he read him, many years before writing the *Critique of Pure Reason* and the *Prolegomena*?[1] What is important for my purposes in this collection of essays is that, however he got there, by the time Kant reached his philosophical maturity at least *one* way he conceived of his philosophical task was that of putting key principles on more secure foundations than all those earlier ones that Hume had shown to rest not on reason but at best on experience and custom, and at worst on mere dogmatism.

[1] See Lewis White Beck, *Early German Philosophy: Kant and His Predecessors* (Cambridge, MA: Belknap Press of Harvard University Press, 1969), 439. In the large literature on both exactly when and exactly how Hume awoke Kant from his slumbers, see especially Manfred Kuehn, "Kant's Conception of 'Hume's Problem,'" *Journal of the History of Philosophy* 21 (1981): 175–94.

What principles? Kant repeatedly stated that Hume had cast doubt on whether the concept of causation expresses a genuine necessity that is "thought through reason *a priori* . . . and has an inner truth independent of all experience" (*Prolegomena*, Preface, 4: 249), and settled instead that it expresses nothing more than our own feeling of necessitation in response to the frequent association or repetition of impressions of external objects. He clearly thought that Hume had raised a genuine problem about the real foundations of the concept of causation and the necessary truth of both the general principle that every event has a cause as well as particular causal laws, and thought that Hume had not sufficiently resolved this problem, although Hume himself may have been content with his solution. But Kant also held that Hume had put his finger on a more general problem without realizing what he had done:

> Thus I first investigated whether **Hume's** objection could be made general, and I soon found that the concept of the connection of cause and effect is far from being the only one by means of which the understanding thinks the connections of things *a priori* for itself, rather that metaphysics consists entirely of such concepts. I sought to assure myself of their number, and since this succeeded according to my wish, namely from a single principle, I went on to the deduction of these concepts, from which I was assured that they were not derived from experience, as **Hume** had worried, but had arisen from the pure understanding. This deduction, which seemed impossible to my acute predecessor, and which no one other than him had ever even thought about, although everyone had confidently used the concepts without asking on what their objective validity is grounded, this, I say, was the most difficult thing that could ever be undertaken in behalf of metaphysics; and what is the worst thing about it is that metaphysics, no matter how much of it is everywhere available, could not give me the least assistance, since this deduction must first establish the possibility of a metaphysics. Now since I was successful in the solution of the Humean problem not just in a special case but with regard to the entire

faculty of pure reason, I could thus take sure although always slow steps in order finally to determine the entire scope of pure reason in its boundaries as well as to determine its content completely and in accordance with universal principles, which was then the very thing that metaphysics needed in order to execute its system in accordance with a secure plan. (*Prolegomena*, Preface, 4: 260–61)

In this statement and others like it (*Pure Reason*, B 19, A 764–68/B 792–96; *Practical Reason*, 5: 13, 5: 50–57), Kant claims that the doubts Hume had raised about the existence of an a priori concept and principle of causation were only an example of the kind of doubts that could be and indeed should be raised about the previously merely dogmatic foundations of all the central concepts of metaphysics, and that none of these concepts and principles could be secure until they had all been given a proper foundation or "deduction" by Kant himself. As Kant rightly points out, Hume had raised no objection to our ordinary *use* of causal concepts and beliefs and, by implication, our ordinary use of the other concepts and beliefs that are in the same boat, nor did Kant himself think that scientists in their laboratories or craftsmen in their shops have to suspend all their activities until their key concepts had been put on a sound footing. But in his view Hume had without realizing it raised a challenge for all of metaphysics that had to be answered before *philosophy* could proceed. Moreover, Kant held that unless the metaphysical concepts at stake were both properly founded *and* properly limited, that is, restricted to the properly demarcated sphere of human experience, perfectly reasonable doubts about their cognitive value *beyond* this sphere could end up undermining our confidence in their use *within* this sphere, and thus cast doubt about our use of these concepts for the purposes of ordinary cognition and ordinary science after all. Thus, in a crucial passage in the *Critique of Pure Reason*, Kant writes about Hume, whom he calls "perhaps the most ingenious of all skeptics" (A 764/B 792), that:

The skeptical aberrations of this otherwise extremely acute man, however, arose primarily from a failing that he had in common with all dogmatists, namely, that he did not systematically survey all the kinds of *a priori* synthesis of the understanding . . . had he done so . . . He would thereby have been able to mark out determinate boundaries for the understanding that expands itself *a priori* and for pure reason. But since he merely **limits** our understanding without **drawing boundaries** for it, and brings about a general distrust but no determinate knowledge of the ignorance that is unavoidable for us, by censuring certain principles of the understanding without placing this understanding in regard to its entire capacity on the scales of critique, and, while rightly denying to understanding what it really cannot accomplish, goes further, and disputes all its capacity to extend itself *a priori* without having assessed this entire capacity, the same thing happens to him that always brings down skepticism, namely, he is himself doubted, for his objections rest only on *facta*, which are contingent, but not on principles that could effect a necessary renunciation of the right to dogmatic assertions. (A 767–68/ B 795–96)

Kant recognized that Hume had been satisfied with his own explanation of key concepts and principles as resting on "nothing but a custom arising from its experience and its law," and thus as "merely empirical, i.e., intrinsically contingent rules, to which we ascribe a supposed necessity and universality" (A 765/B 793), and he recognized that Hume had used his empirical derivation of such concepts and principles to argue that we could not apply them to objects of which we have no experience. Thus, Kant recognized that it was the intended payoff of Hume's philosophy that we cannot use our empirically grounded principle that every event has a cause to infer that the whole world has a unique cause of a sort that we have never directly experienced, namely God.[2] However, Kant also believed that without a clear demar-

---

[2] This is of course the central argument of Section 11 of Hume's *Enquiry concerning Human Understanding* and of his *Dialogues concerning Natural Religion*, the latter as well as the former of which Kant knew well by the time he published the *Critique of Pure Reason*. Kant had read Johann Georg Hamann's partial and never published translation of Hume's *Dialogues* in the summer or fall of 1780, and did not have to wait until Karl Schreiter's full translation appeared in 1781, although

cation between the realm of human experience within which the principle of causation and all the other fundamental principles of human thought apply and the realm beyond experience where we can doubt that those principles apply, there is no barrier to prevent our skepticism about the validity of those principles in the latter realm from splashing back and undermining our confidence in the validity of those principles in the former realm, and with no foundation for those principles within the former sphere but mere "custom and experience," Hume would have no way to resist this gastric reflux of doubt. Thus, although Hume advocated only "mitigated scepticism" as "the limitation of our enquiries to such subjects as are best adapted to the narrow capacity of human understanding" (*Enquiry I*, Section 12, Part 3, p. 120), Kant nevertheless felt justified in calling him the "most ingenious of all skeptics."

As we will see in chapter 2, Hume had raised a more general challenge to our most fundamental concepts and principles than Kant seems to have realized. Kant's acquaintance with Hume's works during the crucial years of his own philosophical development was incomplete: Hume's *Enquiry* (originally *Philosophical Essays*) *concerning Human Understanding*, first published in 1748, was translated into German in 1755,[3] and Kant is known to have owned this early translation of the first *Enquiry* at the time of his death and reasonably presumed to have read it much earlier in his life,[4] in all likelihood very soon after it came out. But

---

he did acquire a copy of that by December 1781, after the *Critique* had appeared. See Gary Hatfield, "The *Prolegomena* and the *Critiques of Pure Reason*," in *Kant und die Berliner Aufklärung: Akten des IX. Internationalen Kant-Kongresses*, ed. Volker Gerhardt, Rolf-Peter Horstmann, and Ralph Schumacher (Berlin: Walter de Gruyter, 2001), 1: 185–208, at 188.

[3] David Hume, *Vermischte Schriften*, edited by Johann Georg Sulzer (translators unknown), 4 vols. (Hamburg and Leipzig: Grund and Holle, 1754–56). The translation of the *Enquiry concerning Human Understanding* appeared in this series in 1755. For information about this publication and especially about Sulzer's editorial comments on Hume's essay, see Eric Watkins, *Kant and the Metaphysics of Causality* (Cambridge: Cambridge University Press, 2005), 364–67.

[4] Arthur Warda, *Immanuel Kants Bücher* (Berlin: Breslauer, 1922), 50. This and the preceding note follow Hatfield, "The *Prolegomena* and the *Critiques of Pure Reason*," 186n6.

under the rubric of "Sceptical Doubts concerning the Operations of the Understanding," Section 4 of the first *Enquiry* focuses almost exclusively on Hume's worries about causation, and under the title of "Sceptical Solution of these Doubts"—a title to which Kant could certainly have appealed for his own characterization of Hume as a skeptic—the first *Enquiry* provides only Hume's empirical account of our belief in causation. Hume's original *Treatise of Human Nature*, by contrast, very clearly raises doubts not only about our concept of and beliefs about causation but also about our concepts of and beliefs in external objects and an enduring self, and moreover notoriously regards those concepts and beliefs as much more problematic than the concept of and belief in causation, with his account of which Hume was entirely satisfied. However, the *Treatise* was not translated into German in its entirety until long after Kant had completed his work on the *Critique of Pure Reason*. At the time that he wrote the *Critique*, Kant is thought to have had anything approximating firsthand knowledge of the *Treatise* only through Johann Georg Hamann's translation of Book I, Part IV, Section 7 of the *Treatise*, published in a Königsberg newspaper in 1771.[5] In this section, Hume gives his famous argument that while "reason is incapable of dispelling" the "clouds" of skeptical doubts, "nature herself," in the form of riverside walks and nice evenings of dinner, backgammon, and conversation, "suffices to that purpose," but he does not restate the particular skeptical doubts about self and object as well as about causation that he had earlier raised.[6] Nevertheless, I will pro-

---

[5] It is traditionally supposed that Kant also knew something of the *Treatise* through James Beattie's citations of it in his 1770 anti-Humean polemic, *An Essay on the Nature and Immutability of Truth, in Opposition to Sophistry and Scepticism*, which was quickly translated into German and present in the Königsberg university library, as well as through various reviews of the *Treatise* in German periodicals; see Manfred Kuehn, *Scottish Common Sense in Germany, 1760–1800: A Contribution to the History of Critical Philosophy* (Kingston, ON: McGill-Queen's University Press, 1987), 169. However, it would certainly be possible that secondhand reports about the *Treatise* did not have the same impact on Kant that firsthand acquaintance with it would have.

[6] See Hume, *Treatise*, I.iv.7, 171–78, quotations from paragraph 9, p. 175.

pose, the philosophical approach Kant developed for showing that our concept of and beliefs about causation have a foundation that Hume denied they have also provides Kant with an approach for addressing the concerns Hume raised about external objects and the self—so even though Kant did not know that Hume had generalized his skeptical doubts about causation as Kant thought he should have, the general approach to grounding metaphysical concepts and principles Kant developed in response to Hume's worries about causations does address the other problems that Hume himself had raised. Thus Kant was wrong to think that Hume had not generalized his problem about causation, but right to think that he himself had developed a general method for addressing the generalization of Hume's problem.

Beyond showing that Kant did indeed generalize Hume's problem about causation and was stirred by his *Erinnerung* of that problem to develop a general foundation for other theoretical concepts such as those of self and object, I will also suggest that much of Kant's philosophy beyond theoretical metaphysics can be read as a response to Hume, specifically that important elements of Kant's moral philosophy, his aesthetics, and his teleology can also be fruitfully read as responses to Hume. By saying this I by no means intend to say that in all these other parts of his philosophy Kant exclusively or even foremost intended to respond to Hume, any more than I mean to suggest that Kant was concerned with Hume alone in this theoretical philosophy. While he was not a learned historian of philosophy, Kant was broadly acquainted not only with the German philosophy of his own century but also with a vast array of European philosophy, science, and thought of both the seventeenth and eighteenth centuries. Thus, his interlocutors and targets in theoretical philosophy include Descartes, Leibniz, Wolff, Baumgarten, Crusius, and Mendelssohn as well as Locke, Berkeley, and Hume; his targets in moral and political philosophy include ancient Stoics and Epicureans, Wolff and Baumgarten, and also Montaigne, Hobbes, Mandeville, and Shaftesbury, Hutcheson, and Adam Smith as well as Hume (see e.g., *Practical Reason*, 5: 40); his targets in aesthetics include Baumgarten, Meier, Mendelssohn, Lessing, and Herder as well as Burke, Gerard, and Hume; and his targets in teleology include Spinoza, Wolff, and Herder as well as Hume—so it would always be a grievous error to reduce Kant's targets in any area of his work to a single figure, no matter how important. Kant's career-long focus on causation, for example, has to be understood as a response to debates within German rationalism that began with Leibniz's claim that genuine substances are "windowless monads" that cannot actually cause changes in each other but merely represent changes in each other because of God's beneficent selection of a coherent set of actual monads from among all those possible.[7] Nevertheless, Kant does mention the name of Hume not only at crucial moments in his theoretical philosophy but also in his moral philosophy (again, *Practical Reason*, 5: 13–14, 50–56), his aesthetics (*Judgment*, §34), and his teleology (*Judgment*, §80), and I will propose that quite apart from any debate about the historical influence of Hume on Kant or Kant's intentions to respond to Hume, it is nevertheless illuminating to think about the ways in which these parts of Kant's philosophy can also be considered as responses to challenges that Hume raised. Just as in the case of theoretical philosophy, where Kant by no means rejected, indeed endorsed Hume's project of criticizing the use of our fundamental concepts and principles in dogmatic metaphysics while nevertheless holding that these concepts and principles required a more secure foundation than Hume had given to them, Kant's relations to Hume in moral philosophy, aesthetics, and teleology are also complex. In the case of moral philosophy, the difference between a philosopher who held that the use of reason is never more than merely instrumental to the realization of goals set entirely by sentiment and one who held that the fundamental principle of morality must be founded in pure reason is obvious, but I will argue that there are also important affinities between Hume's and Kant's models of motivation and their uses of these models in their opposed moral

---

[7] For a detailed account of Kant's response to the debates about causation within German rationalism, see Watkins, *Kant and the Metaphysics of Causality*, chaps. 1 and 2.

theories. In the case of aesthetics, I will suggest that Hume profoundly influenced Kant's conception of the problem of taste, although once again Kant strives for an a priori rather than merely empirical foundation for our claims to agreement in judgments of taste. In the case of teleology, I will argue that Kant fully endorses Hume's criticism of the constitutive or dogmatic use of teleological principles within both natural science and teleology, but also may well derive his conception of the heuristic use of teleology within our investigation of nature from Hume, while he at the same time argues that our naturally teleological conception of nature itself has a use in morality, specifically in moral theology, that Hume entirely failed to recognize. In all these cases, I suggest, reading Kant's philosophy as a response to Hume is a way to elucidate, through both their similarities and their differences, some of Kant's deepest philosophical assumptions and ambitions.

Having stated my intention to look at Kant's treatment of causation as a response to Hume, at his theoretical philosophy as a whole as a response to further problems about objects and the self that Hume had raised even though Kant did not know that, and even at further domains of Kant's philosophy as if they were responses to Hume, I should say something here about some recent arguments against overemphasizing Kant's intentions to respond to Hume in his theoretical philosophy. (Neither of the arguments I am about to discuss go beyond Kant's theoretical philosophy.)

Gary Hatfield has argued that in his few references to Hume in the first edition of the *Critique of Pure Reason*, Kant actually enlisted him as an ally in his own critique of traditional metaphysics, although he also held that Hume did not have a systematic criterion or method for distinguishing between illegitimate pretensions and legitimate claims of reason,[8] and therefore

---

[8] This point in Kant's response to Hume is also emphasized by Robert Stern in "Metaphysical Dogmatism, Humean Scepticism, Kantian Criticism," *Kantian Review* 11 (2006): 102–16, which is a response to the earlier version of chapter 1 of this volume.

did not just suggest a useful "skeptical method" for scrutinizing dogmatic metaphysics but risked lapsing into actual skepticism. According to Hatfield, in the first edition of the *Critique* "Kant did not treat Hume's account of causation as a genuine threat to natural science or ordinary knowledge," but saw "Hume's own attempts as directed primarily against the pretensions of reason," although he also saw "Hume's failure" as lying "in not curbing those pretensions once and for all."[9] Correspondingly, Hatfield sees Kant's own aim in the first edition of the *Critique* not so much as demonstrating the reality of synthetic a priori knowledge and principles in the face of Hume's doubts about that, but instead as providing "an explanation of the possibility of synthetic a priori cognition in order to be able to assess its possibility and impossibility in various metaphysical domains,"[10] thereby making precise and conclusive the criticisms of traditional metaphysics that Hume had left indeterminate and therefore possibly too broad. As Hatfield sums up, "Given that Kant does not mention any skeptical threat to ordinary experience, mathematics, or natural science in the A *Critique*, that he evaluates the skeptical method positively, that he describes the one crucial function of the Deduction and Analytic of Principles as preparatory to limiting the understanding to experience, and that he singles out the possibility (or impossibility) of transcendental metaphysics as his main quarry, there seems little basis for arguing that instead Kant was really out to refute the skeptic and save ordinary knowledge."[11] Hatfield then continues that in the *Prolegomena* Kant "did take a new interest in Hume and skeptical idealism" in response to the charge of the notorious "Garve-Feder" review of the *Critique* that there was no difference between Kant's "transcendental idealism" and the idealism of Berkeley and Hamann's comparison of Kant's skeptical conclusions about metaphysics to those of Hume, but that "a close reading of the Preface" to the *Prolegomena* "reveals that he did not present Hume's problem or Hume's doubt as a

[9] Hatfield, "The *Prolegomena* and the *Critiques*," 194–95.
[10] Ibid., 197.
[11] Ibid., 198–99.

challenge to anything but metaphysics. He certainly did not portray Hume as presenting a skeptical challenge to natural science or to ordinary knowledge of objects."[12] Only in the second edition of the *Critique* (1787), Hatfield concludes, do Kant's added remarks about Hume show that "He related Humean skepticism to ordinary experience; [that] he suggested that his Deduction avoids skepticism"; and did he intend "the latter claim to cover *Humean* skepticism."[13] But, Hatfield also suggests, Kant's new emphasis on refuting Hume's skepticism about our ordinary and scientific knowledge of causation rather than refining Hume's skeptical method in the critique of traditional, dogmatic metaphysics, is a response to external factors, an increased interest in skepticism and charges that Kant's own transcendental idealism leads to skepticism, in the later half of the 1780s, rather than an accurate indication of Kant's original concerns in the *Critique of Pure Reason*. So, Hatfield concludes, for a historically reliable interpretation of Kant, we should not read the *Critique* as really intended to refute skepticism about causation in ordinary knowledge and natural science, let alone skepticism about other fundamental concepts, but should emphasize Kant's original intention to refine Hume's skeptical method for his own critique of metaphysics.

This approach to Kant's relation to Hume is misleading in two regards. First, it is true that Kant recognized that Hume did not mean to argue against our ordinary practices of making causal judgments in science and everyday life—this is why he says that Thomas Reid and other Scottish commonsense philosophers "missed the point of [Hume's] problem . . . proving with great vehemence and, more often than not, with great insolence exactly what it had never entered his mind to doubt" (*Prolegomena*, Preface, 4: 258). It is also true that Kant held that "No critique of reason in its empirical use was needed, since its principles were subjected to a continuous examination on the touchstone of experience; [and] it was likewise unnecessary in mathematics, whose concepts must immediately be exhibited

[12] Ibid., 200.
[13] Ibid., 203.

in concreto in pure intuition, through which anything unfounded and arbitrary instantly becomes obvious," and that a "discipline" of reason is instead necessary "to constrain its propensity to expansion beyond the narrow boundaries of possible experience" "where neither empirical nor pure intuition keeps reason in a visible track" (*Pure Reason*, A 710–11/B 239–40). Kant also, especially in the *Prolegomena* and the Preface to the second edition of the *Critique of Pure Reason* (B x–xiv), appealed to the secure progress of mathematics and science as a model for what needs to be done in metaphysics. Nevertheless, Kant also thought that in the absence of a precise way of demarcating the domain of ordinary experience and normal science where our ordinary practices of causal inference are reliable from the disputable domain of metaphysics where they are not, Hume had no way of preventing his skeptical doubts about the metaphysical use of causal inference from undermining our ordinary use of causal inference. Thus, in Kant's view, Hume was inevitably led into skepticism about the concept and principle of causation in ordinary life and natural science even though he had no intention of being skeptical in those domains. Second, it seems misleading to separate Kant's positive project of grounding the first principles of human thought, including mathematical and scientific thought, from his negative project of eliminating metaphysical dispute by confining those principles to possible experience. To be sure, Kant sometimes stressed the negative rather than the positive side of his project, especially after the first edition of the "Transcendental Deduction of the Pure Concepts of the Understanding," the part of the book that he said in the Preface to the first edition of the *Critique* was of the utmost importance "for getting to the bottom of that faculty we call the understanding, *and at the same time* for the determination of the rules and boundaries of its use" (A xvi, emphasis added), met with rejection from its first readers.[14] This is partic-

---

[14] The attack upon Kant's views about space and time and the assimilation of his transcendental idealism to Berkeleian idealism in the first review of the *Critique*, the so-called Garve-Feder review, is often stressed. But it is equally important to note that Kant's deduction of the categories was also found to be deeply obscured;

ularly so in the Preface to the *Metaphysical Foundations of Natural Science* of 1786, where Kant says that "if we can prove **that** the categories which reason must use in all its cognition can have no other use at all, except solely in relation to objects of possible experience . . . then, although the answer to the question **how** the categories make such experience possible is important enough for **completing** the deduction where possible, with respect to the principle end of the system, namely, the determination of the limits of pure reason, it is in no way **compulsory**, but merely **meritorious**."[15] Yet this seems to have been somewhat of an overstatement on Kant's part: it seems clear that in his original conception of the *Critique* the positive task of establishing the validity of the a priori categories of the understanding and the synthetic a priori principles of judgment (including the concept and principle of causation) within possible experience was every bit as important to him as proving that these concepts and principles cannot yield cognition beyond the limits of possible experience, and that from the outset he considered the former just as much a critical rebuttal of Hume as he considered the latter a critical refinement of Hume. This is evident not just from the nearly equal sizes of the constructive "Transcendental Aesthetic" and "Transcendental Analytic" and the destructive "Transcendental Dialectic" (in the first edition, 273 and 348 pages respectively), but also from Kant's programmatic statements in the first edition of the *Critique*. In the *Critique*'s most extended discussion of Hume, in the "Doctrine of Method" where he is explaining the significance of his position in the history of philosophy, Kant first stresses the inadequacy of Hume's account of causation and then stresses that because of the further inadequacy of Hume's boundary between possible experience and what lies beyond it he has no way of preventing

---

see, for example, the reviews by Selle, Tiedemann, Schultz, and Tittel from 1784–85, translated in *Kant's Early Critics: The Empiricist Critique of the Theoretical Philosophy*, ed. Brigitte Sassen (Cambridge: Cambridge University Press, 2000), part IV. The "Garve-Feder" review and Garve's longer, more favorable original version are translated by Sassen in part I of her volume.

[15] *Metaphysical Foundations of Natural Science*, Preface, 4: 474; translation by Michael Friedman in Kant, *Theoretical Philosophy after 1781*, 189.

his doubts about the use of causation—and other a priori concepts that he should have considered, such as persistence—in metaphysics from casting doubt upon their use everywhere. Kant says that "the most ingenious of all skeptics" raised his doubts about causation because he recognized, although he did not name, the problem of synthetic a priori cognition, but did not know how to solve it:

> Hume perhaps had it in mind, although he never fully developed it, that in judgments of a certain kind we go beyond our concept of the object. I have called this sort of judgment **synthetic**. There is no difficulty about how, by means of experience, I can go beyond the concepts that I possess thus far. Experience itself is a synthesis of perceptions that augments my concept which I have by means of one perception by the addition of others. But we also believe ourselves to be able to go beyond our concepts *a priori* and to amplify our cognition. We attempt to do this either through pure understanding, with regard to that which can at least be an **object of experience**, or even through pure reason, with regard to such properties of things, or even with regard to the existence of such objects, that can never come forth in experience. Our skeptic did not distinguish these two kinds of judgments, as he should have, and for that reason held this augmentation of concepts out of themselves and the parthenogenesis, so to speak, of our understanding (together with reason), without impregnation by experience, to be impossible; thus he held all of its supposedly *a priori* principles to be merely imagined, and found that they are nothing but a custom arising from experience and its laws, thus are merely empirical, i.e., intrinsically contingent rules, to which we ascribe a supposed necessity and universality . . . he made a principle of affinity, which has its seat in the understanding and asserts necessary connection, into a rule of association, which is found merely in the imitative imagination and which can present only contingent combinations, not objective ones at all. (A 764–66/B 792–94)

Kant follows this passage with the paragraph I have already quoted in which he says that Hume has thereby created a "general distrust" of the understanding and "dispute[d] all its capacity to extend itself *a priori*," not just its capacity to extend itself to objects beyond the limits of experience (A 767/B 795). I see no way to interpret this extended discussion of Hume, present in its entirety in the first edition, except as stating Kant's belief that Hume's inadequate foundation for the concept and principle of causation and, by implication, other key categories of thought, could only lead to skepticism about all of the uses of those concepts and principles, and thus that he faced the dual task of rebutting the skepticism to which Hume was led, whether he liked it or not, within the realm of experience, thus the realms of ordinary life and normal science, as well as that of preserving Hume's skepticism about the metaphysical or transcendent use of these concepts and principles by determining the boundary between possible experience and what lies beyond in a way that Hume had not. As Kant understood his situation, he had to rebut what he saw as the general skepticism implied by Hume's approach before he could refine Hume's skepticism about traditional metaphysics. In the terms I will suggest in chapter 1, Kant shared with Hume the project of eliminating Pyrrhonian skepticism arising from conflicting metaphysical dogmas about what lies beyond the bounds of experience, but he did not think that this project could be successful unless what he saw as Hume's own skepticism—Humean skepticism—about the use of first principles even within the realm of possible experience was first rebutted.

Kant also made it clear in the *Prolegomena* that he intended his defense of the principle of causation in the second Analogy of Experience, as already presented in the first edition of the *Critique* just two years earlier, to be aimed specifically at Hume. In the *Prolegomena*, Kant does not restate the details of the Analogies of Experience, saying rather that, "For the most part the reader must be attentive to the method of the proof of the principles that appear under the name of the Analogies of Experience" (*Prolegomena*, §26, 4: 309). He then says:

Here is now the place to remove the ground of the **Humean** doubt. He rightly asserted that we in no way have insight into the possibility of causality, i.e., of the relation of the existence of one thing to the existence of something else, through which the former is necessarily posted, through reason. I add to this that we have just as little insight into the concept of subsistence, i.e., of the necessity that a subject that cannot itself be the predicate of any other thing should underlie the existence of things, indeed that we cannot even form the concept of the possibility of such a thing (although we can point out examples of its use in experience), and that this same incomprehensibility also affects the community of things, in that we have no insight how from the state of one thing an inference to the state of entirely different things outside of it and vice versa can be drawn, and how substances, each of which has its own, separate existence, can depend upon one another, indeed necessarily. Nevertheless I am far from holding these concepts to be merely borrowed from experience and the necessity that is represented in them to be invented and a mere illusion created for us by long experience; rather I have sufficiently shown that they and the principles from them stand firm *a priori* prior to all experience and have their indubitable objective correctness, although to be sure only with regard to experience. (§27, 4: 310–11)

This is an explicit commentary on the first edition of the *Critique of Pure Reason*. Kant thus asserts in 1783 that his constructive theory of causality and the other fundamental concepts of experience had already been aimed against Hume in 1781, although that does not mean that it did not have other targets and sources as well. It would seem very strange not to take this statement written so soon after the original edition of the *Critique* as a sincere statement of Kant's original intentions in that work. So in spite of the fact that Kant did not mention Hume's name in the immediate proximity of the Analogies of Experience, he tells us what is in fact a very short time later, with no indication that he had undergone any major change of heart, that they were directly aimed against Hume.[16] It seems more reasonable to suppose that in the *Critique* he had thought this so obvious that it did not need to be mentioned than that he was revising his intentions for the *Critique* so soon after it had been published.

Another revisionist who downplays the centrality of refuting Hume among Kant's motivations in the *Critique of Pure Reason* is Eric Watkins. The focus of Watkins's concern is indicated by the title of his 2005 book *Kant and the Metaphysics of Causality*.[17] Watkins argues against seeing Kant's treatment of causality as intended to refute Hume's position on causation for both external and internal reasons. The external reasons are that there was already a well-developed debate about the nature and reality of causality within the German rationalist tradition, going back to Leibniz's provocative position that causal relations are merely the appearance of parallel successions of states in different monads whose histories are determined solely by their internal principles, with which Kant had been arguing from very early in his career, and moreover that those in Germany who took Hume seriously, such as Johann Georg Sulzer and Johann Nicolaus Tetens, had not taken Hume's arguments about causality seriously, so there was no reason why Kant should have either. But it hardly follows from these facts that Kant could not have realized that Hume raised more serious concerns about causality than had been raised by Leibniz's fanciful monadology, or that he, even alone among his countrymen, could have realized that Hume's concerns required a far more powerful and general solution than Sulzer or Tetens had offered. That Kant did ex-

---

[16] It is well known that in the *Prolegomena* Kant proposed changing the name of his brand of idealism from "transcendental" to "formal" idealism in order to escape the charge that his idealism was no different from that of Berkeley that had been brought in the first review of the *Critique* in 1782. But that review did not criticize Kant's account of causality, and nothing had happened between the *Critique* and the *Prolegomena* that would make Kant pretend in the later work that the earlier work's account of causation had been directed against Hume when it originally had not been.

[17] Eric Watkins, *Kant and the Metaphysics of Causality* (Cambridge: Cambridge University Press, 2005).

actly that is why, after all, he is remembered as a far greater philosopher than Sulzer or Tetens.

Watkins has three internal reasons for denying that Kant was out to refute Hume. First, he holds that for Kant causality is a relation between enduring objects with active and passive powers rather than between mere events, as he takes Hume to have held. Second, he holds that Kant thought of the change from one state of an object to another that is the effect of the agency of a cause as continuous rather than as an instantaneous succession, as he thinks Hume had held. And finally, he holds that Kant was not out to *refute* Hume because he did not construct an argument for a conclusion that Hume rejected from premises that Hume accepted, so that he instead aimed only to *replace* Hume's treatment of causation with an altogether different approach.[18] But Watkins's claims are problematic. First, Hume often speaks of causes and effects as objects rather than events, especially in the *Enquiry concerning Human Understanding*, Kant's source for Hume's views. There, for example, Hume represents the fundamental problem about causation as explaining how to get from the proposition "*I have found that such an object has always been attended with such an effect*" to the proposition "*that other objects, which are, in appearance, similar, will be attended with similar effects*" (*Enquiry I*, Section 4, Part 2, p. 30). Conversely, since for Kant the role of causation is to allow us to determine "the position of the appearance . . . in time," that is, to determine that one state of affairs has, for example, succeeded rather than preceded another, the invocation of a cause must tell us "that in what precedes, the condition is to be encountered under which the occurrence always (i.e., necessarily) follows" (*Pure Reason*, A 201/B 246). Simply appealing to a certain kind of agent as a cause will not do this; only appealing to the state of an agent *at a certain time*, or more precisely to a particular change in the agent, that is, to an agent's having come to be in a certain state at a certain time, will—and that is to appeal to an event, the event of an object's having come to be in a certain state at a certain time, as the cause. Upon analysis, Hume and Kant both have very much the same conception of

---

[18] See Watkins, *Kant and the Metaphysics of Causality*, 383–85.

a cause, that of an object's being in a certain state at a certain time, which is taken to be the condition of another object's being in a certain state at a certain time. Second, Watkins's claim that Hume and Kant had different and incommensurable conceptions of causation because Hume conceives of an effect as an immediate succession of one state of affairs upon another while Kant conceives of causation as continuous change is misleading. Kant did recognize that the changes we explain causally are often continuous rather than punctiform, and indeed that the effect often appears to be simultaneous with the cause rather than successive to it; but he was so wedded to the Humean model of causation as a necessary succession of one state of an object upon another state of that object triggered by the intervention of a second object at a determinate moment in time, that he went out of his way to explain that even where the effect seems to be simultaneous with the cause there has to be a vanishingly small temporal gap between them so that the effect really is successive on the cause (A 202–3/B 248). He would not have argued this had it not been his larger intention to argue that the very same sort of causation that Hume thought was merely contingent was in fact necessary.

Finally, Watkins's position depends on what is, to say the least, a debatably narrow conception of refutation. As the long quotation from the "Doctrine of Method" has shown, Kant certainly thought of his own treatment of causation as a critical response to Hume, and as chapters 2 and 3 will argue, this response takes the form of explaining that Hume could not explain a cognitive ability that he himself took for granted on the basis of his own view that causal concepts and beliefs are not in any way a priori but are acquired entirely in the course of experience, and never attain genuine necessity. Specifically, Kant will argue that the possibility of our determining of the objective order of states of affairs, or even, ultimately, of our own experiences, a cognitive ability that Hume took for granted as much as anyone else, could not be explained or justified if the reality of causation were doubted or if our concepts of it were derived only from an antecedent experience of successive states of affairs. On my account, Kant and Hume do share a premise, namely that we are capable of determining the temporal order of states of affairs, including at least our own experiences, and the form of Kant's argument is to show that this premise cannot be held consistently with the rest of Hume's claims, but only on the basis of Kant's other claims. This would seem to be entitled to the title of "refutation," unless refutation is to be construed so narrowly that the only thing that counts as one is showing that an opponent holds all the same premises that the refuter holds but has somehow mistaken what follows from those premises. That, I think, is not consistent with the ordinary usage of the term. But however one labels Kant's argument about causation, Watkins is surely right to stress that it is by no means aimed just at Hume, yet just as surely wrong to claim that it is not aimed at rebutting Hume at all. Kant's own account of the goal of the Second Analogy in the *Prolegomena* should put that beyond doubt.

A comprehensive treatment of Kant's philosophy as a response to Hume would require a detailed investigation of all the sources for Kant's acquaintance with Hume's works as well as a thorough discussion of both philosophers on epistemology, the critique of metaphysics, practical philosophy, aesthetics, teleology, and philosophy of religion, the latter including their criticisms of the a priori ontological and cosmological arguments and the empirical argument from design but also of Kant's defense of an "ethicotheology" (*Judgment*, §86) against Hume's rejection of all philosophical theology whatsoever.[19] The chapters of this volume, originally written over a period of six years for a variety of different occasions, have been revised to go together (and to take account of some recent work by myself and others), but will not be that comprehensive or systematic. But I do hope that they demonstrate the fruitfulness of thinking of many aspects of Kant's philosophy, not just his

---

[19] Manfred Kuehn has done much of the necessary historical work in "Kant's Conception of 'Hume's Problem' " and *Scottish Common Sense in Germany*, already cited. Another indispensable source is Günter Gawlick and Lothar Kreimendahl, *Hume in der deutschen Aufklärung: Umrisse einer Rezeptionsgeschichte* (Stuttgart: Fromann-Holzboog, 1987).

treatment of causation, as a response to Hume, although again not as a response to Hume alone.

Chapter 1, "Common Sense and the Varieties of Skepticism," originally written for a conference on skepticism at the Instituto de Investigaciones Filosóficas of the National Autonomous University of Mexico in 2001, argues first for the complexity of Kant's conception of skepticism, in which Pyrrhonian or dialectical skepticism, Humean skepticism about first principles, and Cartesian skepticism about external objects are distinguished, and then argues that refuting the first two forms of skepticism was central to Kant's aims in both his theoretical and practical philosophy, while refuting Cartesian skepticism about external objects was only an afterthought and subsidiary theme in his theoretical philosophy.[20]

Chapter 2, "Causation," written for a special issue of *Philosophical Topics* on early modern philosophy in 2003, distinguishes the three different questions about causation that Hume raised in the *Treatise*, namely, about the origin of our concept of necessary connection, about the basis for our belief in particular causal laws, and about the basis for our belief in the general principle that every event has a cause; it then examines Kant's strategy for answering these different questions, but concludes that although Kant had a plausible account of the origin of our idea of causation itself and a persuasive account of the indispensability of causal belief for the most basic forms of our empirical knowledge, he did not directly reply to Hume's worries about the rational foundation for our claim to know particular causal laws on the basis of induction, even though these worries are particularly prominent in the *Enquiry concerning Human Understanding*, the work of Hume's which, unlike the *Treatise*, Kant did know firsthand.

Chapter 3, "Cause, Object, and Self" written in 2004 for a festschrift for Vere Chappell, takes up the theme of Kant's generalization of Hume's problem about causation and of his own

---

[20] I thus agree with Hatfield in distinguishing Humean and Cartesian skepticism and in deemphasizing the importance of the latter to the largest projects of the *Critique of Pure Reason*; see "The *Prolegomena* and the *Critiques*," 189.

response to it, and shows how the general strategy Kant employs in his treatment of causation also provides an approach to Hume's concerns about our knowledge of both a continuing self distinct from its fleeting impressions of its states and continuing external objects distinct from our fleeting impressions of their states even though Kant remained unaware that in the *Treatise* Hume had raised questions about self and object similar to his questions about causation.

Chapter 4, "Reason, Desire, and Action," written at the invitation of Rachel Cohon and Lorne Falkenstein as a plenary address for the Thirty-Third International Hume Congress in 2006, addresses relations between the moral philosophies of Hume and Kant. However, it does not focus on the obvious contrasts between these two approaches to moral philosophy, namely those between Hume's insistence that reason cannot set ends but merely discovers means to ends set by sentiment, and Kant's insistence that pure practical reason is the source of the end in itself that underlies all moral imperatives. Rather, this chapter brings out affinities between the moral psychologies of Hume and Kant, specifically in the details of their models of moral motivation and in their conceptions of the psychological results of moral conduct. The point of this approach is to show that Kant has a more complex model of the motivation of human action than is usually supposed, and to intimate that there is much in this model that remains worthy of consideration even if his transcendental idealist insistence that we are always free to act in accordance with the moral dictates of pure practical reason in spite of all empirical circumstances cannot be accepted.

Finally, chapter 5, "Systematicity, Taste, and Purpose," written for the *Cambridge Companion to Kant and Modern Philosophy* published in 2006, shows how Kant's treatments of the systematicity of science, of judgments of taste, and of teleology in the *Critique of the Power of Judgment* can all usefully be read as responses to Hume's treatments of natural law, taste, and the argument from design.

1

COMMON SENSE AND
THE VARIETIES OF
SKEPTICISM

Is Kant Responding to Skepticism?

Is the refutation of skepticism a central objective for Kant? Some commentators have denied that the refutation of either theoretical or moral skepticism was central to Kant's concerns. Thus, in *Kant and the Fate of Autonomy*,[1] Karl Ameriks rejects "taking Kant to be basically a respondent to the skeptic." According to Ameriks, who here has Kant's theoretical philosophy in mind,

> What Kant goes on to propose is that, instead of focusing on trying to establish with certainty—against skepticism— that the objects of common sense exist, let alone that they have philosophical dominance, or, in contrast, on explaining that it is only the theoretical discoveries of science that determine what is objective, one can rather work primarily to determine a positive and balanced philosophical relation between the distinct frameworks of our manifest and scientific images.[2]

---

[1] Karl Ameriks, *Kant and the Fate of Autonomy: Problems in the Appropriation of the Critical Philosophy* (Cambridge: Cambridge University Press, 2000). The argument of this book goes back to Ameriks's earlier work, such as "Kant's Transcendental Deduction as a Regressive Argument," *Kant-Studien* 69 (1978): 273–87.

[2] Ameriks, *Kant and the Fate of Autonomy*, 43.

In invoking the famous contrast of Wilfrid Sellars,[3] Ameriks seems to claim that Kant's task is to reconcile common sense and Newtonian science, and that such a reconciliation has nothing to do with responding to skepticism. On his account, Kant always assumes "that there are legitimate empirical judgments," and asks only how we can "make sense of ordinary practices of justifying" them. The answer to this question then lies in demonstrating simply that "Principles such as causality . . . for example, . . . function both as necessary conditions for particular empirical judgments and as framework postulates for specific higher sciences."[4] Apparently, once the objects of common sense and science and the principles of common sense and science have been shown to be the same, neither the assumption of those common objects nor the assertion of those common principles needs any further defense against skepticism.

It has also been argued that Kant should not be seen as responding to any sort of moral skepticism. John Rawls has bluntly stated:

> I don't see Kant as at all concerned with moral skepticism. It is simply not a problem for him, however much it may trouble us. His view may provide a way to deal with it, but that is another matter. He always takes for granted, as part of the fact of reason, that all persons (barring the mentally retarded and the insane) acknowledge the supreme principle of practical reason as authoritative for their will.[5]

Thomas E. Hill Jr. had earlier offered a more nuanced caution against reading Kant's practical philosophy as a reply to a skepticism about the need to be moral that he portrays as peculiarly modern, but that was already the target of Plato's *Republic*. Re-

[3] See Wilfrid Sellars, "Philosophy and the Scientific Image of Man," originally in *Frontiers of Science and Philosophy*, ed. Robert Colodny (Pittsburgh: University of Pittsburgh Press, 1962), reprinted in Sellars, *Science, Perception, and Reality* (London: Routledge and Kegan Paul, 1963), 1–40.

[4] Ameriks, *Kant and the Fate of Autonomy*, 59.

[5] John Rawls, *Lectures on the History of Moral Philosophy*, ed. Barbara Herman (Cambridge, MA: Harvard University Press, 2000), 149.

ferring to Kant's attempt to prove in Section III of the *Groundwork for the Metaphysics of Morals* that we are obligated by the moral law analyzed in its Sections I and II by demonstrating that we are free and that our freedom entails our obligation under the moral law, Hill writes that Kant's argument

> Amounts to an answer to the contemporary question "Why be moral?" But Kant's aim is easily obscured by the fact that his imagined audience is not the sort of moral skeptic with which we are most familiar today. Kant does not see himself as addressing, for example, those who are indifferent to morality and demand that philosophy supply them with a motive to be moral; for Kant's own theory denies that anyone rational enough to ask the question could really be so indifferent. . . . The intended audience, I think, is rather those whose moral commitment is liable to be called into question by philosophical accounts of practical reason which imply that morality could not be grounded in reason.[6]

On Hill's account, Kant's aim is not to prove that we should conceive of moral precepts as categorical imperatives, as if we did not know *that*, but rather to demonstrate that we have a faculty of reason that makes it possible for us to both acknowledge and act upon such principles, thereby saving our presumption in favor of the categorical imperatives of morality not from a moral skeptic tout court but rather from anyone who fails to see that both the binding force of the categorical imperative and the possibility of our complying with it are grounded in the nature of our own reason, and reason alone.

Ameriks is right that Kant's project in theoretical philosophy involves demonstrating that both common sense and science share common principles, but it is wrong to infer that this has nothing to do with refuting skepticism as Kant understood it. Rawls and Hill are right to suggest that the project of the

---

[6] Thomas E. Hill Jr., "The Rationality of Moral Conduct," originally published in *Pacific Philosophical Quarterly* 66 (1985): 3–23, reprinted in his *Dignity and Practical Reason in Kant's Moral Theory* (Ithaca, NY: Cornell University Press, 1992), 97–122, at 98–99.

Groundwork is not to justify the universal and binding demands of morality to someone who alleges no presumption in their favor, but it would be wrong to conclude from this that Kant's argument is not intended as an answer to moral skepticism as Kant understood it. Further, while Hill is also right in suggesting that Kant's objective is instead to save a preexisting commitment to morality from being undermined, he is especially wrong to assume that Kant's aim is only to save this commitment from being called into question by inadequate *philosophical* accounts of freedom and practical reason. Kant stresses from the outset of the *Groundwork* that he is concerned to save our moral innocence from a certain *natural dialectic*, a "propensity" that lies in us *prior* to any philosophy "to rationalize against those strict laws of duty and to cast doubt upon their validity, or at least upon their purity, and, where possible, to make them better suited to our wishes and inclinations, that is, to corrupt them at their basis and to destroy all their dignity" (*Groundwork*, 4: 405). The threat to the commitment to morality, a commitment that is itself inherent in common sense, does not arise from mere philosophy, but from a source within common sense itself and a philosophy that reflects this source, and can only be averted by a philosophy which remains true to what is best in common moral sense but also exposes its weakness:

> In this way **common human reason** is impelled, not by some need of speculation . . . but on practical grounds themselves, to go out of its sphere and to take a step into the field of **practical philosophy**, in order to obtain there information and distinct instruction regarding the source of its principle . . . so that it may escape from its predicament about claims from both sides and not run the risk of being deprived of all genuine moral principles through the ambiguity into which it easily falls.

As Kant makes explicit, "a **dialectic** . . . constrains" moral common sense "to seek help in philosophy, just as happens in its theoretical use" (*Groundwork*, 4: 405). Likewise, Kant introduces his theoretical philosophy by asserting that "there has always been some metaphysics or other to be met with in the world . . . because dialectic is natural to reason," and philosophy is necessary precisely because dialectic is natural: "Hence it is the first and most important occupation of philosophy to deprive dialectic once and for all of all disadvantageous influence, by blocking off the source of the errors" (*Pure Reason*, B xxxi).

What does Kant's claim that dialectic is natural to both common sense and reason, in both the theoretical and the practical domain, have to do with skepticism? Plenty, because for Kant dialectic is one of the chief sources of skepticism. Kant often stressed this point, as in his lectures on metaphysics when he characterized the ancient skeptics as "subtle and dialectical" (*Metaphysik L2*, 28: 538; *LM*, 305), and conversely asserted that "as soon as the contradiction and the existence of . . . wholly conflicting propositions"—propositions concerning whether "each space and bodies consists [*sic*] of simple parts" or not, whether "the world has a beginning" or not—"there arose that **party** which doubted the certainty of either," which "took the opportunity thereby to declare all truths of reason as uncertain" (*Metaphysik Vigilantius (K3)*, 29: 958; *LM*, 429). But if a dialectic that is natural to human reason is a chief source of skepticism, then in resolving that dialectic philosophy is responding to skepticism.

But this is only part of the picture. Kant recognizes three different forms of skepticism. There is, as we have just seen, the skepticism about reason itself that inevitably arises from any natural but apparently irresolvable dialectic. Following Kant's association of this form of skepticism with the Greek skeptics and their founder Pyrrho, we may call this form of skepticism Pyrrhonian.[7] Such natural dialectic produces confusion in the theoretical sphere, but even worse it produces corruption in the moral sphere, and for this reason it is imperative that this form of skepticism be resolved by philosophy. Second, there is a skepticism about the first principles of both theory and practice that will inevitably arise, even in the absence of dialectic, if we at-

---

[7] The importance of this form of skepticism for Kant may be reflected by the fact that Hume saw this as the dangerous form of skepticism (*Enquiry I*, Section 12, Part 2), and that Hegel subsequently saw it as the most important and dangerous form of skepticism; see Michael N. Forster, *Hegel's Idea of a Phenomenology of Spirit* (Chicago: University of Chicago Press, 1998), 128–29.

tempt to justify such principles by a mere appeal to experience. This form of skepticism can be called Humean, for in his published works Kant repeatedly states that if they are unresolved Hume's doubts about the a priori origins of the concept and principle of causation must inevitably lead to skepticism about all first principles of cognition.[8] Common sense inherently recognizes universal and necessary principles in both inquiry and conduct, but will come to doubt the validity of those principles unless an adequate account of their origin and thus the possibility of our knowledge can be given. This account will certainly be part of philosophy, not common sense, although it must be accessible and ultimately acceptable to common sense.[9] Finally, Kant does recognize what has in recent decades often been thought of as the paradigmatic form of skepticism, Cartesian skepticism about our knowledge of the existence and character of objects external to our representations of them, or as he calls it in his early lectures on metaphysics the "skeptical test about the reliability of my senses" (*Metaphysik L1*, 28: 206; *LM*, 29). In the *Critique of Pure Reason* he calls this form of skepticism "a scandal of philosophy and of universal human reason," and sets out to refute it too, although the small number of pages he devotes to it could well give the impression that he is not very much concerned with it.[10]

---

[8] See *Critique of Pure Reason*, B 127–28, and *Prolegomena*, "Preamble," 4: 262. Kant did not always distinguish Humean skepticism about first principles from Pyrrhonian or dialectical skepticism; in the early (ca. 1770) Blomberg logic lectures, he characterizes Hume as "a *scepticus* who had an overwhelming, indeed, a somewhat extravagant inclination to doubt," displayed in his practice of considering, "first, all of one side of a thing," searching "for all possible grounds for it," and then "tak[ing] up the other side, present[ing] it for examination, as it were, completely without partisanship," and "in conclusion [appearing] in his true form as a real skeptic" (*Blomberg Logic*, 24: 217, in *LL*, 172). This is a characterization of the classical procedure of Pyrrhonian skepticism.

[9] Here the substance of my account is not that different from that of Ameriks and Hill; the difference is in my insistence that Kant clearly intends his position as a response to what he conceives of as a major form of skepticism.

[10] In a subtle response to the original publication of this chapter, Robert Stern has argued that my distinction between Humean and Pyrrhonian skepticism obscures the fact that Hume attempted to resolve Pyrrhonian skepticism by his empir-

Far from being indifferent to skepticism, then, Kant organized his entire philosophy as a response to the varieties of skepticism *as he understood them.* The refutation of Cartesian skepticism, to be sure, is by far the predominant concern of Kant's theoretical philosophy, although neither is it entirely ab-

icism about first principles—which is what for Kant gives rise to Humean skepticism on my account—by demonstrating that irresolvable conflicts over first principles arise from trying to extend first principles beyond the limits of experience; he then argues that there is a structural similarity between Hume's project and Kant's, because Kant too attempts to overcome Pyrrhonian skepticism by this theory of first principles, although in Kant's case it is specifically the transcendental idealist distinction between appearance and things in themselves that is entailed by his account of our knowledge of first principles that undercuts the paradoxes of Pyrrhonian skepticism. See Robert Stern, "Metaphysical Dogmatism, Humean Skepticism, Kantian Criticism," *Kantian Review* 11 (2006): 102–16. Stern may be right about this parallelism between the projects of the two philosophers, but I think it is nevertheless worth separating Humean and Pyrrhonian skepticism as I have, first for the historical reason that it is not clear that Kant saw this parallel, and more importantly for the philosophical reason that Kant's arguments for the certainty of first principles (of both theoretical and practical reason) may, in my opinion, be separated from the transcendental idealism that he thinks they entail and that he uses to resolve Pyrrhonian skepticism.

In a number of publications, Karl Ameriks has argued that Kant never felt the need to refute Cartesian skepticism, because he did not think that his "formal" idealism, the denial that space and time are real mind-independent forms of objects, takes anything away from the real existence of the objects that we represent as spatial and/or temporal, or leads to "material" or Cartesian idealism that actually doubts the existence of those objects, and thus did not consider the latter as a view needing refutation. See, for example, Ameriks, *Interpreting Kant's* Critiques (Oxford: Clarendon Press, 2003), Introduction, 1–48, especially 29–33, and "Idealism from Kant to Berkeley," in his *Kant and the Historical Turn* (Oxford: Clarendon Press, 2006), 67–88, especially 74–74. I agree with Ameriks that Kant started with the commonsense assumption that objects external to us exist, and saw his own arguments for transcendental idealism as merely relocating certain (though fundamental) properties from such objects to our representations of them; but that did not stop him from attempting to demonstrate that we must believe that such objects exist, thus responding to Cartesian skepticism, when his approach met with incomprehension. That is why he specifically labeled the "Refutation of Idealism" that he added to the second edition of the *Critique of Pure Reason* and further elaborated in subsequent years a refutation of Cartesian idealism (see *Pure Reason*, B 275, and Reflections 6311–17, in *Notes and Fragments*).

In chapter 3, I will argue that Hume raised a problem about external objects to which Kant's account of substance can be interpreted as an (unwitting) response.

sent. More importantly, it would be wrong to infer from the minor role of Cartesian skepticism in his thought that Kant is not centrally concerned with refuting skepticism more generally in this theoretical philosophy. The whole of the *Critique of Pure Reason* is organized around the dual tasks of, first, in the "Analytic," refuting Humean skepticism about first principles, and then, second, in the "Dialectic," resolving Pyrrhonian skepticism engendered by the natural dialectic of human reason. It would likewise be wrong to infer that Kant's practical philosophy is not concerned with the refutation of moral skepticism, at least as he understands it. While there is no parallel to Cartesian skepticism about the objects of the senses in Kant's moral philosophy—he certainly takes the existence of moral subjects for granted, and also our awareness of the content of the moral law, not only in the *Critique of Practical Reason* as a "fact of reason" but also in the *Groundwork* as a matter of "common rational moral cognition"—this moral philosophy is likewise organized around the two central tasks of revealing the a priori origin of the moral law in pure practical reason, a parallel to the refutation of Humean skepticism in theoretical philosophy, and then resolving several natural dialectics that threaten our commitment to morality, in parallel to the theoretical task of resolving Pyrrhonian skepticism.

It All Depends on How You Define Skepticism

Far from being unconcerned with skepticism, as I have suggested, Kant addresses no fewer than three forms of skepticism. Of these, Cartesian skepticism about external objects is the least

---

This does not entirely blur the line between Cartesian and Humean skepticism, however, because Descartes and Hume raised quite different problems about external objects, Descartes about the certainty of any inference from inner experience to outer reality and Hume about the coherence of any idea or concept of the outer in which to believe. In the "Refutation of Idealism," Kant took himself to be responding to Cartesian skepticism, or as we would say, to the inadequacy of Descartes' resolution of doubts about the certainty of our knowledge of the external world as far as Kant is concerned.

central to the organization of the *Critique of Pure Reason*. Kant does not address skeptical doubts about the existence of external objects at the outset of the first *Critique*, nor does he organize the structure of the book as a whole around this issue. In the first edition, "skeptical idealism," or Cartesian doubt about the certainty of the existence of matter (as opposed to "dogmatic idealism," the Berkeleian denial of the very possibility of matter or coherence of its concept), is addressed only midway through the book, in the fourth "Paralogism of Pure Reason" (*Pure Reason*, A 366–80), and there the relation of skepticism about external existence to the chief issues of the paralogisms, the substantiality, simplicity, and immortality of the soul, is tenuous. In the second edition, Kant inserts a refutation of what he there calls not skepticism but "problematic idealism," although he still associates the problem with Descartes, into his discussion of the second "Postulate of Empirical Thinking," the postulate that sensation is the criterion or evidence of actuality, which he did not in the first edition think needed any defense against skepticism (*Pure Reason*, B 275–79). His famous statement that skepticism about external objects is "a scandal to philosophy and universal human reason," although it occurs in the Preface to the second edition, occurs only in a footnote amplifying this "Refutation of Idealism" that had been inserted into the second "Postulate." However, none of this implies that the refutation of Cartesian skepticism was unimportant to Kant; it obviously was, as, apparently still dissatisfied with the published "Refutation," he returned to the topic and drafted numerous further versions of the argument in the following years.[11] But this form of skepticism, unlike what I have dubbed Humean and Pyrrhonian skepticism, was not central to the organization of the

[11] See especially Reflections 5653–55, 18: 306–16, and 6311–17, 18: 607–29. I discussed these notes in "Kant's Intentions in the Refutation of Idealism," *Philosophical Review* 92 (1983): 329–83, and *Kant and the Claims of Knowledge* (Cambridge: Cambridge University Press, 1987), part IV, 279–329. Eckart Förster also discussed them in "Kant's Refutation of Idealism" in *Philosophy, Its History and Historiography*, ed. A. J. Holland (Dordrecht, the Netherlands: D. Reidel, 1985), 295–311. See Guyer, *Kant and the Claims of Knowledge*, 454, note 19, for several earlier discussions in German.

Critique of Pure Reason nor paralleled by the forms of skepticism that are central to the organization of Kant's chief works in practical philosophy.

The prominent reference to skepticism in the Preface to the first edition of the *Critique of Pure Reason* is a reference to the skepticism that inevitably arises in response to the natural dialectic of human reason. Here Kant writes that metaphysics was initially dogmatic and despotic, degenerated into anarchy, and inevitably called forth attacks from "skeptics, a kind of nomads who abhor all permanent cultivation of the soil." The debates between dogmatists and skeptics can give rise to "indifferentism," which might have referred to the position of Hume himself, who notoriously argued, in the conclusion to Book I of the *Treatise* that was the only part of that book to which Kant had direct access, that even though skepticism could not be refuted, it could and would simply be ignored once we left the solitude of the study for the company of the dining room and gaming table,[12] although Kant probably meant it to refer to the German "popular philosophers" of his time such as Moses Mendelssohn and Johann Georg Sulzer, who thought that (Humean) skepticism did not have to be taken very seriously. Either way, for Kant the metaphysical issues about which the skeptics raise doubts are "inquiries, to whose object human nature **cannot** be **indifferent**," and so "the **critique of pure reason** itself" is required precisely to determine whether any of the natural claims of metaphysics can be rescued from skeptical doubt and if so how that can be done (*Pure Reason*, A ix–xii). What it is that calls forth skepticism about traditional metaphysics is not

---

[12] Hume, *Treatise of Human Nature*, I.iv.7, 171–78. Kant has traditionally been assumed not to have read the *Treatise* at the time he wrote the *Critique of Pure Reason*, because he did not read English and the *Treatise* had not yet been translated into German. However, it has been demonstrated that this chapter of the *Treatise* was translated into German by Kant's then close friend Johann Georg Hamann and published in a Königsberg journal in 1771, so it is actually inconceivable that Kant did *not* know it. See Manfred Kuehn, "Kant's Conception of 'Hume's Problem,'" *Journal of the History of Philosophy* 21 (1983): 175–93, at 185–86. Kuehn supports the interpretation of Kant's "indifferentism" as an allusion to Hume's position at pp. 181–82.

merely its "obscurity" but above all its "contradictions" and "endless controversies," the perplexities into which human reason falls "through no fault of its own" (A vii–viii). This form of skepticism is the inevitable response to the conflicts between doctrines each of which seems to have reason fully on its side—in other words, Pyrrhonian skepticism. Indeed, Kant will later identify the critical procedure of the second half of the first *Critique*, in which he describes dialectical conflicts between metaphysical assertions on the matters of the most fundamental concern to human reason, that is, the soul, the cosmos, and God, and then seek to resolve them by appeal to the transcendental idealism that he takes to be a central result of the first half of the work, as the "skeptical method." For Kant, such a "method" is not a mere suspension of judgment, but a resolution of dialectically opposed theses that unmasks their common but fallacious assumptions. But it will only be employed once skepticism itself is directly confronted:

> This method of watching or even occasioning a contest between assertions, not in order to decide it to the advantage of one party or the other, but to investigate whether the object of the dispute is not perhaps a mere mirage at which each would snatch in vain without being able to gain anything even if he met with no resistance—this procedure, I say, can be called the **skeptical method**. It is entirely different from **skepticism**, a principle of artful and scientific ignorance that undermines the foundations of all cognition, in order, if possible, to leave no reliability or certainty anywhere. For the skeptical method aims at certainty, seeking to discover the point of misunderstanding in disputes that are honestly intended and conducted with intelligence by both sides . . . (*Pure Reason*, A 423–24/B 451–52)

Two points should be noted here. First, Kant always insists that these dialectical controversies of metaphysics are never a product of mere bad philosophical theory, but are natural and unavoidable products of human reason reflected in common sense, the source of which must be diagnosed and cured in order to render human reason itself and its expression in common

sense consistent. At the outset of the "Transcendental Dialectic" he says that

> What we have to do with here is a **natural** and unavoidable
> **illusion** which itself rests on subjective principles and passes
> them off as objective. . . . Hence there is a natural and un-
> avoidable dialectic of pure reason, not one in which a bungler
> might be entangled through lack of acquaintance, or one that
> some sophist has artfully arranged in order to confuse rational
> people, but one that irremediably attaches to human reason.
> (*Pure Reason*, A 298/B 354)

Thus, although Kant sometimes claims that "**idealism** and
skepticism . . . are more dangerous to the schools and can
hardly be transmitted to the public" (B xxxiv), this cannot apply
to the skepticism that is the natural response to the natural
dialectic of human reason, and everyone, not just the philosopher, needs an answer to it. Second, Kant's insistence that the
dialectic that calls forth skepticism is natural and not artificial
means that no *simple* appeal to common sense can defend the
most fundamental principles of human thought, whether theoretical or, as we will also see, practical.[13] Common sense recognizes the fundamental and a priori principles of human reason,
at least tacitly, that is, by properly making particular judgments
that depend upon these principles, but common sense is also
inherently liable to controversies that can be resolved only by
the appeal to transcendental idealism, which is without question philosophical.

---

[13] Hence Kant's contemptuous dismissal of the Scottish "common sense" philosophers Reid, Oswald, Beattie, and Priestley at *Prolegomena to Any Future Metaphysics*, Preface, 4: 248: they did not recognize that Hume could not be refuted simply
by appealing to common sense, but that common sense itself had to be liberated
from the contradictions or dialectic to which it is naturally liable through sound
philosophy. In spite of the interesting parallels between the views of Kant and Reid
on the issues of a priori first principles and realism that Karl Ameriks points out
in "A Common Sense Kant?" in *Kant and the Historical Turn*, 108–33, the fact that
Reid did not think that common sense is inherently liable to dialectics that must
be resolved and that Kant did remains a fundamental difference between them.

The other main form of skepticism to which the *Critique of Pure Reason* responds is doubt about the universality and necessity of the primary concepts and first principles of human cognition, such as the concept of causation and the universal principle that every event has a cause. To be sure, the name of David Hume is not actually mentioned in either of the versions of the Prefaces to the first *Critique*. But the "Doctrine of Method," the concluding section of the *Critique* that remained unchanged from the first to the second edition, makes it clear that rebutting Humean skepticism was central to Kant's project in the work. The first chapter of the "Doctrine of Method" is titled "The discipline of pure reason," and its final section is "On the impossibility of a skeptical satisfaction of pure reason that is divided against itself" (A 758/B 796). In this section Kant states that "Hume is perhaps the most ingenious of all skeptics" (A 764/B 792). He then diagnoses the core of Hume's skepticism as his failure to recognize that in addition to the conceptual or analytical judgments that may be known through the merely logical use of reason and the factual or synthetic a posteriori judgments that can be known through empirical means, all of our experience must rest on a body of synthetic a priori cognitions through the kind of examination of the conditions of the possibility of experience that Kant has provided. Referring to synthetic a posteriori and synthetic a priori judgments, Kant says,

Our skeptic did not distinguish these two kinds of judgments, as he should have, and for this reason held that the augmentation of concepts out of themselves and the parthenogenesis, so to speak, of our understanding (together with reason), without impregnation by experience, to be impossible; thus he held all of its supposedly *a priori* principles to be merely imagined, and found that they are nothing but a custom arising from experience and its laws, thus are merely empirical, i.e., intrinsically contingent rules, to which we ascribe a supposed necessity and universality. . . . In the transcendental logic, on the contrary, we have seen that although of course we can never **immediately** go beyond the content of the concept which is given to us, nevertheless we can still cognize the law of the connection with other things completely *a priori*, although in relation to a third thing, namely **possible** experience, but still *a priori*. (A 765–66/B 793–94)[14]

Kant continues that Hume was lulled into his skepticism by confining his scrutiny of first principles to the case of causation: "The skeptical aberrations of this otherwise extremely acute man . . . arose primarily from a failing that he had in common with all dogmatists, namely, that he did not systematically survey all the kinds of *a priori* synthesis of the understanding," for had he done this, Kant claims, he would necessarily have seen that there are other principles, such as the principle of the persistence of substance, that are indispensable to our experience but cannot themselves be proven by merely empirical means, and he would have been forced "to mark out determinate boundaries for the understanding that expands itself *a priori*" (A 767/B 795). Since Hume did not develop his problem about causation into a general problem about the synthetic a priori principles of the possibility of experience and therefore did not see that such a general problem could not be left unsolved, Kant, as he sees it, had to do this for him.

Many other passages make it plain that Kant always understood his general project of establishing synthetic a priori cognition as that of refuting the generalization of Hume's skepticism about the principle of causation. As we saw in the Introduction, Kant claims in the *Prolegomena to Any Future Metaphysics* that it was Hume who had awakened him from his "dogmatic slumbers," and presents the project of the *Critique* precisely as that of answering for a whole range of central concepts the kind of doubts or objections that Hume had raised about the specific concept "of the **connection of cause and effect** (and of course also its derivative concepts, of force and action, etc.)" (*Prolegomena*, 4: 257, 4: 261). Kant goes on to say that unlike Hume, who "deposited his ship on the beach (of skepticism)," "it is important to me to give it a pilot, who, provided with complete

---

[14] Kant uses similar metaphors of procreation at *Prolegomena*, Preface, 4: 257–58.

sea-charts and compass, might safely navigate the ship wherever seems good to him" (4: 262). In the *Critique of Practical Reason*, Kant again characterizes the objections that Hume had raised to the necessity and apriority of the concept and principle of cause and effect as skepticism, and thus presents his own project of establishing the objective and a priori validity of causation and the other categories of the pure understanding as a project of refuting skepticism. In his words:

> David Hume, who can be said to have really begun all the assaults on the rights of pure reason which made a thorough investigation of them necessary, concluded as follows. The concept of **cause** is a concept that contains the **necessity** of the connection of the existence of what is different just insofar as it is different. . . . But necessity can be attributed to a connection only insofar as the connection is cognized *a priori*; for, experience would enable us to cognize of such a conjunction only that it is, not that is necessarily so. Now it is impossible, he says, to cognize *a priori* and as necessary the connection between one thing and **another** . . . if they are not given in perception. Therefore the concept of a cause is itself fraudulent and deceptive. . . . So, with respect to all cognition having to do with the existence of things (mathematics thus remaining excepted) **empiricism** was first introduced as the sole source of principles, but along with it the most rigorous **skepticism** with respect to the whole of natural science (as philosophy). (*Practical Reason*, 5: 50–51)[15]

In Kant's view, to attack the apriority of a fundamental concept of human thought, one used by common sense at every turn even if common sense itself would not call it a priori, is a form of skepticism, and the critical philosophy certainly aims to refute this form of skepticism.

Kant's confidence that Hume would have been forced to solve the problem of synthetic a priori knowledge if only he had

---

[15] Kant explicitly claims here that Hume's empiricism necessarily leads to skepticism about the "whole of natural science," contrary to the interpretation of Gary Hatfield discussed in the Introduction to this volume.

realized that this problem extends beyond the single principle of causation, and especially if he had considered mathematical knowledge, which is self-evidently synthetic a priori (see *Prolegomena*, §2(c), 4: 272) is touching, and also proves that Kant was not fully acquainted with Hume's *Treatise*, for there Hume did extend his doubts about the rational foundations of our belief in causation to the cases of the external object and the enduring self as well, and indeed explicitly applied his empiricism—in Kant's eyes, skepticism—to mathematics as well (see *Treatise*, Book I, Part II, on "The Ideas of Space and Time"). We shall see in this chapter and chapter 3, however, that although he was unaware that Hume had generalized his problem about causation without being shaken in his skepticism, Kant did address, whether successfully or not, all of the skeptical topics that Hume had actually raised: Kant did address Humean empiricism—or, as he sees it, skepticism about synthetic a priori first principles—regarding causation, enduring selves and objects, and mathematics.

Kant did not exaggerate, however, when he wrote in the *Critique of Practical Reason* that "my labor in the *Critique of Pure Reason* . . . was occasioned by that Humean skeptical teaching but went much further and included the whole field of pure theoretical reason in its synthetic use and so too the field of what is generally called metaphysics" (*Practical Reason*, 5: 52.). Refuting Humean skepticism about the universality and necessity of first principles is primarily the project of only the first half of the *Critique*, while the second half is devoted to the resolution of Pyrrhonian skepticism about the metaphysical claims of pure reason. Thus, the *Critique of Pure Reason* is organized almost entirely around the tasks of responding to these two forms of skepticism—to the first in the "Transcendental Analytic" and to the second in the "Dialectic." After outlining Kant's answer to these forms of skepticism in theoretical philosophy (which will be treated in more detail in the following two chapters), I will then argue that he is concerned with very much the same two forms of skepticism in his practical philosophy, that is, a skepticism about the apriority of the fundamental principle of morality and a skepticism engendered

by a natural dialectic inherent in the practical rather than theoretical use of human reason, and that just as the first *Critique*
is largely organized around the task of refuting the two forms
of theoretical skepticism with which Kant is concerned, so his
chief works in practical philosophy can be seen as organized
largely around the task of refuting the two forms of moral skepticism that he recognizes.

Kant's Response to Theoretical Skepticism

This chapter will provide an outline of his approach to theoretical skepticism that can then be used as a guide for an analysis
of Kant's response to moral skepticism; further details about
Kant's reply to theoretical skepticism will be provided in the
next two chapters. As we have seen, Kant is chiefly concerned
about two forms of skepticism, Humean doubt about the universal and necessary validity of such fundamental concepts as
causality raised by Hume, and the Pyrrhonian skepticism about
reason itself that is the inevitable response to the natural dialectic of metaphysical dogmas. The two parts of the *Critique of
Pure Reason* respond to these two forms of skepticism in turn.
Kant does not present the "Transcendental Aesthetic" as a response to skepticism, but he pursues a common strategy in the
"Aesthetic" and the "Analytic," arguing in these two divisions
of the *Critique* that the existence of a priori forms of intuition
and concepts is the only possible basis for several basic cognitive
capacities that common sense certainly takes for granted, even
if it hardly has a theory of them, but then that our a priori
knowledge of the universality and necessity of these forms of
intuition and concept can only be defended on the supposition
that they express the structure the human mind imposes on its
experience of appearances rather than revealing the structure of
the objects of our experience as they are in themselves, in other
words, by the doctrine of transcendental idealism. In the "Transcendental Dialectic," Kant then argues that the distinction between the cognitive capacities of sensibility and understanding
for which he has argued as well as transcendental idealism's

contrast between appearances and things in themselves undermine the apparent conflicts of traditional metaphysics, and
thereby resolve the second form of skepticism with which he
is concerned.

The first part of Kant's argument, his response to Humean
skepticism, then, itself consists of two stages, his demonstration
that ordinary cognitive capacities presuppose a priori cognition
and the explanation of such a priori cognition by transcendental
idealism. His response is also divided into two parts by his argument that there are two distinct components in all cognition,
whether a priori or empirical, namely, intuitions and concepts,
and the two main stages of his argument are repeated for each
of these. Thus, although the "Transcendental Aesthetic" is not
explicitly described as part of the response to Humean skepticism, its arguments that a variety of ordinary cognitive capacities reveal the existence of a priori forms of intuition and that
only transcendental idealism can explain such a priori forms of
cognition are an unwitting response to Hume's extension of his
empiricism to our ideas of space and time in the *Treatise*; the
"Transcendental Analytic," which is billed as the response to
Humean skepticism (*Pure Reason*, B 127–28), then follows the
same strategy in arguing that ordinary cognition also presupposes a priori concepts and principles of judgment (which arise
when the a priori concepts are applied to experience through
the a priori forms of intuition), and that these too entail transcendental idealism. In the second edition of the first *Critique*,
the first stage of the argument of the "Aesthetic" is divided
into two further parts, which Kant calls the "metaphysical" and
"transcendental expositions" of the concepts of space and time.
In the metaphysical exposition, Kant pursues the antiskeptical
strategy of arguing that what he clearly assumes to be several
ordinary and fundamental cognitive capacities, namely the ability to represent objects as numerically distinct from one another
and from ourselves (*Pure Reason*, A 23–24/B 37–38) and the ability to represent states of affairs, whether external or internal, as
successive or simultaneous (A 30–31/B 46), as well as the perhaps less commonsensical disposition to represent space and
time as single infinite wholes of which particular, bounded

spaces and times are parts rather than instances (A 24–25/B 39–
40, A 31–32/B 47–48), can all be explained only on the supposition that we have a priori representations of space and time as
the forms of all empirical intuitions, that is, immediate representations of particular objects in experience.[16] In expounding
this argument, Kant makes no explicit reference to either skepticism or common sense, but it seems clear that the abilities to
distinguish objects and moments from one another as well as
the disposition to treat individual spaces and times as parts of
single all-encompassing wholes are taken for granted in common sense, and the concept of a priori forms of intuition is thus
introduced as the necessary philosophical basis for a piece of
common sense. In the transcendental expositions of space and
time, Kant then argues that the universality and necessity of
the synthetic rather than merely analytic propositions of geometry and other branches of mathematics, or our synthetic a priori cognition of the structure of the pure objects of mathematics
as well as the empirical objects of ordinary experience, can only
be explained by the same supposition that we have a priori cognition of space and time as the fundamental forms of all intuition (*Pure Reason*, A 24, replaced by B 40–41, and A 31/B 47).[17]
Here Kant's supposition seems to be that while common sense
may never explicitly assert either the syntheticity or the universality and necessity of mathematical propositions, mathematics
certainly does, and common sense goes along.

Kant presents mathematics as if it is immune from skepticism. Mathematicians, he suggests, neither have nor should
have any qualms about their ordinary practice; instead, how
synthetic a priori cognition is possible is a question for the philosopher, and it is the philosopher who answers this question

---

[16] For the definition of empirical intuition, see *Critique of Pure Reason*, A19–20/
B 33–34, A 320/B 376–77.

[17] The title "transcendental exposition" is, as mentioned, introduced only in the
second edition, where Kant removes the argument from the synthetic a priori cognition of geometry to space as an a priori form of intuition to a separate section
under this rubric (B 40–41). In the case of time, the added section carrying this
title repeats material that is also left in its original position (A 31/B 47). But the
substance of both arguments is the same in both editions.

by demonstrating the existence of a priori forms of intuition. As Kant says much later in the *Critique*, when he is distinguishing the method of mathematics from that of philosophy, "it seems to" mathematicians "to be useless to investigate the origin of pure concepts of the understanding and the scope of their validity; rather, they merely use them. In all of this they proceed quite correctly, as long as they do not overstep their appointed boundaries, namely those of **nature**" (A 725/B 753). The undisputed success of mathematics apparently frees it from the need of justification from philosophy. Nevertheless, what is offered merely as a philosophical explanation rather than justification of the possibility of mathematics in the "Transcendental Aesthetic" follows the same strategy that Kant will use to confront Humean skepticism in the "Analytic," grounding a human cognitive capacity that is unquestioned in the case of mathematics but doubted in the case of causal reasoning, in an analysis of the underlying capacities of human intuition and thought.

The second stage of Kant's argument in the "Transcendental Aesthetic" is then that our a priori cognition of these fundamental forms of intuition can itself be explained only by transcendental idealism, the thesis that we impose the a priori forms of cognition on our experience but that they do not reveal the real nature of the objects of this experience as they are in themselves. The basis for this startling claim is Kant's supposition that nothing else can explain how we can have a priori cognition of objects, that is, knowledge of the necessary features of all objects prior to the experience of any particular object. As Kant puts it in the case of space, it "represents no property at all of any things in themselves nor any relation of them to each other . . . that would remain even if one were to abstract from all subjective conditions of intuition. For neither absolute nor relative determinations can be intuited prior to the existence of the things to which they pertain, thus be intuited *a priori*" (A 26/B 52). Here, if not sooner, one is certainly impelled to object to Kant's argument. Even if we were inclined to concede that our a priori cognition of the structure of space and time in everyday life as well as mathematics can only be explained by positing some sort of innate mental representations of the structure of space and time to which we have immediate access, why couldn't we suppose that these mental structures serve merely as reliable filters for the objects of experience, allowing us to experience only objects that have the very properties we are inherently able to detect? Why shouldn't the a priori forms of intuition be like colored glasses, which screen out any light that does not have the right wavelength to pass through them but do allow us to see whatever light does have the right wavelength?[18] Kant's answer to this question comes only some pages later, when he argues that if the forms of intuition were thought to characterize not only our own minds, which is necessary to explain our a priori knowledge of them, but also the objects we perceive, then while they might be necessary features of our representations of objects, they could at best be only contingent features of the objects themselves: "how could you say that what necessarily lies in your subjective conditions for" representing an object, for example, "constructing a triangle[,] must also necessarily pertain to the triangle itself?" (A 48/B 65). Kant repeats this argument when he says in the *Prolegomena* that "if the senses had to represent objects as they are in themselves,"

> Then it absolutely would not follow from the representation of space, a representation that serves *a priori*, with all the various properties of space, as foundation for the geometer, that all of this, together with which is deduced from it, must be exactly so in nature. The space of the geometer would be

---

[18] The formulation of the objection to Kant's argument for transcendental idealism in terms of colored glasses goes back at least as far as H. J. Paton, *Kant's Metaphysic of Experience* (London: George Allen and Unwin, 1936), 1: 168. It is a way of putting the objection of the "excluded alternative," that is, that Kant has failed to consider that spatiality and temporality could be properties of *both* our representations and of things as they really are, that goes back to August Trendelenburg in the 1840s. For a detailed discussion of Trendelenburg's objection and the reply to it by Kuno Fischer, see Hans Vaihinger, *Commentar zur Kants Kritik der reinen Vernunft*, vol. 2 (Stuttgart: Union Deutsche Verlagsgesellschaft, 1892), 136–51 and 290–326; Norman Kemp Smith, *A Commentary to Kant's "Critique of Pure Reason,"* 2nd ed. (London: Macmillan, 1923); and most recently, Graham Bird, "The Neglected Alternative: Trendelenburg, Fischer, and Kant," in *A Companion to Kant*, ed. Graham Bird (Oxford and Malden: Blackwell, 2006), 486–99.

taken for mere fabrication and would be credited with no objective validity, because it is simply not to be seen how things would have to agree necessarily with the image that we form of them by ourselves and in advance. If, however, this image—or better, this formal intuition—is the essential property of our sensibility by means of which alone objects are given to us, and if this sensibility represents not things in themselves but their appearances, then it is very easy to comprehend, and at the same time to prove incontrovertibly, that all objects in our sensible world must necessarily agree, ... (*Prolegomena*, §13, Note I, 4: 287)

Kant's claim is that only the supposition of transcendental idealism can explain the necessity of any synthetic a priori cognition throughout its entire domain. Of course, one can object to this that Kant is not entitled to the supposition that any synthetic cognition is necessarily true throughout its entire domain, and with the rejection of that supposition at least one of the foundations for transcendental idealism would certainly collapse. But I will not pursue that objection here.[19]

Kant's explicitly antiskeptical argument about the a priori concepts of the understanding in the "Transcendental Analytic" has the same two-staged construction as his argument about the a priori forms of intuition, with similar complexity in its first stage and simplicity in its second stage. In the first stage of his argument, where Kant argues that we must have a priori cognition of the concept of causality and the universal principle of causation that Hume had doubted, as well as of the other concepts and principles that Kant thought Hume should have

---

[19] I have pursued it in *Kant and the Claims of Knowledge*, chap. 16, especially 354–59 and 362–69. For endorsement of my claim that the argument from the apriority of geometry to the ideality of space is central to Kant's transcendental idealism, see James van Cleve, *Problems from Kant* (New York: Oxford University Press, 1999), 37. For a very different approach to Kant's transcendental idealism, which argues that it is based in Kant's conception of a thing in itself as defined only by its intrinsic properties, not by its relational properties and for that reason not by the forms of its epistemic relations to us, see Rae Langton, *Kantian Humility: Our Ignorance of Things in Themselves* (Oxford: Clarendon Press, 1998).

doubted had he applied his own method in its full generality, such as the concepts of substance and interaction and their associated principles, Kant argues that a priori cognition of the pure concepts of the understanding and of the associated principles of empirical judgment is the necessary condition of the possibility of cognitive capacities assumed without question in both common sense and natural science. Thus, in the "Transcendental Deduction" Kant bases his general argument for the objective validity of the categories on the premise that "The **I think** must **be able** to accompany all my representations" (*Pure Reason*, §16, B 131; cf. A 116), an ability to make an a priori judgment that can only be explained by a priori cognition of the fundamental forms of judgment and their associated categories. Common sense might never explicitly formulate this proposition, but it always assumes it in practice—we accept the slide from saying "*p*" to saying "I think that *p*" all the time, even if we do not realize everything this entails. In the "System of all principles of pure understanding," Kant then argues that a variety of specific cognitive capacities, in particular the capacity to judge that a change in the objects of our representations, and not just a change in our representations, has occurred and the capacity to judge that two objects are simultaneous even when our representations of them are not, presuppose a priori cognition of the synthetic principles that the quantum of substance is constant, that every event has a cause, and that all objects in space are in interaction with one another, principles that common sense may never explicitly enunciate but that both common sense and natural science use all the time.

We will consider these arguments in more detail in the next two chapters;[20] here I observe only that Kant repeatedly illustrates them with examples drawn from common sense. In the First Analogy, to be sure, he says that it is a philosopher who assumes the principle of the conservation of substance when he infers that the weight of the smoke released by a burning log must equal the difference between the weight of the original log less that of the remaining ashes, but the example is ordinary

---

[20] See also Guyer, *Kant and the Claims of Knowledge*, chaps. 8 through 11.

enough (*Pure Reason*, A 185/B 228). In the Second Analogy, which argues that our judgments about the succession of states of affairs in events depends upon the ubiquitous validity of causal laws, Kant argues that we assume causal laws even in making such judgments as that a ship is moving downstream rather than upstream, that a room has become warm, or that a previously plumped pillow has become dented (A 192/B 237, A 202–3/B 247–48)—the kind of judgments we all make every day. In the Third Analogy, he says that the sorts of judgments about simultaneous existence that depend upon the universal interaction of objects in space are easy to make:

> From our experience it is easy to notice that only continuous influence in all places in space can lead our sense from one object to another . . . and that we cannot empirically alter any place (perceive the alteration) without matter everywhere making the perception of our position possible[,] and only by means of its reciprocal influence. (A 213/B 260)

Throughout these arguments, Kant's claim is not that common sense explicitly formulates or asserts the principles that are also the foundations of natural science, but that it constantly *uses* these principles in making judgments that nobody has thought to doubt. Finally, when at last Kant does explicitly address the "problematic idealism" of Descartes in the "Refutation of Idealism," he argues that the existence of objects in space outside of me is not an inference from but a presupposition of "the mere, but empirically determined, consciousness of my own existence" (B 275). By the latter he means nothing other than the ability to make determinate judgments about the sequence of my own experiences merely as such, the most ordinary of cognitive capacities. Throughout the "Transcendental Analytic," then, Kant does not argue that common sense explicitly recognizes or asserts that we have a priori cognition of the concepts and principles he aims to defend from Hume, let alone that philosophy can simply appeal to common sense to defend these principles, but he does assert that philosophical analysis can reveal the contested concepts and principles to be the conditions of the possibility of the most ordinary and uncontested sorts of cognitive accomplishments.

The second stage of Kant's argument in the "Analytic," that is, his argument from a priori cognition to transcendental idealism, differs from the second stage of the argument in the "Aesthetic" in two ways. First, since Kant always argues that we must apply the categories of the understanding to empirical intuitions, and he has already argued for the transcendental ideality of space and time in both pure and empirical intuitions in the "Aesthetic," he does not need to develop any novel argument for transcendental idealism in the "Analytic": since the categories must apply to intuitions, they in fact apply to appearances. Second, since Kant will ultimately argue that in the practical use of pure reason we must postulate the existence of objects such as God and the immortal soul that we cannot prove in the theoretical use of reason, he needs to be able to maintain that we can conceive of such objects, and we can conceive of objects only by means of the categories; he therefore denies only that we can *know* things in themselves by means of the categories, but not that we can *think* of them in such terms. Nevertheless, the basic argument remains the same: if we are to explain how we can have a priori cognition of the most basic laws of nature, as he typically puts it, or, as we might better put it, of the general forms of the laws of nature, we cannot suppose that there is a merely contingent correspondence between the forms of our experience and those of its objects, but must instead assume that we impose the former upon the latter.

Thus we ourselves bring into the appearances that order and regularity in them that we call **nature**, and moreover we would not be able to find it there if we, or the nature of our mind, had not originally put it there. For this unity of nature should be a necessary, i.e., *a priori* certain unity of the connection of appearances. But how should we be able to establish a synthetic unity *a priori* if subjective grounds of such a unity were not contained *a priori* among the original sources of cognition in our mind, and if these subjective conditions were not at the same time objectively valid, being the grounds of the possibility of cognizing any object in experience at all? (*Pure Reason*, A 125–26)[21]

As before, Kant argues that ordinary cognitive capacities presuppose *a priori* cognition, and then that *a priori* cognition can only be explained by transcendental idealism.

This is the outline of Kant's response to Humean skepticism. His response to the second form of theoretical skepticism, that which is the natural response to the contradictions of equally natural dogmatic metaphysics, is presented in the "Transcendental Dialectic." In general, Kant argues that metaphysical confusion arises from the natural assumption of reason "that when the conditioned is given, then so is the whole series of conditions subordinated to one another, which is itself unconditioned, also given" (A 307–8/B 364).[22] It is natural for reason to assume this, Kant argues, because it is the proper task of reason to strive for completeness in understanding or explaining anything that is conditioned, but it is also a mistake for reason to assume this, because the distinction between sensibility and understanding that philosophy has shown to be necessary means that the conditions under which intuitions are *given* are distinct from those by which they are *understood*, and that we have no reason to suppose that they are congruent, that is, that sensibility can satisfy all the demands of the intellect. The philosophical reflection upon space and time undertaken in the "Transcendental Aesthetic" has already revealed that nothing given in intuition is ever unconditioned in the sense that Kant has in mind, that is, free of essential relations to something beyond itself: every space and time, and thus everything *in* space and time, is always given as part of a larger space and time, and thus nothing unconditioned by further relations

---

[21] See also the interesting note that Kant added to this passage in his own copy of the *Critique*, at 23: 26–27, translated in Paul Guyer and Allen W. Wood, trans., *Critique of Pure Reason* (Cambridge: Cambridge University Press, 1998), 241n. See also B 166–68.

[22] For a recent work emphasizing the importance of this principle to Kant's diagnosis of the natural illusions of metaphysics, see Michelle Grier, *Kant's Doctrine of Transcendental Illusion* (Cambridge: Cambridge University Press, 2001).

beyond its spatial and/or temporal limits can ever actually be given in sensibility. Here philosophy criticizes one part of what it is natural for us to believe—what it is natural for our reason to assume—by clarifying the implications of another part of what it is natural for us to believe—what is inherent in our sensibility. This is emblematic of what is absolutely central to Kant's conception of common sense: it is a source of skepticism as well as of belief, and ultimately always needs philosophy to sort things out.

The diagnosis of the dialectic of metaphysical beliefs stated thus far does not depend specifically upon transcendental idealism, but Kant does employ that doctrine in his full resolution of the "natural dialectic" of metaphysics. Kant sees skepticism as the inevitable response to the antinomies of pure reason, and uses transcendental idealism to dissolve the antinomies and thus remove the object and motivation for skepticism. He describes four conflicts, based on the four concepts of quantity, substance, causal relation, and modality: the opposition between the thesis that the world is bounded in space and time and the antithesis that it is not (*Pure Reason*, A 426–27/B 454–55); that between the thesis that the world consists of simples and the antithesis that it does not (A 434–35/B 462–63); that between the thesis that world includes the spontaneous origination of events or a "causality through freedom" and the antithesis that "There is no freedom, but everything in the world happens solely in accordance with laws of nature" (A 444–45/B 472–73); and finally that between the thesis that the world consists of contingencies dependent upon a necessary being and the antithesis that there are only the contingencies but no necessary being (A 452–53/B 480–81). In each conflict, Kant argues, both positions seem to follow from sound arguments of reason, yet they can hardly both be true, and skepticism about reason itself is the inevitable result. But the conflicts can be dissolved by transcendental idealism, Kant argues, and skepticism about reason averted. In the case of the first two antinomies, which Kant calls the "mathematical" antinomies, the solution lies in realizing that reason is arguing about properties of syntheses of representations of objects in sensibility—extent and divisibility—

which because of the structure of our pure representations of space and time are always only carried to an indefinite point, and are thus never either actually finite or actually infinite. Thus both sides of the antinomies are ill founded, and there is no need for us to be caught in skeptical suspension between them. In the case of the latter two antinomies, which Kant calls the "dynamical" antinomies, the solution is different: one side, namely the antithesis, accurately describes the structure of empirical intuition, but the other side, the antithesis, describes a conception of things in themselves that can and indeed must be coherently formulated by reason even if it can never be confirmed in sensibility. Yet once again there is no reason for us to be caught in skeptical suspension between two contradictory assertions about the same things, for we are not talking about the same things in the theses and antitheses. So Pyrrhonian skepticism about reason is undercut: it is a response to a problem that is natural for us to imagine, but that can be dissolved by philosophical analysis.

Thus, although Kant calls the presentation and resolution of this dialectic the "skeptical method," he does not mean by this the same thing that Hume means in calling his own response to his doubts about causation a "Sceptical Solution of these Doubts" (*Enquiry I*, Section 5). Hume calls his psychological explanation of our possession of the idea of necessary connection and of our practice of induction from past to future a skeptical solution because he explains our belief in causality in the external world with an appeal to mechanisms of the imagination, that is, causality in the mind, without ever refuting his own doubts about induction: he produces no argument that the imagination must behave in the future as it has in the past, nor does he think that he should. Thus his skeptical doubts, at least about induction, remain valid in theory even if they do not move us in practice. For Kant, however, transcendental idealism conclusively undercuts skepticism, that is, shows it to rely upon either a conflict between ill-formulated propositions (in the case of the mathematical antinomies) or an ill-formulated conflict between coherent propositions (in the case of the dynamical antinomies). For Hume, skepticism remains coherent even if psychologically unmoving, but for Kant it is shown to be incoherent from the outset.

Robert Stern has recently argued that Hume attempted to undermine Pyrrhonian skepticism by weakening our confidence in the principles, such as the principle of causation, that dogmatists try to use in order to extend our knowledge beyond what we have actually observed, but that for Kant, this is to throw the baby out with the bath water. As Stern puts it, "The key to Kant's strategy is to offer a way of allowing 'ordinary consciousness' "—what I have been calling common sense—"to hang on to principles such as the principle of causality and the principle of permanence . . . but to argue that these principles are only valid for objects as they appear to us within experience, and so cannot be employed within any metaphysical speculations, which concern objects that lie outside our experience (such as God)."[23] As we have already seen, Kant holds that since Hume "merely *limits* our understanding without *drawing boundaries* for it," he inevitably "brings about a general distrust but no determinate knowledge of the ignorance that is unavoidable for us" (*Pure Reason*, A 767–68/B 795–96). Thus, Hume had attempted to undermine Pyrrhonian skepticism with Humean skepticism, but for Kant this only redoubles skepticism: doubts about the universality and necessity of fundamental principles means that there can only be doubt about how far these principles can extend—thus, for example, whether we can use the principle of causality to infer to the existence of an unseen God—and not certainty; thus, fruitless debates between dogmatists are free to go on after all.

Kant's critical philosophy, by contrast, is supposed to put the certainty of the fundamental principles of experience beyond doubt, while at the same time making it certain, through transcendental idealism, that there cannot be any theoretical knowledge of the application of these principles beyond the limits of experience, to things in themselves, although things in themselves can be conceived for practical purposes. Thus, as Stern

---

[23] Stern, "Metaphysical Dogmatism, Humean Scepticism, Kantian Criticism," pp. 110–11.

argues, Kant sees himself as overcoming Pyrrhonian skepticism in a way that Hume could not. Nevertheless, even though Hume could be seen as having attempted to overcome empirical skepticism as well as Kant, it is still important to distinguish between Humean skepticism and Pyrrhonian skepticism for at least two reasons: one, because the specter of Pyrrhonian skepticism would have threatened Kant even without Hume; and second, because if the doctrine of transcendental idealism should turn out *not* to be a necessary consequence of Kant's strategy for securing the certainty of the first principles of experience, then Kant's strategy for rebutting Humean skepticism might be a success even if his own strategy for rebutting Pyrrhonian skepticism should turn out to fail. Since, as I have suggested above and argued at length elsewhere, transcendental idealism may not be an inevitable consequence of Kant's transcendental deductions of the fundamental forms and principles of sensibility and understanding,[24] it thus seems important to maintain the distinction between "Humean" skepticism about first principles and "Pyrrhonian" skepticism engendered by unresolved metaphysical disputes.

Kant's Response to Moral Skepticism

I now turn to the parallels between Kant's response to theoretical skepticism and his response to moral skepticism. As noted earlier, Kant begins his practical philosophy by claiming that it is necessary to combat a "**natural dialectic,** that is, a propensity to rationalize against . . . strict laws of duty and to cast doubt upon their validity, or at least upon their purity and strictness, and, where possible, to make them better suited to our wishes and inclinations" (*Groundwork*, 4: 405). A natural dialectic is what induces one of the two forms of skepticism with which Kant is obsessed, Pyrrhonian skepticism, so to resolve a natural dialectic about the strict laws of duty is itself to respond to one

---

[24] See Guyer, *Kant and the Claims of Knowledge*, part V.

form of moral skepticism. But in morality, skepticism is not just a theoretical problem, a scandal to philosophy. Rather,

> A metaphysics of morals is . . . indispensably necessary, not merely because of a motive to speculation—for investigating the source of the practical basic principles that lie *a priori* in our reason—but also because morals themselves remain subject to all sorts of corruption as long as we are without that clue and supreme norm by which to appraise them correctly. (*Groundwork*, 4: 389–90)

An unresolved dialectic about the fundamental principle of morality will not just leave us in a theoretical quandary, it will undermine our commitment to morality by letting us identify its principles with our own inclinations, thereby corrupting those principles at their basis and destroying all their dignity (4: 405).

A clear formulation of the fundamental principle of morality, which may not be explicit in common sense but which can be reached and confirmed by philosophical reflection upon commonsense moral beliefs and judgments and which must remain accessible to common sense, is certainly the first step toward averting the corruption with which Kant is concerned. The identification of a pure principle for morality that is implicit in common sense yet that has its source in pure reason is analogous to Kant's response to Humean skepticism about the a priori principles of cognition. But the formulation of the a priori principle of morality and the discovery of its source does not complete its defense; there is a second stage, analogous to Kant's response to the natural, Pyrrhonian dialectic of theoretical reason, in which natural but conflicting beliefs about morality that can threaten our commitment to it must be resolved—and indeed, if Kant's resolution of the dialectic of theoretical reason is to be any clue, it must be resolved by being properly understood within the framework of transcendental idealism.

However, what makes the structure of Kant's practical philosophy even more complicated is that there is not just one but two natural dialectical conflicts about morality that must be resolved. The dialectic of the first *Critique* already included a conflict about the possibility of freedom, the conflict between the thesis that there must be a "causality through freedom" and the antithesis that "There is no freedom, but everything in the world happens solely in accordance with laws of nature" (*Pure Reason*, A 444–45/B 472–73), and this of course is an issue, at least in Kant's view, that bears directly on the possibility of morality. The *Groundwork* suggests that it is precisely this conflict that is the natural dialectic threatening to corrupt morality:

> Hence freedom is only an **idea** of reason, the objective reality of which is in itself doubtful, whereas nature is a **concept of the understanding** that proves, and must necessarily prove, its reality in examples. From this there arises a dialectic of reason since, with respect to the will, the freedom ascribed to it seems to be in contradiction with natural necessity; and . . . reason **for speculative purposes** finds the road of natural necessity much more traveled and more usable than that of freedom; yet **for practical purposes** the footpath of freedom is the only one on which it is possible to make use of our reason in our conduct; hence it is just as impossible for the most subtle philosophy as for the most common human reason to argue freedom away. Philosophy must therefore assume that no true contradiction will be found between freedom and natural necessity in the very same action. (4: 455–56)

The threat of corruption is not made explicit here, but surely Kant is supposing, first, that if we are to remain committed to acting upon a pure principle of morality that requires of us something other than the mere gratification of our own inclinations, we must believe that we are always free to act upon such a principle regardless of what our inclinations are, and, second, that such a freedom is apparently incompatible with natural necessity; so unless philosophy can show that it is not, our commitment to act on the principle of morality will give way before our belief in our powerlessness always to do so. Section III of the *Groundwork* and the "Analytic" of the *Critique of Practical Reason* each attempt to show how philosophy does resolve this apparent contradiction, differing in their tactics but aimed at the same strategic objective, and thus attempt to remove a fundamental source of moral skepticism, in the sense of skepticism about the possibility of our acting morally.

In spite of Kant's clear indication in the passage just quoted that Section III of the *Groundwork* is aimed at resolving our natural dialectic about freedom and determinism, he does not actually label this section a dialectic, and the explicitly labeled "Dialectic" of the *Critique of Practical Reason* is not concerned with the conflict between freedom and determinism. Instead, it deals with the highest good, or the relation between virtue and happiness in the complete good for human beings, and with the existence of God and immortality as postulates of pure practical reason necessary for the possibility of the highest good. This raises a series of questions: Why is the highest good the subject of a dialectic? How would such a dialectic threaten to corrupt our commitment to morality, and thus count as a source of moral skepticism? Further, does this dialectic have anything to do with the dialectic about freedom and determinism?

As answers to these questions, I would suggest the following: There is a dialectic about happiness because it is natural for us, part of common sense if you will, to believe both that morality has nothing to do with happiness and yet that morality must have something to do with happiness, and these beliefs apparently conflict. This dialectic must be resolved because if we believe that morality has nothing to do with happiness it will come to seem pointless to us, and our motivation to live up to its stringent demands will be undermined; yet if we believe that morality is simply about our individual happiness, that will surely corrupt it, and us, as well. But this dialectic can be resolved by showing that while our individual happiness is not the *motive* nor *first principle* of morality, yet the collective happiness of mankind as a product of universal virtue, that is, the highest good, at least insofar as that can be the aim of our own efforts, while still not the motive for morality, is the proper *object* or *goal* for it. And this resolution of the dialectic of happiness is linked to the resolution of the dialectic of freedom and determinism because the realization of such a form of happiness depends upon nature, to suggest through its inclinations the

individual objects of happiness for each of us, but also on freedom, the freedom of each of us to subordinate his individual
and indeed unstable conception of his or her own happiness to
the end of the collective and enduring happiness of all, an object
of the free rather than merely natural will—so we need to explain how nature and freedom fit together. Toward the very end
of the *Groundwork*, Kant says that it is of "great importance" to
"all moral inquiry" that reason "not, on the one hand, to the
detriment of morals search about in the world of sense for the
supreme motive and a comprehensible but empirical interest,
and that it may not, on the other hand, impotently flap its wings
without moving from the spot in the space, which is empty for
it, of transcendent concepts called the intelligible world, and so
lose itself among phantoms" (4: 462). This can be read to mean
that transcendental freedom must find both a motive that is
pure and an object that is realizable in the natural world, and
thus that the resolution of the natural dialectic of freedom and
determinism must go hand in hand with the resolution of the
natural dialectic of virtue and happiness. Only when we put the
two strands of Kant's argument in practical philosophy together
in this way, I suggest, can we understand the full scope of his
intended response to the dialectical or, as it were, Pyrrhonian
form of moral skepticism.

Here there will be room only for brief comments on each of
the three main points of this diagnosis of Kant's strategy in
practical philosophy. The first stage of this philosophy, the clar-
ification of the content of the fundamental principle of morality
and of its relation to common sense on the one hand and pure
reason on the other, is Kant's response to Humean-style skepticism about the first principles of practical rather than theoretical reason. However, although Hume had indeed formulated a
skepticism about the rationality of moral principles in Book III
of the *Treatise of Human Nature* to parallel his skepticism about
theoretical principles in Book I—his argument that moral principles are grounded in sentiment rather than pure reason—Kant
does not explicitly cast his foundation of the fundamental principle of morality as a response to Hume nor take up the details
of Hume's argument. Next, Kant attempts to resolve two dis-

tinct but ultimately connected natural dialectics, the one between freedom and determinism and the other between virtue
and happiness, in order to avert the second, Pyrrhonian style of
moral skepticism, the response to conflict that in this case
would not lead to mere theoretical confusion or indifference
but to the actual corruption of our morals.

As in his theoretical philosophy, Kant's response to the first
form of skepticism, skepticism about the pure principle of morality, consists of two parts, first the derivation of the principle
and then the analysis and defense of its origin in the faculty of
pure reason. The first of these steps in turn has a complex structure. The key to Kant's argument here is that the fundamental
principle of morality cannot be directly derived from empirical
examples of human conduct, but that it is implicit in common
beliefs about morality and must remain accessible to common
sense once philosophy has properly formulated and derived it.
The principle cannot be derived from actual examples of human
conduct, of course, because, at least in Kant's view, whether this
be coldly realistic or excessively pessimistic, these are hardly
ever fully virtuous.[25] Yet, Kant also claims, that there must be
"a pure moral philosophy . . . is clear of itself from the common
idea of duty and of moral laws" (*Groundwork*, 4: 389). From
these two assumptions, Kant then proceeds by arguing that the
fundamental principle of morality can be derived both from
common assumptions about the nature of duty (*Groundwork* I)
and from philosophical assumptions about the nature of rational agency (*Groundwork* II), although more completely from
the latter, and that the correctness of the principle thus derived
can then be confirmed by analysis of the everyday practice of
making moral judgments as well as by the derivation of the
commonly accepted system of duties from the philosophical
principle. That the fundamental principle of philosophy must
first be derived from analysis and then confirmed by examples

---

[25] *Groundwork*, 4: 407: "It is absolutely impossible by means of experience to
make out with complete certainty a single case in which the maxim of an action
otherwise in conformity with duty rested simply on moral grounds and on the
representation of one's duty."

of its application is what Kant has in mind in saying in the Preface to the *Groundwork* that the method of the argument in the *Groundwork* is first analytic and then synthetic (4: 392), although this use of the distinction is different from what he has in mind later in the work when he states that the derivation of the principle in the first two sections is analytic and then the proof in the third that it is actually binding upon us is synthetic (e.g., 4: 444–45). The fundamental principle of morality can be derived from the analysis of both common practices of moral judgment and philosophical concepts, which is why there are two analytical sections of the *Groundwork*, one a "transition from common rational to philosophical moral cognition" and the other a "transition from popular moral philosophy to metaphysics of morals" (4: 392).

The first step in this argument, in *Groundwork* I, is not uncomplicated. Kant begins this section with his polemic against a straightforward derivation of the principle of morality from the pursuit of happiness, arguing as a matter of common rational cognition that the unconditional value of a good will is something quite different from the conditional value of individual happiness or any means to it (4: 393–97). He then proceeds to his analysis of common views about duty, which consists of three propositions: first, that actions do not have their moral worth by being done from inclination, no matter how selfless or benevolent inclination might sometimes be (4: 398); second, that, since moral worth does not lie in inclination it also cannot arise directly from any goal suggested by mere inclination, that is, "an action from duty has its moral worth **not in the purpose** to be attained by it but in the maxim in accordance with which it is decided upon" (4: 399); and third, since the moral worth of an action cannot lie either in an inclination to it nor in the goal of that inclination, all that remains is that "duty is the necessity of an action from respect for law" (4: 400). The premise of this argument, that there is no moral worth in mere inclination, is supposed to be a matter of common sense, and Kant supports it not with philosophical arguments but with examples such as that of the philanthropist whose mind has become clouded with grief but who can still act from duty (4: 398): any normal person is supposed to recognize that there was no special moral worth in the philanthropist's beneficence as long he was moved by mere inclination, but that if he was moved by the thought of duty—his only possible motivation once he had lost all inclination toward beneficence—then surely his action had moral worth.[26] Then Kant argues that these conditions recognized by common sense can be satisfied only by what will become the first formulation of the categorical imperative:

> But what kind of law can that be, the representation of which must determine the will, even without regard for the effect expected from it . . . ? Since I have deprived the will of every impulse that could arise for it from obeying some law, nothing is left but the conformity of actions as such with universal law, which alone is to serve the will as its principle, that is, **I ought never to act except in such a way that I could also will that my maxim should become a universal law.** (4: 402)

This proposition might never be enunciated in everyday life, but it is, Kant holds, the only principle that can satisfy the conditions on a moral principle imposed by the common conception of duty.[27] Moreover, he claims, "Common human reason also agrees completely with this in its practical judgments and always has this principle before its eyes." He illustrates this claim by describing how anyone contemplating making a promise he did not intend to keep would ask himself "would I indeed

---

[26] This diagnosis of Kant's example draws upon Barbara Herman's discussion in "On the Value of the Motive of Acting From Duty," *Philosophical Review* 90 (1981): 359–82, reprinted in her *The Practice of Moral Judgment* (Cambridge, MA: Harvard University Press, 1993), chap. 1, 1–22.

[27] I omit here discussion of the objection that there is a "gap" in Kant's derivation of the moral law, because he may show that our maxim must conform to *some* universal law but not specifically to the formal law that it must be universalizable; see Bruce Aune, *Kant's Theory of Morals* (Princeton: Princeton University Press, 1979), e.g., 32. I agree with the response of Samuel Kerstein to this allegation of a gap that it fails to recognize that at least in Kant's eyes the exclusion of any inclination as a basis for the moral law excludes any law that could be recommended only by inclination, such as the utilitarian principle, and leaves only the requirement of the universalizability of maxims as such. See Kerstein, "Deriving the Formula of Universal Law," in Bird, ed., *A Companion to Kant*, 308–21.

be content that my maxim (to get myself out of difficulties by a false promise) should hold as a universal law (for myself as well as for others)?" (4: 403). The claim is thus that this moral principle is one we all use in our ordinary practice even if we have not asserted it in philosophical form.

Kant then argues that the same principle, although ultimately in a much fuller formulation, can also be reached from philosophical premises. This argument is made both in *Groundwork* II and in the second *Critique*. In *Groundwork* II, Kant begins from the philosophical premise that the fundamental principle of morality would present itself to us as a categorical imperative, and then derives from the mere concept of the categorical imperative the same formulation of this principle that was previously reached from the analysis of duty (4: 413–21). In the *Critique of Practical Reason*, Kant reaches the same formulation of the principle of morality by an analysis that starts with the concept of a practical law, assuming that the formal characteristics of a practical law will be sufficient to determine the content of the fundamental principle of morality (*Practical Reason*, 5: 19). In the *Groundwork* Kant adds a further philosophical premise, namely that a rational will must be determined not only by a universal law but also by a necessary end in order to reach the second formulation of the moral law, the requirement that humanity always be treated as an end and never merely as a means (4: 427–29). Kant presents this premise as part of the analysis of the concept of a rational agent—a rational agent does not act without an end in view, so if it is to act in accordance with a necessary law then it must have a necessary end in view—but this premise is also necessary to correct what would otherwise be a gaping hole in the analysis of duty in *Groundwork* I, namely, its assumption that the only possible ends of action are the contingent ends suggested by mere inclination.[28] Kant then combines these two results in the idea that what fills this role of an end in itself is precisely the legislative

---

[28] For a fuller account of this point, see my article "The Derivation of the Categorical Imperative: Kant's Correction for a Fatal Flaw," *Harvard Review of Philosophy* 10 (2002): 64–80.

capacity of rational beings to derive the formula of autonomy, that is, the requirement that every rational being regard himself and every other rational being as "giving universal law through all the maxims of his will." This in turn yields the imperative that the object of morality be a realm of ends, that is, a condition in which each rational being is regarded as an end in itself and for that very reason, namely that they have been freely chosen by ends in themselves, the particular ends set by each rational being are regarded as ends by all rational beings, to the extent that those ends are consistent with each other and with the treatment of the rational beings themselves as ends (4: 431–33).

Next, although Kant has now derived the principle of morality from philosophical concepts and premises rather than from any direct appeal to common sense, he amplifies his philosophical derivation by showing, twice, that the formulations of the categorical imperative give rise to examples of duties "in accordance with the usual division of them into duties to ourselves and to other human beings and into perfect and imperfect duties" (4: 421–22). Clearly this is meant to *illustrate* his principle for the common understanding, in accordance with his earlier statement "that the doctrine of morals is first **grounded** on metaphysics and afterwards, when it has been firmly established, is provided with **access** by means of popularity" (4: 409). I would suggest that it is also meant to *confirm* his philosophical analysis, by showing that philosophy and common sense lead to the same results. The philosophical conception of the fundamental principle of morality is not derived directly from common experience, which presents no conclusive examples of action in accordance with it, nor from common wisdom, which does not speak at such a level of generality, although common concepts of duty and common practices of moral judgment point the way to it. Only philosophy explicitly formulates the moral law. And subsequently common sense will also be shown to contain contradictions about morality that only philosophy can resolve. Yet although philosophy can reach its formulation of the principle of morality independently of common sense, it also seeks confirmation of the validity of its result in common sense. Moral philosophy does not resist skepticism simply by clarifying common sense, but its response to skepticism must ultimately be accessible to common sense.

The second stage of Kant's answer to skepticism about the existence of an a priori principle of morality, analogous to his location of the a priori forms of intuition and judgment in the faculties of sensibility and understanding, would seem to require its location in the faculty of pure reason and the proof of the existence of such a faculty. However, since the existence of such a faculty has already been amply demonstrated in theoretical philosophy, both positively in its identification as the source of our capacity for performing inference generally and negatively in its identification as the source of the dialectical inferences of metaphysics, it is not the existence of pure reason that needs to be established. Rather, what particularly needs to be done within practical philosophy, beyond simply characterizing the moral principle as an assertion of unconditioned universality that, at least for Kant, wears its origin in pure reason on its face, is to prove, first, that pure reason can have an effect on the will and, second, that in its postulation of the necessary conditions for morality "it is possible to think of an extension of pure reason for practical purposes without thereby also extending its cognition as speculative" (*Practical Reason*, 5: 134).

The former of these points is argued for in Section III of the *Groundwork* and the "deduction of the principles of pure practical reason" in the second *Critique* (*Practical Reason*, 5: 42–57). Although there is a tactical change in the direction of Kant's argument between these two texts,[29] in both cases Kant estab-

---

[29] In the *Groundwork*, Kant argues that we have a transcendentally free will and are therefore governed by the moral law as the law of reason, not just by laws of nature; in the *Critique of Practical Reason*, Kant argues that we are immediately conscious of our obligation under the moral law and can infer the transcendental freedom of our will only from our awareness of that obligation. See Dieter Henrich, "Kants Deduktion des Sittengesetzes," in *Denken im Schatten des Nihilismus*, ed. Alexander Schwan (Darmstadt, Germany: Wissenschaftliches Buchgesellschaft, 1975), 55–112, translated in Paul Guyer, ed., *Kant's Groundwork of the Metaphysics of Morals: Critical Essays* (Lanham, MD: Rowman and Littlefield, 1998), 303–41; and Karl Ameriks, "Kant's Deduction of Freedom and Morality," *Journal of the*

lishes the same kind of complex relationship between common sense and philosophy that he does elsewhere in his response to skepticism. That is, he does not look to common sense for an explicit assertion of the thesis that he wants to defend against skepticism, but rather argues philosophically that this thesis is presupposed by a capacity exercised in common life, which he assumes no skeptic will seriously challenge. In the *Groundwork*, he argues that "no subtle reflection" is necessary to hit upon the distinction between appearances and things in themselves in reflecting upon any experience of the external world, and then that this must yield "a distinction, although a crude one, between a **world of sense** and the **world of understanding**"; from there he argues to the further realization that the latter must have its laws as well as the former, and that while the former is governed by the laws of nature, the latter can only be governed by the law of reason, that is, pure reason must be effective on the will. In Kant's words, "the rightful claim to freedom of will made even by common human reason is based on the consciousness and the granted presupposition of the independence of reason from merely subjectively determining causes" (*Groundwork*, 4: 457).

After 1785, Kant must have written a new *Critique of Practical Reason* to replace *Groundwork* III at least in part because he came to be dissatisfied with this argument,[30] but his revisions do not fundamentally affect the epistemic character of his argument, which is, as I said, not a direct appeal to common sense but rather an inference from an alleged capacity of common sense to a philosophical analysis of its presuppositions: Kant uses the same general form of argumentation in the second *Critique* when he argues that consciousness of the obligatory force of the moral law is universal, that is, recognized by anyone, but that its ability to obligate us depends upon our capacity to

---

History of Philosophy 19 (1981): 53–79, revised as chapter 6 of his *Kant's Theory of Mind*, new ed. (Oxford: Clarendon Press, 2000), 189–233.

[30] I have diagnosed the problems with this argument in my *Kant's Groundwork for the Metaphysics of Morals: A Reader's Guide* (London: Continuum Books, 2007), chap. 6.

choose to comply with it regardless of our history and circumstances, that is, our absolute freedom of the will, even though
the latter is hardly something that would be asserted by common sense. And again, as in his defense of his initial formulation of the categorical imperative, Kant appeals to example to
confirm that common sense implicitly acknowledges in its
practice what it might not immediately assert in theoretical
form. Ask anyone, Kant says, whether he would necessarily vio-
late the moral law in order to save his own life, and you will
discover that "he must admit without hesitation that it would
be possible for him" to refrain from violating the law even at the
cost of his life. "He judges, therefore, that he can do something
because he is aware that he ought to do it" (*Practical Reason*, 5:
30). As in his arguments for the analogies of experience, for
example, Kant does not turn to common sense for the assertion
of theoretical propositions that the skeptic could easily attack,
but rather uncovers the philosophical presuppositions of everyday judgments which, at least in his view, no skeptic could
seriously question.

The second stage of Kant's response to the Humean form of
moral skepticism, that is, the proof that we have an efficacious
faculty of pure reason that is the origin of the universal and
necessary law of morality, obviously slides seamlessly into
Kant's response to the second form of moral skepticism, that
is, the Pyrrhonian skepticism and ensuing threat of corruption
that would follow from the natural dialectic of conflicting but
apparently reasonable opinions on matters indispensable for
morality; so I now turn to this "natural dialectic." As I noted
earlier, the *Groundwork* does not have a section titled "Dialectic," but it does make it plain that its Section III is meant to
resolve the "dialectic of reason . . . with respect to the will" (4:
455), and so is a dialectic in everything but name. This dialectic
is the one already stated in the third Antinomy of the first *Critique* between the antithesis that everything in nature is governed by natural necessity and the thesis that causality through
freedom must be possible even in nature, and also already resolved there by transcendental idealism, which allows us to see
that revised versions of these two reasonable but apparently

conflicting doctrines can both be entertained when we recognize that one and the same event can be both enmeshed in the network of natural necessity at the phenomenal level but yet also be a spontaneous act of freedom at the noumenal level. So the question to ask now is, what does the *Groundwork* add to the earlier treatment of this issue? In addition to the (remarkable) claim that any "reflective human being" (4: 451) must hit upon transcendental idealism and thus upon the solution to the antinomy, a claim that Kant did not make in the first *Critique*, the *Groundwork* chiefly provides a motivation for resolving the antinomy beyond the purely theoretical interest in avoiding contradiction and the theoretical skepticism that provokes. It makes clear that even though all scientific inquiry presupposes causal determinism, freedom is presupposed by the validity of the moral law (4: 455–56), and thus that we could not simply give up one side of the antinomy in favor of the other. And it makes clear what the danger of failing to find a way to hold on to the assertion of freedom would be, namely, that reason would then, "to the detriment of morals[,] search about in the world of sense for the supreme motive and a comprehensible but empirical interest" in all of our actions (4: 462). In other words, failure to solve the antinomy of freedom would lead not just to theoretical skepticism but also to the corruption of morals, because in that case we would convince ourselves that everything is a matter of natural necessity and that natural necessity can only lead to the pursuit of the satisfaction of particular inclinations that comprise individual happiness, so that we can and should seek to do nothing other than to satisfy such inclinations. The theoretical failure to resolve the antinomy of freedom would thus provide us with a colossal excuse for our practical failure to live up to the demands of morality.

This mention of happiness brings us to the dialectic of the *Critique of Practical Reason*. Although the "Analytic" of the second *Critique* is devoted to the problem of freedom of the will, which was addressed in the explicitly titled "Dialectic" of the first *Critique* and the not explicitly titled dialectic of *Groundwork* III, the section of this work that Kant explicitly titles its "Dialectic" concerns not freedom but the highest good, or the relation between virtue and happiness, and the postulates of God and immortality on which the possibility of the highest good is supposed to depend. Formally, this dialectic consists in the opposition between two views of the relation between virtue and happiness, one on which it is supposed to be analytic, the other on which it will be synthetic. The first is any view, such as that of the Stoics or Epicureans, on which the pursuit of virtue and the pursuit of happiness are supposed to be identical; the second would be a view on which the pursuit of virtue is distinct from the pursuit of happiness but in which the achievement of virtue is nevertheless supposed to bring happiness in its train. The first of these views is to be rejected as "**absolutely** impossible because . . . maxims that put the determining ground of the will in the desire for one's happiness are not moral at all," while the second is to be rejected "because any practical connection of causes and effects in the world . . . does not depend upon the moral dispositions of the will but upon knowledge of the laws of nature and the physical ability to use them for one's purposes; consequently no necessary connection of happiness with virtue in the world . . . can be expected from the most meticulous observance of moral laws" (*Practical Reason*, 5: 113). But a synthetic connection between virtue and happiness can be saved when we postulate the existence of God, a postulation made possible by transcendental idealism, and consider that the laws of morality and the laws of nature must have a common author (5: 125), which will in turn allow us to see that the connection between virtue and happiness that we might think could not be brought about by the exercise of our physical abilities if those are considered without respect to their divine origin may in fact be able to be brought about after all once we understand the origin of those powers and their place in nature.

There are numerous problems with this argument, beginning with the fact that Kant does not trouble to explain why the two propositions that are initially opposed necessarily result from unavoidable inferences of either reason or common sense—he leaves it up to us to figure out how we would arrive at just these two conflicting positions in attempting to see both virtue and happiness as complete and unconditioned. But leaving aside this problem as well as the details of Kant's argument for the postulates of pure practical reason,[31] we can think of the dialectic about the highest good as part of a larger and indeed more natural dialectic concerning the relation between virtue and happiness. This would be the opposition between the natural view that virtue has nothing to do with the pursuit of one's own happiness, because there is nothing morally praiseworthy about acting for the sake of one's own happiness, and the equally natural view that virtue must have something to do with human happiness, because otherwise it is hard to see why and how humans could be motivated to take any interest in virtue. Failure to resolve this natural dialectic would also lead to a corruption of morality, because it would either simply undermine our motivation to fulfill the demands of morality or lead us, in the very name of morality, to accept our own merely personal inclinations as the supreme and sufficient motive of morality. The dialectic can be resolved, however, by distinguishing between the *motive* and the *object* of morality, that is, between our reason for striving to fulfill the demands of morality and the state of affairs that we would bring about by fulfilling those demands. Once we have recognized this distinction, the pursuit of duty for its own sake can remain as the pure motive for morality while happiness can become the object of morality, as long, that is, as we further distinguish between our own individual happiness and the collective happiness of mankind, including but not limited to our own, and rigorously exclude our own happiness alone as a permissible object of morality but identify the collective happiness of mankind as the obligatory object of morality, the state of affairs that would be brought about under ideal conditions by the effort of all to achieve virtue. This, I suggest, is what is actually suggested by Kant's concept of the highest good.

[31] For some discussion of the latter, see "From a Practical Point of View: Kant's Conception of a Postulate of Pure Practical Reason," in my *Kant on Freedom, Law, and Happiness* (Cambridge: Cambridge University Press, 2000), chap. 10, 333–71.

Documenting this approach to the highest good would be the task of another paper, or book.[32] The point to be made here is simply that the doctrine of the highest good can be interpreted as a response to a natural dialectic between two views of the relation between virtue and happiness, and thus as a response to that form of moral skepticism that would be the inevitable response to such a dialectic. It also seems reasonable to interpret it as an anticipatory response to skepticism about Kant's own moral theory: no intelligent reader in the eighteenth century could have been anything but skeptical of a moral theory that seemed to make no place for happiness at all, so Kant would indeed have had to make a place for happiness to allay skepticism about his own theory. Can we say anything more than this by way of conclusions about Kant's approach to skepticism as a whole?

Conclusion

A number of different traits run through Kant's responses to the various forms of skepticism that he diagnoses. One key feature of his approach is to argue that the principles the skeptic attacks, whether in theory or in practice, may not be explicitly asserted by common sense but are presupposed by common practices that it would be very hard for any sane person to forego. Another characteristic of his approach is essentially to argue that the skeptic's doubts are ill formed, or are engendered only by an assumption, such as that space and time are things in themselves, which is itself baseless, so that the skeptic's doubts should ultimately be dismissed rather than refuted. The first of these tactics might be considered a move to raise the costs for the skeptic, one that makes his arguments for doubt more com-

---

[32] Kant's clearest exposition of his concept of the highest good is perhaps that in Section I of the 1793 essay "On the common saying: That may be correct in theory but it is of no use in practice." For further discussion, see my essay "Ends of Reason and Ends of Nature: The Place of Teleology in Kant's Ethics," in my *Kant's System of Nature and Freedom* (Oxford: Clarendon Press, 2005), chap. 8, 169–97.

plicated but not impossible. But Kant does not just establish linkages from less obvious to more obvious claims to knowledge, as the opening quotation from Karl Ameriks, for instance, might suggest. Rather, his antiskeptical strategy also includes demonstrating that all of the connected beliefs, for example, those of both common sense and abstract science, are grounded in fundamental faculties of the mind and their interaction. Thus the skeptic who would continue to doubt either first principles or assertions of the existence of objects based on this analysis of the mind must be prepared to attack Kant's analysis of the capacities of the mind itself. This is by no means impossible, but would certainly raise the bar for skeptical arguments to a philosophical level beyond common sense. Kant's second tactic, showing that the skeptic's questions are ill formed because when fully unpacked they turn out to depend on assumptions that are baseless or incoherent, is always a good method to use against skepticism. Yet since Kant's particular claims that the dialectic that engenders at least one form of theoretical skepticism is merely apparent depends on his controversial doctrine of transcendental idealism, we might judge the general strategy promising, but his own execution of it doomed. At the same time, we should also recognize that since Kant's conception of empirical knowledge depends upon a view of sensibility in which our knowledge of objects in space and time can always be indefinitely further refined or extended, there is no room in this conception for any illusion that particular empirical hypotheses and classifications can ever be completely immune from revision. To this extent, Kant's response to skepticism is free of the illusionism of Cartesianism, or at least of a traditional caricature of Cartesianism, and is instead committed to the view that we should live with at least a certain kind of skepticism, namely Lockean skepticism about the completability of science, rather than vainly attempting to refute it.[33] Indeed, per-

---

[33] For elaboration of this suggestion, see my "Transcendental Idealism and the Limits of Knowledge: Kant's Alternative to Locke's Physiology," in *Kant and the Early Moderns*, ed. Daniel Garber and Béatrice Longuenesse (Princeton University Press, forthcoming).

haps Kant's conviction that the indubitable first principles of natural science can never yield a completed system of particular scientific concepts and laws but that such a system must remain a regulative ideal of reason (as in the first *Critique*) or reflecting judgment (as in the third),[34] is analogous to his conviction (stressed in the *Groundwork*) that we must temper our unwavering certainty of the moral law with our uncertainty that there has ever been a single case of action performed wholly and solely from respect for this law (4: 407).

These few reflections are hardly meant to constitute an adequate assessment of Kant's response to skepticism. My purposes in this chapter have only been to show, contrary to some influential contemporary interpretations, that Kant is profoundly concerned with skepticism, only not predominantly Cartesian skepticism, but skepticism as he understands it, consisting primarily in Humean and Pyrrhonian skepticism, and that recognizing that both his theoretical and practical philosophies are structured around the task of responding to these two forms of skepticism as he understands it may be a useful way to analyze his method throughout philosophy.[35]

---

[34] See *Critique of the Power of Judgment*, Introduction §§IV and V; for some discussion, see my articles "Reason and Reflective Judgment: Kant on the Significance of Systematicity," *Noûs* 24 (1990): 17–44 and "Kant's Conception of Empirical Law," *Proceedings of the Aristotelian Society, Supplementary Volume LXIV* (1990): 221–42, both reprinted in *Kant's System of Nature and Freedom*.

[35] I would like to thank Faviola Rivera Castro and Plínio Junquiera Smith for their helpful comments on the version of this paper presented at the conference on skepticism organized by the Instituto de Investigaciones Filosóficas, UNAM, August 27–29, 2001.

2

CAUSATION

IN THE *Enquiry concerning Human Understanding*, Hume presents his discussion of causation under the section titles "Sceptical Doubts concerning the Operations of the Understanding" and "Sceptical Solution of these Doubts"; since the work was first published readers have naturally enough taken him to question the truth of our beliefs about causation. A problem about the rationality of induction is particularly prominent in Hume's discussion, the problem, namely, that although our particular beliefs about causal connections are evidently based not on any a priori reasoning from the concept of the cause to the concept of the effect, but on repeated prior experience of sequences of states of affairs (events), which leads us to expect the imminent experience of one member of such a sequence when we have a new experience of the other, this expectation apparently has no rational basis: if our expectation of a future repetition of what we have experienced in the past were to have a rational basis, it would have to be founded on the premise that the future will resemble the past, but this premise is not self-evidently true—its denial would not be a self-contradiction—nor can it itself be noncircularly induced from past experience (*Enquiry I*, Section 4, 30–31). So Hume's "Sceptical Doubts" about causation seem above all to be doubts about the rationality of induction.

As we have already seen, when Kant claimed that it was the recollection of Hume that first interrupted his dogmatic slumber (*Prolegomena*, Preface, 4: 260), he made it clear that it was Hume's doubts about causation that he had in mind: "Hume

started mainly from a single but important concept in metaphysics, namely, that of the connection of cause and effect . . .
and called upon reason, which pretends to have generated this
concept in her womb, to give him an account of by what right
she thinks: that something could be so constituted that, if it is
posited, something else necessarily must thereby be posited as
well" (*Prolegomena*, Preface, 4: 257).[1] "The question was not,"
Kant continued, "whether the concept of cause is right, useful,
and, with respect to all cognition of nature, indispensable, for
this Hume had never put in doubt; it was rather whether it is
thought through reason a priori, and in this way has an inner
truth independent of all experience" (4: 258). But it is not clear
that by these general remarks Kant meant to refer to Hume's
particular question about the rationality of induction, nor is
it clear that Kant ever explicitly addressed this question. So it
is natural for us to ask how Kant did understand Hume's
"Sceptical Doubts" and what questions about causation he did
mean to answer.

In the *Prolegomena*, Kant ascribes two different problems
about causation to Hume. In the Preface, from which I have
just been quoting, he suggests that Hume's problem is that we
cannot make an a priori inference from the concept of a cause
to the necessary occurrence of its supposed effect:

---

[1] There is a large literature on just how Hume aroused Kant from his dogmatic
slumbers. Lewis White Beck represented the traditional view that it was Hume's
doubts about causation that aroused Kant from his dogmatic slumber; see, for example, "A Prussian Hume and a Scottish Kant," in Beck, *Essays on Kant and Hume*
(New Haven, CT: Yale University Press, 1978), 111–29. Lothar Kreimendahl, by
contrast, has argued that Hume aroused Kant from his dogmatic slumber by getting
him to see that pure reason is liable to antinomies; see his *Kant—Der Durchbruch
von 1769* (Cologne: Jürgen Dinter, 1990), and the earlier Günter Gawlick and
Lothar Kreimendahl, *Hume in der deutschen Aufklärung: Umrisse einer Rezeptionsgeschichte* (Stuttgart: Fromann Holzboog, 1987). Manfred Kuehn attempted to mediate between these two positions by arguing that it was specifically an antinomy
about causation that Kant found in Hume—that everything must have a cause yet
that the world as a whole cannot have a cause—that aroused him from his dogmatic
slumber; see his "Kant's Conception of Hume's Problem," *Journal of the History of
Philosophy* 21 (1983): 175–93, where he also gives further references to literature
on this issue.

He indisputably proved that it is wholly impossible for reason to think such a connection *a priori* and from concepts, because this connection contains necessity; and it simply is not to be seen how it could be, that because something is, something else necessarily must also be, and therefore how the concept of such a connection could be introduced *a priori*. From this he concluded that reason completely and fully deceives herself with this concept, falsely taking it for her own child, when it is really nothing but a bastard of the imagination . . . impregnated by experience . . . (Preface, 4: 257–58)

This sounds like what is only the first stage of Hume's considerations in the *Enquiry*, where he denies that we can infer its effect from a single experience or idea of a putative cause, prior to his introduction of the problem about the rational basis for induction, which arises only once it has been established that any causal inference must be based on repeated rather than unique experience. This remark makes it sound as if Kant had just not read very far in Hume's *Enquiry*.

In the body of the *Prolegomena*, however, Kant tells a different story about the "Humean doubt" (§27, 4: 310). Here he says that Hume "rightly affirmed: that we in no way have insight through reason into the possibility of causality, i.e., the possibility of relating the existence of one thing to the existence of some other thing that would necessarily be posited through the first one," and then adds that Hume should have generalized this problem to the concept of "subsistence" and "the community of things as well" (4: 310) and thus argued that we cannot infer a priori from the concept of a thing why it should endure or interact with any other things. However, Kant argues, it does not follow from the fact that we cannot make such a priori inferences that our concepts of causation, subsistence, and community are bastards of the imagination, "falsely imputed and a mere illusion through which long habit deludes us." Instead, he claims, "I have sufficiently shown that they and the principles taken from them stand firm *a priori* prior to all experience, and have their undoubted objective correctness, though of course only with respect to experience" (4: 311). He goes on to state that although the restriction of the validity of these concepts and principles to experience means that "I therefore do not have the least concept of such a connection of things in themselves," the crucial question is not "how things in themselves but how the cognition of things in experience is determined with respect to said moments of judgments in general, i.e., how things as objects of experience can and should be subsumed under those concepts of the understanding" (§28, 4: 311). Hume's problem is then described as arising from a doomed attempt to gain insight "into the possibility of a thing in general as a cause," a problem "indeed because the concept of cause indicates a condition that in no way attaches to things, but only to experience" (§29, 4: 312). The solution to this problem is simply to recognize that the concept of causation and the other fundamental concepts of metaphysics are meant to hold only for experience and not things in general, that is, for appearances and not for things in themselves:

> The complete solution of the Humean problem, though coming out contrary to the surmise of the originator, thus restores to the pure concepts of the understanding their *a priori* origin, and to the universal laws of nature their validity as laws of the understanding, but in such a way that it restricts their use to experience only, because their possibility is founded solely in the relation of the understanding to experience: not, however, in such a way that they are derived from experience, but that experience is derived from them, a completely reversed type of connection that never occurred to **Hume**. (§30, 4: 313)

Kant's thesis that experience depends upon the concepts of the understanding rather than those concepts being derived from experience, which he develops at length in both the *Critique of Pure Reason* and the *Prolegomena*, is a fundamental alternative to Hume's approach to such concepts. But Kant's main thesis here, that Hume's doubt about causation arose because he assumed that our concept of causation should give insight into things in general or things in themselves, and that this doubt is groundless because we should never raise such pretensions for the concepts of our understanding in the first place, does not sound like anything said by Hume, to whom after all Kant's distinction between appearances and things in themselves was unknown. So now it seems as if Kant did not address what we take to be central to Hume's questions about causation, namely, the problem of induction, and that he instead addressed a problem that Hume did not even raise.

Should we infer from the comedy of errors described thus far that Hume and Kant were ships passing in the night, that Kant's vaunted attempt to answer Hume was doomed to failure from the outset? That would be premature. A full account of Hume's questions about our concept of and beliefs in causation and of Kant's own treatment of the concept and principle of causation as well as of the epistemic basis of our cognition of particular laws of nature will show that Kant certainly offered plausible alternatives to several key features of Hume's treatment of causation. Above all, Kant responded to Hume's claim that causal inferences have no basis in reason with a radically revised conception of the nature of judgment, concepts, and reason itself. Yet we will also see that Kant never directly responded to Hume's concern about the rationality of induction, and that if we are inclined to take Hume's problem about induction as a genuine "Sceptical Doubt" then we should not think that Kant has provided a satisfactory resolution of it.

Hume's Questions

We need to begin with an exposition of Hume's arguments about causation. It might seem natural to base our account on the *Enquiry concerning Human Understanding*, since, as we have seen, Kant owned a German translation of this work and can safely be presumed to have known it, whereas the whole of the *Treatise* was not translated into German until after Kant had already published the *Critique of Pure Reason*, and he is presumed not to have been familiar with its treatment of causation in Book I, Part III when "responding" to Hume.[2] But, even

---

[2] As Kuehn notes, "Hume's first *Enquiry* appeared in German as the second volume of the *Vermischte Schriften* in 1755," edited but apparently not translated by

if only serendipitously, Kant's central argument in the second "Analogy of Experience" most directly addresses a problem about causation that Hume explicitly raises in the *Treatise of Human Nature* and does not even mention in the *Enquiry*. For this reason, as well as for the obvious chronological reason that the *Treatise* preceded the *Enquiry*, I will first discuss Hume's treatment of causation in the *Treatise* and only then comment on his account in the *Enquiry*.

THE *TREATISE*

In the *Treatise*, Hume raises what appear to be three distinct questions about causation. (1) The first seems to be a question about the content of the *idea* of causation, or as we would no doubt say, about the *meaning* of this concept. Hume asserts that there are three relations that are not relations of ideas only, and that of these three causation is "the only one that can be trac'd beyond our senses, and informs us of existences and objects, which we do not see or feel" (*Treatise*, I.iii.2, 53); in a theory of

---

Johann Georg Sulzer (Kuehn, "Kant's Conception," 179). Kant owned this edition. A German translation of the *Treatise* did not appear until 1790–92, long after Kant had completed the *Critique of Pure Reason* and *Prolegomena* (Ibid., 179), although Kant is presumed to have known something of the *Treatise* much earlier through a translation of the final chapter of Book I that appeared in the *Königsberger Zeitung* in July, 1771, and through his (stormy) friendship with the translator, Johann Georg Hamann (Ibid., 185), as well as through James Beattie's *Essay on the Nature and Immutability of Truth* (1770), which was reviewed in the *Göttingische Anzeigen von gelehrten Sachen* in January, 1771, and translated into German in 1772 (Ibid., 184, and Robert Paul Wolff, "Kant's Debt to Hume via Beattie," *Journal of the History of Ideas* 21 [1960]: 117–23). However, Beattie's treatment of Hume on causation (Part I, Chapter II, Section 5) does not detail either any of Hume's questions about the rational basis for our idea of and beliefs in causation or Hume's alternative psychological explanation for this idea and these beliefs, and could not have allowed Kant to have discerned any differences between Hume's treatments of the issue of causation in the *Treatise* and the *Enquiry*. See Beattie, *Essays on the Nature and Immutability of Truth, On Poetry and Music*, etc. (Edinburgh: William Creech, 1776), 63–76. So I cannot accept Lewis White Beck's suggestion that the translation of Beattie can have added very much to the knowledge of Hume that Kant already had from the earlier translation of the *Enquiry*; see Beck, "A Prussian Hume and a Scottish Kant," 111–29, at 118–19.

"Knowledge and Probability," as Hume entitles Part III of Book I of the *Treatise*, the idea of the causation is thus the first thing that must be considered. "To begin regularly," as Hume states, "we must consider the *idea* of causation, and see from what origin it is deriv'd." This consideration will, of course, be based on the principle Hume has earlier introduced that every simple idea is a copy of an antecedent impression, and thus that in a complex idea, which is a combination of simple ideas, each of the latter must originate from a corresponding impression even if there has not been any antecedent experience of all those impressions in just that combination (*Treatise*, I.i.i, 2–9). Hume begins by maintaining that the idea of causation cannot be based on the impression of any particular quality of objects, because "which-ever of these qualities I pitch on, I find some object, that is not possest of it, and yet falls under the denomination of cause and effect." From this he infers that "The idea, then, of causation must be deriv'd from some *relation* among objects" (*Treatise*, I.iii.2, 53–54), a relation that could be instantiated by objects no matter how diverse their particular qualities may be. As Hume continues, however, it quickly becomes apparent that the idea of causation must be a complex idea consisting of ideas of several simple ideas of relations. Two are readily identified: "in the first place, whatever objects are consider'd as causes or effects are *contiguous*," or in close physical proximity; second, "PRIORITY of time in the cause before the effect" is "essential to causes and effects" (54). Hume does not explicitly say so, but presumably he takes it to be obvious that we have impressions of the relations of both spatial contiguity and temporal priority, so that the simple ideas of these relations have an obvious source. However, the relations of contiguity and succession are not sufficient criteria for the relation of causation, or a sufficient analysis of its concept, because "An object may be contiguous and prior to another, without being consider'd as its cause." For causation, there must be a "NECESSARY CONNEXION to be taken into consideration" as well as contiguity and succession. This in turn means that for us to have a satisfactory complex idea of causation we must be able to find an impression that is the source of the idea of necessary connection that it includes. However, Hume now says that even if he turns "the object on all sides," he cannot find among our impressions of the qualities and relations of any object one that can be the basis for our idea of necessary connection (55).

It might thus seem as if the attempt at an analysis of the concept of causation, that is, the search for impressions that can ground all the simple ideas combined in this complex idea, has thus ended in a skeptical impasse, an insuperable doubt about the very meaningfulness of this concept. However, Hume does not assert such a skeptical conclusion. He merely says that at this point we might do better "to leave the direct survey of this question concerning the nature of that *necessary connexion* . . . and endeavour to find some other questions, the examination of which will perhaps afford a hint, that may serve to clear up the present difficulty" (55). He then introduces two new questions that might serve this purpose, (2) the question of the basis for our belief in the general principle that every event has some cause, and (3) that about the basis for our particular causal beliefs, or inferences of particular effects from particular causes:

> *First,* for what reason we pronounce it *necessary,* that every thing whose existence has a beginning, shou'd also have a cause?
> *Secondly,* Why we conclude, that such particular causes must *necessarily* have such particular effects; and what is the nature of that *inference* we draw from the one to the other, and of the *belief* we repose in it? (55)

These are questions we should be able to answer in their own right, as well as questions the answers to which should also answer the pending question about the impression of necessary connection that we need to complete the explanation of the content of the idea of causation.

(2) However, the attempt to explain our belief in the "general maxim in philosophy, that *whatever begins to exist, must have a cause of existence*" runs into difficulty as quickly as did the attempt to find an impression as the source of our idea of necessary connection. Because the idea of what we consider a cause is logically distinct from the idea of its effect, there can be

"no contradiction or absurdity" in separating the idea of any effect from the idea of its supposed cause, and thus no demonstrative proof that every event must have a cause. With only a brief look at some arguments for the general maxim of causation offered by Thomas Hobbes, Samuel Clarke, and John Locke, Hume confidently asserts that "we shall find upon examination, that every demonstration, which has been produc'd for the necessity of a cause, is fallacious and sophistical" (*Treatise*, I.iii.3, 56–57). Again, however, Hume does not draw the skeptical conclusion that this general principle is either dubious or false. He says only that, "Since it is not from knowledge or any scientific reasoning, that we derive the opinion of the necessity of a cause to every new production, that opinion must necessarily arise from observation and experience." But instead of immediately explaining how "observation and experience" might ground this opinion, Hume says, "it will be more convenient to sink this question in the following, *Why we conclude, that such particular causes must necessarily have such particular effects, and why we form an inference from one to another?*" (58). To this point in his exposition, then, Hume has drawn no skeptical conclusions about causation, but only placed the burden of answering our questions about the bases for (1) our idea of necessary connection and (2) our belief in the universal principle of causation on (3) his forthcoming account of the basis for our particular causal inferences.

(3) This account occupies much of the remainder of Book I, Part III of the *Treatise*. Hume starts by claiming that "the inference we draw from cause to effect, is not deriv'd merely from a survey of these particular objects, and from such a penetration into their essences as may discover the dependence of the one upon the other." His basis for this claim is, as in his discussion of the general principle of causation, that the ideas of the purported cause and effect are distinct from each other, and thus there can be no "absolute contradiction and impossibility of conceiving" of the occurrence of one without that of the other (*Treatise*, I.iii.6, 61). In other words, particular inferences from cause to effect are not grounded in any purely deductive reasoning.

Again, however, this conclusion is not intended to cast any doubt on our practice of making particular causal inferences, but only to show that it must therefore be "by EXPERIENCE only, that we can infer the existence of one object from that of another." But what kind of experience? It cannot be merely a present experience of a purported cause that leads to the idea of its effect, let alone belief in the reality of the object of that idea, because as Hume has just asserted, the idea of the cause and that of the effect are logically distinct and therefore separable from each other. Instead, Hume claims, what makes us "pronounce any two objects to be cause and effect" in addition to their necessary but not sufficient relations of spatial contiguity and temporal succession is "their CONSTANT CONJUNCTION," or the fact that "We remember to have had frequent instances of the existence of one species of objects; and also remember that the individuals of another species of objects have always attended them, and have existed in a regular order of contiguity and succession with regard to them" (61). However, Hume is quick to point out, the repeated past conjunction of impressions of two species of objects or events cannot imply as a matter of "reason" that they must be conjoined in the future unless reason can "proceed upon the principle, *that instances, of which we have had no experience, must resemble those, of which we have had experience, and that the course of nature continues always uniformly the same.*" But here is where Hume raises his question about the rationality of induction: this premise, he argues, which is necessary to ground any particular inference from repeated past experience to future experience, cannot be grounded on any "*demonstrative* arguments," because "We can at least conceive a change in the course of nature" sufficient to prove that a change in any particular recurring pattern "is not absolutely impossible." Thus Hume concludes that "even after experience has inform'd us of [the] constant conjunction" of any particular causes and effects, "'tis impossible for us to satisfy ourselves by our reason, why we shou'd extend that experience beyond those particular instances, which have fallen under our observation" (62).

Once again, however, Hume does not draw a skeptical conclusion that our practice of induction is dubious or in any ordinary sense *unreasonable*; instead, he merely says that "When the mind, therefore, passes from the idea or impression of one object to the idea or belief of another, it is not determin'd by reason, but by certain principles, which associate together the ideas of these objects, and unite them in the imagination" (62), and then proceeds to offer his account of the principles of the imagination that do lead the mind to pass from the idea or impression of one object to the idea or belief of another when it has had past experience of their constant conjunction. This account is Hume's theory of belief. He argues first that a belief is nothing other than "A LIVELY IDEA RELATED TO OR ASSOCIATED WITH A PRESENT IMPRESSION" (*Treatise*, I.iii.7, 67) or "*a more vivid and intense conception of any idea*" (I.iii.10, 82), second that the liveliness or "force and vivacity" of an impression can be communicated to an idea associated with it, thus that we can come to believe in the reality of (the object of) an idea on the basis of the liveliness communicated to it by another impression (I.iii.8, 69), and finally that the effect of repeated past experience of a conjunction of certain species of objects or states of affairs is nothing other than to set up a disposition for a new impression of one instance of that sort of conjunction (typically, that of the cause) both to call up and to communicate its liveliness to an idea of the other conjunct (the effect) and thereby create a belief in the reality of that effect. "After a frequent repetition, I find, that upon the appearance of one of the objects, the mind is *determin'd* by custom to consider its usual attendant, and to consider it in a stronger light upon account of its relation to the first object" (I.iii.14, 105). Hume's answer to our question (3) then, is that this operation of the imagination or custom, and not any demonstrative inference of reason, is the basis of our practice of making particular causal inferences.

Whatever his readers have thought, in the *Treatise* Hume does not intend to cast any doubt on the reasonableness and value of this practice, but only to argue that it is grounded in the faculty of imagination rather than that of reason, understood specifically as our capacity for demonstrative inference.[3] Having in this way answered question (3), Hume now returns to question (1), lifting his original suspension of the search for the impression that is the basis for our idea of necessary connection and making good on his suggestion that "Perhaps 'twill appear in the end, that the necessary connexion depends on the inference, instead of the inference's depending on the necessary connexion" *(Treatise, I.iii.6, 62)*.[4] What he claims is that "'Tis this impression, then, or *determination*" of the mind "which affords me the idea of necessity" (I.iii.14, 105): that is, when I have repeatedly experienced instances of a certain type of pair of impressions, and now experience a new impression of one member of such a pair, I am not only aware of a lively idea of the other member and thus believe in its reality, but I am also actually aware of the forceful transition of my mind from the one impression to the other idea, and it is my impression of this transition itself which is the basis for my idea of necessary connection. As Hume puts it,

> Tho' the several resembling instances, which give rise to the idea of power, have no influence on each other, and can never produce any new quality *in the object*, which can be the model of that idea, yet the *observation* of this resemblance produces a new impression *in the mind*, which is its real model. . . . Necessity, then, is the effect of this observation, and is nothing but an internal impression of the mind, or a determination to carry our thoughts from one object to another. (I.iii.14, 111)

As Hume famously adds, "the mind has a great propensity to spread itself on external objects, and to conjoin with them any

---

[3] On the point of Hume's attitude toward particular causal inferences in the *Treatise*, I am obviously aligning myself with the long line of "naturalistic" interpreters of him, from Norman Kemp Smith, *The Philosophy of David Hume* (London: Macmillan, 1941) to Barry Stroud, *Hume* (London: Routledge and Kegan Paul, 1977), rather than with "skeptical" interpreters such as Robert J. Fogelin, *Hume's Skepticism in the Treatise of Human Nature* (London: Routledge and Kegan Paul, 1985), e.g., 46.

[4] On this point, see also Fogelin, *Hume's Skepticism*, 47–48.

internal impressions, which they occasion" (112); by means of this additional propensity of the mind, again a matter of imagination or custom, the idea of necessary connection that is based on an impression that is internal to the mind is added to our ideas of external objects, and thus an idea of necessary connection is formed that can stand alongside of the ideas of spatial contiguity and temporal succession in our complex idea of the relation of causation among objects. Hume's original question (1) is now answered, on the same basis as his question (3), in a way that shows that the idea of causation is grounded in a faculty of the mind other than demonstrative reason, but that also shows that we need have no skeptical doubt about this idea.

What about Hume's question (2), however, that is, the question about the basis for our belief in the general principle that every event or "beginning of existence" has some cause? Hume had originally argued that this belief has no basis in demonstrative reason, thus that this "opinion must necessarily arise from observation and experience" (*Treatise*, I.iii.3, 58), but had deferred giving the explanation of how it does so until he had addressed question (3) about the experiential basis for particular causal inferences. After having thus "sunk" question (2) into question (3), does Hume ever return to it? It can easily seem that he never does,[5] but a careful reading of the conclusion of his discussion "Of the idea of necessary connexion" will show not only that he does return to this question, but also that for the first time he here reaches a skeptical conclusion about causation. This happens in his discussion of the two definitions of causation, which Hume employs precisely in order to show that we have no basis whatever—neither demonstrative nor experiential—for our belief in the general maxim that every event has a cause. The passage is worth quoting in full:

[5] Thus, Beck, in "A Prussian Hume and a Scottish Kant," 121. Beck argues that Hume kept the principle "every event, some cause" on "dry land" to appeal to when recalcitrant experience threatens our commitment to particular laws formed on the basis of prior inductions. He appeals to Hume's case of the suddenly appearing porter who was not heard ascending the stairs to the chamber (Ibid., 122–23). I think it is questionable whether Hume must be relying on the general principle

We may now be able fully to overcome all that repugnance, which 'tis so natural for us to entertain against the foregoing reasoning, by which we endeavour'd to prove, that the necessity of a cause to every begining of existence is not founded on any arguments either demonstrative or intuitive. Such an opinion will not appear strange after the foregoing definitions. If we define a cause to be, *an object precedent and contiguous to another, and where all the objects resembling the former are plac'd in a like relation of priority and contiguity to those objects, that resemble the latter*, we may easily conceive, that there is no absolute nor metaphysical necessity, that every beginning of existence shou'd be attended with such an object. If we define a cause to be, *An object precedent and contiguous to another, and so united with it in the imagination, that the idea of the one determines the mind to form the idea of the other, and the impression of the one to form a more lively idea of the other*, we shall make still less difficulty of assenting to this opinion. Such an influence on the mind is in itself perfectly extraordinary and incomprehensible; nor can we be certain of its reality, but from experience and observation. (I.iii.14, 115–16)

Hume here enlarges his earlier brief against the general principle of causation, saying now that it is proven neither by demonstrative nor intuitive arguments,[6] but also suggesting no way in which "experience and observation" could confirm the general principle. For our particular causal beliefs are always based on repeated past experiences, and we obviously cannot have repeated past experiences of every sort of event we might ever encounter, or that we can imagine existing, thus we can have no basis for making a causal inference about every such event.

"every event, some cause" rather than simply well-entrenched prior particular inductions to explain our beliefs in such a case.

[6] The term "intuitive" is presumably being used in the Lockean sense, to connote an immediate inference based on direct comparison of two ideas, as contrasted to a longer inference that proceeds through a sequence of comparisons of ideas; see John Locke, *An Essay concerning Human Understanding*, ed. P. H. Nidditch (Oxford: Clarendon Press, 1975), Book IV, chap. ii, §§1–2.

The principles of the imagination suffice to explain the particular causal inferences that we do make, but not to produce belief in the general maxim that every event has a cause. Hume does not label this conclusion a skeptical one, but it would surely appear so to anyone convinced that we are justified in asserting this general maxim.

THE ENQUIRY

As noted previously, Kant read not Hume's *Treatise* but his *Enquiry concerning Human Understanding*, originally published a decade later than the *Treatise* but translated into German far earlier. Hume's discussion of causation in the later work differs from that in the earlier book in several respects, some of which help explain Kant's characterization of the "Humean problem" but others of which make Kant's responses to this "problem" puzzling.

(1) The *Enquiry* adopts the style of an essay rather than a treatise,[7] and Hume does not commence his presentation with the series of three questions he raised in the *Treatise*. Instead, after his initial reiteration of his view that ideas must always have their origin in impressions (Section 2) and his statement that the "relations of *Resemblance, Contiguity,* and *Causation*" are the basis for all associations of ideas (Section 3) (23), he proceeds immediately to argue that "All reasonings concerning matter of fact seem to be founded on the relation of *Cause* and *Effect*," but that "the knowledge of this relation" is not, in any instance, "attained by reasonings *a priori*; but arises entirely from experience, when we find, that any particular objects are constantly conjoined with each other" (Section 4, 25). In other words, as his language—"in any instance," "any particular ob-

---

[7] Indeed, in its first editions it was titled *Philosophical Essays concerning Human Understanding*, and Hume did not give it the title *An Enquiry concerning Human Understanding* until the 1758 edition of his *Essays and Treatises on Several Subjects*, thus until after the German translation edited by Sulzer in 1755. On the titles of the several editions of the *Enquiry*, see the edition by Beauchamp here cited, xlv–lvii.

jects"—makes clear, Hume begins by raising the question of the basis for our particular causal beliefs and inferences. He then argues, as in the *Treatise*, that because "every effect is a distinct event from its cause," there cannot be any a priori inference from the cause to the effect because there can be no contradiction in imagining that the one obtains without the other (Section 4, 27). However, in the *Enquiry* Hume writes as if our inability to discover causal connections by a priori "reasonings" also has something to do with the limited acuity of human observation or our inability to penetrate much beyond the superficial appearance of objects:

> [T]he utmost effort of human reason is, to reduce the principles, productive of natural phænomena, to a greater simplicity, and to resolve the many particular effects into a few general causes, by means of reasonings from analogy, experience, and observation. But as to the causes of these general causes, we should in vain attempt their discovery; nor shall we ever be able to satisfy ourselves, by any particular explication of them. These ultimate springs and principles are totally shut up from human curiosity and enquiry. . . . Thus the observation of human blindness and weakness is the result of all philosophy, and meets us, at every turn, in spite of our endeavours to elude or avoid it. (27–28)

There is no direct connection between the logical thesis that effects cannot be inferred a priori from the ideas of their causes because the ideas of cause and effect are distinct and the epistemological thesis that our knowledge of causal connection is limited by the fact that we cannot observe the most fundamental aspects of objects: even if we could observe causal connections at the level of the most fundamental aspects of objects, causes and effects would still be logically distinct and thus there could be no a priori inference from causes to their effects. Hume's Lockean invocation of the limited scope of human observation is a just a bit of rhetoric that does not add anything to the original argument of the *Treatise*.

It could be just such a passage, however, that led Kant to think that Hume's problem about causation arises from the attempt to gain causal knowledge about things in themselves rather than appearances. For Kant, there are no a priori limits on the acuity of our observations of appearances, because our natural senses can always be supplemented by both instrumentation and scientific theory.[8] Perhaps charitably thinking that Hume could not have been unaware of this obvious fact, Kant took him to have been making the subtler mistake of confusing appearances and things in themselves, thereby unnecessarily inferring limitations on our knowledge of causal connections among appearances from our genuine ignorance of things in themselves. This might explain why Kant thought that the distinction between appearances and things in themselves offers a resolution of Hume's problem, as he insisted in the *Prolegomena*. But as Hume's appeal to the "secret structure of parts" and "ultimate springs and principles" of objects seems to be merely a rhetorical addition to his original argument from the logical separability of the ideas of any cause and its effect to the impossibility of any a priori reasoning from one to the other, it is implausible that his insistence that causal inference must be based on experience rather than reason has anything to do with a confusion between appearances and things in themselves.

(2) Having argued that causal inferences must be based on experience of constant conjunction rather than a priori reasoning, Hume then proceeds to ask why "past *Experience* . . . should be extended to future times, and to other objects, which, for aught we know, may be only in appearance similar" (*Enquiry I*, Section 4, 30). The final reservation in this quotation might again suggest that Hume now thinks his problem has something to do with the limitation of our observation to more superficial aspects of objects, but here too this seems to be just a rhetorical flourish. Hume's main argument is that "the supposition that the future will be conformable to the past" (31) cannot be proven by "any demonstrative argument or abstract reasoning *a priori*" *or* by any appeal to experience, so that our

---

[8] I take this to be the implication of Kant's inclusion of magnetic fields inferred from patterns of iron filings within the scope of the empirical knowledge of appearances; see *Pure Reason*, A 226/B 273.

projection of previously observed regularities into the future must be a "propensity" of the mind or a "CUSTOM OR HABIT" that is not "impelled by any reasoning or process of the understanding" (Section 5, 37). Here Hume significantly amplifies the *Treatise*'s treatment of the premise that would be needed to make induction from past experience a matter of reason by arguing not only that this premise is not founded in demonstrative reasoning but also that any attempt to infer that the future must resemble the past from any amount of past experience alone would be circular:

> We have said, that all arguments concerning existence are founded on the relation of cause and effect; that our knowledge of that relation is derived entirely from experience; and that all our experimental conclusions proceed upon the supposition, that the future will be conformable to the past. To endeavour, therefore, the proof of this last supposition by probable arguments, or arguments regarding existence, must be evidently going in a circle, and taking that for granted, which is the very point in question. (31)

The central negative claim of Hume's discussion of causation in the *Enquiry* is the claim that the premise that would be needed to convert inferences from prior to future experience into valid syllogisms cannot be proven by demonstrative reasoning *or* induction from experience. This work thus seems to go further than does the *Treatise* in questioning the rationality of induction.

(3) However, Hume is no less satisfied with his psychological resolution of the problem of induction in the *Enquiry* than he was in the *Treatise*. Rather, having concluded that induction is not an operation of the understanding, that is, demonstrative reason, Hume proceeds to restate his explanation of our "custom or habit" of causal inference in terms largely unchanged from the *Treatise*: he explains that "belief is nothing but a more vivid, lively, forcible, firm, steady conception of an object, than what the imagination alone is ever able to attain" (*Enquiry I*, Section 5, 40–41), and asserts that belief so understood is simply "the necessary result of placing the mind in . . . circumstances"

in which it has experienced the constant conjunction of "any two kinds of objects" (39); and then he reiterates the *Treatise*'s account of the impression that is the basis of the idea of necessary connection as the feeling of the "customary transition in the mind from one object to its usual attendant" (Section 7, 59), although this time after a fuller canvas and elimination of alternative accounts than he had earlier provided (49–57). "All these operations" of the mind, he says, "are a species of natural instincts, which no reasoning or process of the thought and understanding is able, either to produce, or to prevent" (Section 5, 39).

Although Hume's accounts of the basis of our particular causal inferences and of our idea of necessary connection in the *Enquiry* thus do not differ substantively from those in the *Treatise*, there are nevertheless several striking features of the later exposition of the theory. First, although Hume *titles* the sections (4 and 5) in which he argues that causal reasoning is not demonstrative and then explains how it is instead based in custom or habit "Sceptical Doubts concerning the Operations of the Understanding" and "Sceptical Solution of these Doubts" respectively, there is *no* skepticism about the truth of particular causal beliefs in the *contents* of these sections. Hume simply replaces one account of the nature of causal inference with another account that he apparently does not find inadequate in any way. He certainly does not argue that we should *suspend* our belief in causality, as a genuine skeptic might; on the contrary, as we have just seen, he claims that "no reasoning or process of the thought and understanding" is capable of preventing the operation of our natural instinct to form causal beliefs.

This position is only reinforced in the final section of the *Enquiry*, "Of the Academical or Sceptical Philosophy." Here Hume immediately rejects as "extravagant" all "antecedent" attempts "to destroy *reason* by argument and ratiocination" (*Enquiry I*, Section 12, 116), for the obvious reason that any attempt to undermine the reliability of reason by ratiocination would presuppose the reliability of reason, and therefore be incoherent. However, he seems to allow that skepticism about claims to knowledge based on more concrete peculiarities of our cognitive condition might be coherent. Thus he says that the skeptic

> *seems* to have ample matter of triumph; while he justly insists, that all our evidence for any matter of fact, which lies beyond the testimony of sense or memory, is derived entirely from the relation of cause and effect; . . . and that nothing leads us to this inference but custom or a certain instinct of our nature; which it is indeed difficult to resist, but which, like other instincts, may be fallacious or deceitful. While the sceptic insists upon these topics, he shows his force, or rather, indeed, his own and our weakness; and *seems, for the time at least*, to destroy all assurance and conviction. (119, emphasis added)

But Hume immediately adds that "Nature is always too strong" for such skepticism, that the skeptic must confess "that all his objections are mere amusement, and can have no other tendency than to show the whimsical condition of mankind, who must act and reason and believe." This is a restatement of his earlier thesis that ratiocination is incapable of either producing or preventing our practice of causal inference. Thus Hume dismisses the possibility of any enduring skepticism about causal belief. He does add that a "mitigated" form of skepticism, which, "avoiding all distant and high enquiries, confines itself to common life, and to such subjects as fall under daily practice and experience," is a "salutary" attitude of mind; but this is merely to reiterate the Lockean "limitation of our enquiries to such subjects as are best adapted to the narrow capacity of human understanding" (120–21),[9] not to assert that we have any ground for doubt about the existence of causation within the sphere of subjects that are adapted to our capacity for understanding.

(4) In the *Treatise*, as we saw, Hume also gave no hint that he regarded his psychological explanations of our practice of causal inference and our idea of necessary connection as giving any ground for doubting the veracity of our causal beliefs, but

---

[9] See, for example, Locke, *Essay concerning Human Understanding*, Book I, chap. i, §4.

he did conclude that experience can give no more ground for belief in the general principle that every event has some cause than does reason. This did seem like a skeptical conclusion in spite of the fact that in that work Hume did not there label his account of causation "sceptical." In the *Enquiry*, as we have just seen, Hume does label his treatment of our belief in causation "sceptical," but he actually dismisses skepticism about particular causal belief, at least in any domain of objects that we can actually experience. How does he avoid his earlier skepticism about the general principle of causation? *Simply by not mentioning it*: in the *Enquiry*, Hume does not raise the question about the general principle of causation prior to asking for the basis of our particular causal beliefs, he does not propose to sink the former question into the latter, and therefore he has no need to conclude that his explanation of our particular causal beliefs is inadequate to explain our belief in the general principle of causation. Even when Hume comes in Section 11 to foreshadow the doubts about arguments from analogy for the existence of God, "Of a Particular Providence and of a Future State," which he would develop more fully in the *Dialogues concerning Natural Religion*, he never mentions and therefore does not, at least explicitly, raise a doubt about the principle that every object or event must have some cause; he only says that cause must always be in "just proportion" to their effects, thus that we can never "mount up from the universe, the effect, to JUPITER, the cause, and then descend downwards, to infer any new effect from the cause" (*Enquiry I*, Section 11, 103).

(5) So the text of the *Enquiry*, as contrasted to its section titles, raises no skeptical doubts about particular causal beliefs, and it avoids raising any skeptical doubts about the general principle that every effect has some cause by the simple expedient of not mentioning this principle. Indeed, so far is Hume from being a skeptic about causation in the *Enquiry* that he even allows himself to conclude his supposedly "Sceptical resolution" of his doubts about causation with the suggestion, unparalleled in the *Treatise*, that we can safely assume a "pre-established harmony" between the mechanisms of the mind that

produce our causal beliefs on the basis of prior experience and the course of the world beyond our mind:

> Here, then, is a kind of pre-established harmony between the course of nature and the succession of our ideas; and though the powers and forces, by which the former is governed, be wholly unknown to us; yet our thoughts and conceptions have still, we find, gone on in the same train with the other works of nature. Custom is that principle, by which this correspondence has been effected; so necessary to the subsistence of our species, and the regulation of our conduct, in every circumstance and occurrence of human life. (*Enquiry I*, Section 5, 44)[10]

No doubt Hume's use of the expression "pre-established harmony" is aimed at Leibniz's view that God is necessary to ensure correspondence between any monad's internal representation of the course of the universe and the actual course of the universe (constituted in some way by all the rest of the monads); Hume's view is that the disposition of the human mind to correspond to the external circumstances and occurrences of human life needs no further, especially no theological, explanation.[11] But a true skeptic would not allow himself to assume a preestablished harmony even merely between the mechanisms that generate our beliefs and the objects of those beliefs. The Hume of the *Enquiry* whom Kant is supposed to have known is even less of a skeptic about causation than is the Hume of

---

[10] Juliet Floyd assumes that this passage is "tongue-in-cheek"; see "The Fact of Judgment," in *From Kant to Davidson: Philosophy and the Idea of the Transcendental*, ed. Jeff Malpas (London: Routledge, 2003), 22–47, at 25. But unless there is independent evidence of Hume's skepticism about particular causal beliefs in the *Enquiry* or elsewhere in Hume, one has no reason to assume that this passage is meant to be ironic—and as I have argued, the *Treatise* is not skeptical about such beliefs, and the *Enquiry* does not manifest any skepticism in its contents, as contrasted to its section titles.

[11] Hume explicitly refers to the "celebrated *Monsieur Leibnitz*" in his anonymous *Abstract* of the *Treatise of Human Nature*, although in support of Leibniz's view that previous systems of logic have not adequately dealt with probability rather than in reference to Leibniz's doctrine of preestablished harmony; see *Treatise*, 408.

the *Treatise*, whom Kant is not supposed to have known, but who did raise a skeptical doubt about the general principle that every event has some cause.

Skeptics were not the only philosophers who raised Kant's ire; dogmatic believers in preestablished harmony in any form actually stood lower in his esteem than skeptics. Maybe Hume really aroused Kant from his own dogmatic slumber by this casual hint of dogmatism, that is, by an easy assumption of good fit between our own faculties and the world around us, rather than by any clear commitment to skepticism. Such a conjecture, as we will now see, would be compatible with much of what Kant explicitly says about Hume's problem in the first *Critique* and the *Prolegomena*.

Kant's Answers?

In this section, I will make three points about Kant's response to the problems about causation that he takes Hume to have raised. First, although Hume was satisfied with his psychological explanation of the origin of our idea of necessary connection in the feeling of the mind's transition from one idea to another, Kant was not satisfied with a restriction of the resources for the explanation of the idea of causation to the realm of impressions; instead, in his theory of the pure concepts of the understanding and their schematism he appealed to both logic as expressing the pure form of thought and space and time as the pure forms of intuition in order to provide the foundations for an a priori concept of causation. But he never suggests that this a priori concept of causation by itself provides a priori knowledge of particular causal laws, and to this extent he does not controvert Hume's argument that our particular causal inferences are not made on the basis of "*a priori* reasonings," whether from the ideas of particular causes or from the idea of necessary connection. Second, even though Hume raised a skeptical doubt about the general principle that every event has some cause only in the *Treatise*, of which Kant had very limited knowledge, and not in the *Enquiry*, which he clearly knew well, Kant neverthe-

less took Hume to have raised such a problem and attempted
to answer it in the second "Analogy of Experience" by demonstrating that "the principle of sufficient reason is the ground of
possible experience" and is thus valid if not for all objects without qualification then at least for all objects that we can experience. Moreover, he tried to do this by showing precisely that
the general principle of causation is the ground of the possibility
of something that Hume, at least in Kant's view, must have
taken for granted, "namely the objective cognition of appearances with regard to their relation in the successive series of
time" (*Pure Reason*, A 201/B 246). But while Kant's argument
for the general principle of causation works by demonstrating
that our cognition of particular sequences of objective states of
affairs in the successive series of time depends upon our knowledge of the determination of those sequences by particular
causal laws, and thus that we must presuppose the availability
of some particular causal law applying to any event that we can
experience, hence that every experienceable event has some
cause, he does not explain our knowledge of particular causal
laws any more in the "Second Analogy" than he did in the
"Transcendental Deduction" or the "Schematism." So Kant's argument in the "Second Analogy" provides an answer to the
problem that Hume does not raise in the *Enquiry*, the problem
of the general principle of causation, only by presupposing but
not providing an answer to the question that Hume does raise
in the *Enquiry*, but which Kant clearly believed he had inade-
quately answered, namely, the question of our cognition of particular causal inferences. Finally, Kant does attempt to provide
an account of our knowledge of particular causal laws in the
extended theory of reason and judgment that he subsequently
develops, not in the "Transcendental Analytic" of the *Critique
of Pure Reason* or in the *Prolegomena to Any Future Metaphysics*
but only in the Introduction to the *Critique of the Power of Judgment* (perhaps preceded by the Appendix to the "Transcendental
Dialectic" of the first *Critique*)—but even there he never explicitly formulates, let alone answers Hume's specific question about
the basis for the premise that the future must resemble the past
on which, according to Hume, any strictly rational justification

of the practice of inductions must rest. So Kant never really answers the question about induction that the *Enquiry* suggests is the most fundamental of Hume's problems about causation, even if it did not lead Hume to skepticism. Thus, Kant does not have a complete answer to the "Humean skepticism" that Hume did not think was unmitigatedly skeptical.

THE "TRANSCENDENTAL DEDUCTION" AND "SCHEMATISM"

Kant's answer to Hume's question about the origin of our idea of necessary connection is part of his larger theory of the a priori concepts of the understanding and the synthetic a priori principles that they yield by means of their schematism. Kant makes this clear in the Preface to the *Prolegomena* when he writes that "I tried first whether **Hume's** objection might not be presented in a general manner, and I soon found that the concept of the connection of cause and effect is far from being the only concept through which the understanding thinks connections of things *a priori*; rather, metaphysics consists wholly of such concepts"; and it is precisely because the concept of cause and effect is only one of a number of concepts that must be shown to be a priori yet objectively valid that "the **elaboration** of" Kant's answer to "the Humean problem in its greatest possible amplification" is nothing less than the entirety of the constructive theory of the *Critique of Pure Reason* (*Prolegomena*, 4: 260, 261).

Kant concludes the second-edition version of the "Transcendental Deduction of the Pure Concepts of the Understanding" with a swipe at believers in preestablished harmony, or as he calls it there "a kind of **preformation-system** of pure reason" (*Pure Reason*, B 167); and although Kant does not mention Hume there, since, as we have just seen, Hume explicitly appealed to the idea of a preestablished harmony between the mechanisms of custom and imagination on the one hand and the course of nature on the other in order to express his complete confidence in causal beliefs generated from experience, Kant could just as well have had that passage from the *Enquiry* as anything in Leibniz in mind—after all, Leibniz is not men-

tioned by name in this passage either—in suggesting that the
"Transcendental Deduction" solves a problem that the theory
of pre-established harmony does not. And what problem would
that be? The problem

> that in such a case the categories would lack the **necessity**
> that is essential to their concept. For, e.g., the concept of
> cause, which asserts the necessity of a consequent under a
> presupposed condition, would be false if it rested only on a
> subjective necessity, arbitrarily implanted in us, of combining
> certain empirical representations according to such a rule of
> relation. I would not be able to say that the effect is combined
> with the cause in the object (i.e., necessarily), but only that I
> am so constituted that I cannot think of this representation
> otherwise than as so connected; which is precisely what the
> skeptic wishes most . . . (B 167–68)

This sounds more like a criticism of Hume than a criticism of
Leibniz—the criticism that a preformation system of pure reason, at least when pure reason is interpreted, on Humean lines,
as nothing but certain typical operations of the imagination,
leaves the correspondence between our causal way of conceiving
of nature and the course of nature itself contingent rather
than necessary.

And this is precisely the problem that Kant highlighted in
the introduction to the second-edition version of the "Transcendental Deduction" as well. The paragraphs that Kant added
just before completely rewriting the core of the deduction contain the following: in order to be able "to make attempts at
cognitions that go far beyond the boundary of all experience,"
Hume recognized,

> it is necessary that these concepts would have to have their
> origin *a priori*. But since he could not explain at all how it is
> possible for the understanding to think of concepts that in
> themselves are not combined in the understanding as still
> necessarily combined in the object, and it never occured to
> him that perhaps the understanding itself, by means of these
> concepts, could be the originator of that experience in which

its objects are encountered, he thus, driven by necessity, derived them from experience (namely from a subjective necessity arisen from frequent association in experience, which is
subsequently falsely held to be objective, i.e., **custom**. . . . The
empirical derivation, however, . . . cannot be reconciled with
the scientific cognition *a priori* that we possess . . . (B 127–28)

In this passage, Kant makes it clear that he thinks Hume's explanation of our concept of necessary connection fails to justify
the necessity of our use of that concept in "scientific cognition,"
and that the deduction of the pure concepts of the understanding on which he is about to embark will be both necessary and
sufficient to remedy that deficiency.

There are really two issues raised by these passages at the
beginning and the end of Kant's "Transcendental Deduction."
For one, Kant clearly thinks that Hume's explanation of the
origin of our idea of necessary connection from our impression
of the customary transition of the mind from one species of
idea to another rests on an inadequate inventory of our mental
capacities, and has to be remedied with the vastly richer account
of the resources of the mind that he begins to provide in the
"Deduction." But he also suggests that Hume's account suffers
from an an inadequate conception of the relation between the
mind and the objects of experience: if Hume thinks that the
relation between our idea of necessary connection and necessary
connections in nature itself is merely a matter of preestablished
harmony, and therefore, in Kant's eyes, inevitably contingent,
that must be because he thinks of the objects of experience as
entirely independent of experience and its subjective sources.
That must be the real reason, after all, why Kant claims, as he
does in the *Prolegomena*, that the "Humean problem" arises
from failing to distinguish appearances from things in themselves, and that the answer to it therefore lies in transcendental
idealism, which rethinks this relationship.

So there are two parts to Kant's answer to Hume's worries
about the idea of necessary connection. First, Kant shares
Hume's strategy of finding the basis of our ideas in the structure
of our own experience, but he has a far richer conception of the

sources of that structure than does Hume. Second, while Hume is ultimately content to assume a preestablished harmony between the structure of our own thought and the course of nature in order to explain our success in causal inference, Kant thinks that we must be able to assert a necessary connection between thought and nature, and that only his own theory of transcendental idealism can allow us to do this. I comment on these two points in turn.

(1) Hume's problem about the complex idea of causation, as we saw, is that although we can readily explain the origin of the simple ideas of spatial contiguity and temporal succession in our impressions of those relations, we cannot find an impression in our experience of objects to serve as the basis for the idea of necessary connection that is also crucial for our idea of causation, but must instead turn inward to our impression of the mind's forcible transition from its idea of the cause to its idea of the effect—an explanation with which, as we also saw, Hume was quite satisfied. From Kant's point of view, however, it must have seemed as if in this analysis Hume had confined himself to the resources of our a priori forms of intuition, without availing himself of the resources of the a priori functions of judgment and the principles that result from the schematism of those functions of judgment onto our forms of intuition. That is, for Kant the ideas of spatial contiguity and temporal succession could certainly be derived from the most basic structures of space and time as pure forms of intuition, and Hume would have been relying on the availability of these forms of intuition in helping himself to these two ideas, although without realizing that he was relying on a priori rather than merely empirical forms of intuition; but the idea of necessary connection would have its basis in our pure forms of thought, not our pure forms of intuition, and Hume would have to have been overlooking the pure forms of thought and their schematism in order even to have found an initial problem about the idea of necessary connection. Specifically, in Kant's eyes Hume failed to recognize that the idea of ground and consequence, as a logical function or structure of judgment, comes from the pure forms of thought, not from any intuition, whether empirical or pure, and

that the idea of causation, as "the succession of the manifold insofar as it is subject to a rule" (*Pure Reason*, A 14/B 183), is the result of the interpretation of the logical idea of ground and consequence into the spatiotemporal terms it must have in order to be applicable to our experience with its necessarily spatiotemporal structure (that is, the schematism of this concept).

The logical functions of judgment include far more than the idea of the relation of ground to consequence; they provide the basis for the general theory of a priori concepts of objects that Kant thought would be the complete answer to the generalization of the problem about necessary connection that Hume should have undertaken. For Kant, every judgment has a quantity—it is either universal, particular, or singular; a quality—it is either affirmative, negative, or infinite; a relation—it is either an atomic, categorical judgment, predicating an accident of a subject, or a hypothetical or disjunctive judgment, linking two categorical judgments, in the first case as ground and consequence, in the second, as alternatives;[12] and, finally, a modality— it is either problematic, that is possibly true, assertoric, that is, actually true, or apodictic, that is, necessarily true (*Pure Reason*, A 70/B 95). But if we are to be able to make judgments with these structural features about the *objects* of our experience, then the general forms of our *concepts* of those objects must reflect these functions of judgments in order to make those objects suitable objects of judgment. Thus our concepts must represent the objects of our experience as unities, pluralities, and totalities; they must ascribe to them the qualities of reality, negation, and limitation; they must ascribe to them the relations of inherence and subsistence, causality and dependence, and community or reciprocity; and they must also ascribe to them the modal properties of possibility or impossibility, existence or nonexistence,

---

[12] This is a simplification: once hypothetical or disjunctive judgments have been compounded out of categorical judgments, further hypothetical or disjunctive judgments could be formed out of such first-order hypothetical or disjunctive judgments. And Kant omits any mention of conjunctive judgments, although this perhaps is no grave omission, since conjunction can be defined by the use of disjunction and negation (or vice versa).

and necessity or contingency (A 80/B 106). In particular, Kant claims, in order to employ (all) the relational functions of judgment we must conceive of the *objects* of our experience as substances with accidents that can stand in relations of causality or community with one another—thus, for Kant the category of substance is certainly as indispensably rooted in the logic of judgments as is the category of causality, and had he known of the problem about the concept of substance that Hume raises in Book I, Part IV of the *Treatise* but omits from the *Enquiry*, he could certainly have argued that his theory of the logical functions of judgment and the categories that correspond to them would explain the origin of this concept as well.[13]

Here I will not question Kant's assumption that we do have a priori knowledge of the logic of judgment and through that of the basic concepts of ontology. But two problems specific to his treatment of the idea of causation within this general framework should be noted. First, while Kant directly associates the relational category of causality and dependence with the logical function of the hypothetical judgment, that is, compound judgments of the "if *p* then *q*" form, this seems a mistake: there are a variety of kinds of judgments that can be linked as ground and consequence in hypothetical judgments, thus a variety of kinds of properties that can support such judgments, not all of which properties and therefore not all of which judg-

---

[13] Kant says that Hume *should* have generalized his problem about causation, and then he would inevitably have seen how his problem had to be answered; in fact, what Kant did not realize is that Hume *had* to some extent generalized his problem in the *Treatise*, in his dilemma about the idea of enduring objects, but still had not seen that the answer to his problems lay in the functions of judgment. Yet, even if we accept the general outlines of Kant's argument that we must conceive of objects in certain ways if we are to be able to make judgments about them by means of the functions of judgment available to us, we can still ask why we should need to use *all* of these functions of judgment and thus use *all* the categories of objects that allow us to apply these functions of judgment to them. For discussion of this question, see my essay "Space, Time, and the Categories: Kant's Project in the Transcendental Deduction," in *Idealismus als Theorie der Repräsentation?* ed. Ralph Schumacher (Paderborn, Germany: Mentis, 2001), 313–38. The form of Kant's answer to the generalization of Hume's problem will be discussed further in the next chapter.

ments are causal. For although causal judgments (on both Hume's and Kant's analyses) concern relations of states of affairs that are both spatially contiguous and temporally successive, some hypothetical judgments express relations between states of affairs or properties that are not both spatial and temporal. For example, there are hypothetical judgments in geometry that express relations of ground and consequence between objects that are spatial but not temporal, such as "If a figure is a triangle then the sum of its interior angles equals two right angles" or "If a figure is a circle then its circumference is its diameter times π." These are not causal judgments. We can also at least formulate hypothetical judgments concerning objects that are neither spatial nor temporal, such as "If two is added to two then the sum is four,"[14] and these too are not causal judgments. So Kant should have said that the category that corresponds to the hypothetical form of judgment is the category of *ground and consequence*, and then argued that the relation of causality and dependence is *one form* of the relation of ground and consequence, that which obtains between states of affairs that are spatially contiguous and temporally successive. However, this is not a serious problem for Kant; after all, in order to answer Hume, he has no need to prove that all relations of ground and consequence are causal relations, but needs to prove only that from the logical idea of ground and consequence we can derive the idea of causation, as succession in accordance with a rule, by schematizing the logical idea, that is, applying it to the idea of states of affairs that are both spatially contiguous and temporally successive. Kant's fundamental point, after all, is only that the conjunction of the pure forms of intuition and the pure forms of thought offer sufficient resources for a complete idea of causation, so that we do not need to resort to subjective impressions associated with our experience of causation, as Hume does, in order to find the impression of necessary

---

[14] Here I am ignoring Kant's assumptions that *we* can individuate objects only in space and/or time and that addition is itself a temporal process, and helping myself to an entirely difference conception of number and addition, such as a Fregean or set-theoretic one.

connection that we cannot find in our external experience of objects. To make this point Kant does not need to argue that logic requires us to think of every relation of ground and conse- quence as a relation of cause and effect.

The second point to be noted here is that Kant includes ne- cessity and contingency as the categories of modality that corre- spond to the logical status of apodictic judgments, and thus it might seem as if it is to these modal categories rather than to the schematism of the relational category of ground and conse- quence that he should have turned for his answer to Hume's problem about the origin of the idea of necessary connection. If he were to have done so, however, then it might also seem as if his answer to Hume is just question-begging, that is, as if he simply includes in his list of categories the idea of necessity that Hume questioned. But this is not a real problem, for Kant subsequently makes clear that the application of the category of necessity to the objects of our experience often depends on the application of the category of causality, rather than vice versa. In the "Schematism," obviously thinking about the idea of a necessary being, Kant says that "The schema of necessity is the existence of an object at all times" (*Pure Reason*, A 145/B 184); but in the chapter on "The postulates of empirical thinking in general," Kant says that, "That whose connection with the actual is determined in accordance with general conditions of experience is (exists) **necessarily**" (A 218/B 266), and then makes clear in his elucidation that as far as "material necessity in existence" is concerned, "the necessity of existence can . . . never be cognized from concepts but rather always only from the connection with that which is perceived, in accordance with general laws of experience"—but "there is no existence that could be cognized as necessary under the condition of given appearances except the existence of effects from given causes in accordance with the laws of causality" (A 227/B 280). In other words, our basis for applying the concept of necessity to the existence of a state of affairs is precisely that we take it to be connected to another in accordance with a law, that is, caused by it. The a priori concept of causality, used to formulate particular causal laws that can connect particular states of affairs in space and time with one another, is thus the basis for the application of the a priori concept of necessary existence, not vice versa. Here Kant's thought parallels Hume's suggestion that "the necessary connexion depends on the inference, instead of the inference's depending on the necessary connexion" (*Treatise*, I.iii.6, 62), although his idea is not that the *idea* of necessary connection arises from the observation of constant conjunctions, but rather that the *use* of the category of necessity depends upon the use of the category of cause and effect.

While thus arguing that the a priori concept of causation is derived from the schematism of the pure concepts of the understanding and is in turn the basis for the application of the pure concept of necessity, however, Kant never argues that particular causal laws are known a priori. If the application of the pure concept of necessity is dependent upon the subsumption of appearances under particular causal laws, obviously those causal laws cannot themselves be derived in any way from the mere concept of necessity. But more generally, Kant makes clear that the necessary subsumption of all of our experience to the whole system of the pure concepts of the understanding does not by itself yield cognition of particular laws of nature. Thus in each of the two editions of the *Critique*, he concludes the "Transcendental Deduction," which is supposed to show that the very possibility of the transcendental unity of apperception, or the recognition that all of one's experiences as such constitute the experiences of a numerically identical self, presupposes and therefore entails the subsumption of those experiences under the categories, with the express statement that the categories do not by themselves yield particular causal laws. In the first edition he writes:

> Thus as exaggerated and contradictory as it may sound to say that the understanding is itself the source of the laws of nature . . . such an assertion is nevertheless correct. . . . To be sure, empirical laws, as such, can by no means derive their origin from the pure understanding, just as the immeasurable manifoldness of the appearances cannot be adequately conceived through the pure form of sensible intuition. But all

empirical laws are only particular determinations of the pure
laws of the understanding, under which and in accordance
with whose norm they are first possible . . . (*Pure Reason*, A
127–28)

By saying that empirical (causal) laws are "particular determinations of the pure laws of the understanding" Kant means precisely that such particular laws cannot be derived from the general concepts or principles of the understanding because the
former must make the latter more determinate, that is, add information to them. Similarly, Kant concludes the second-edition version of the deduction by stating that

. . . all possible perceptions, hence everything that can ever
reach empirical consciousness, i.e., all appearances of nature,
as far as their combination is concerned, stand under the categories, on which nature (considered merely as nature in general) depends, as the original ground of its necessary lawfulness. . . . The pure faculty of understanding does not
suffice, however, to prescribe to the appearances through
mere categories *a priori* laws beyond those on which rests a
nature in general, as lawfulness of appearances in space and
time. Particular laws, because they concern empirically determined appearances, **cannot** be **completely derived** from the
categories, although they all stand under them. (B 165)

Here Kant states that the unity of consciousness presupposes
the subsumption of our experience under the concepts and principles of "nature in general" but that this is not enough to produce cognition of "particular laws," for which we must therefore
require some additional basis.

(2) It might seem natural to interpret these remarks to mean
that since the unity of consciousness presupposes the subsumption of our experiences under the categories as general concepts
of nature, while the use of the categories in turn presupposes
but does not by itself generate the cognition of particular laws
of nature, including particular causal laws, the use of the categories and therefore the transcendental unity of apperception
must be contingent upon the discovery of particular causal laws.

Such a result, however, would yield just the sort of merely pre-supposed harmony between our own forms of thought and the actual course of nature for which Kant criticizes Hume and himself desperately wants to avoid. He thinks that he can avoid it by the doctrine of transcendental idealism, that is, the doctrine that the mind imposes the form it requires upon the appearances of nature while leaving unknown what the objects of nature might be like in themselves. Whether by means of this doctrine Kant can successfully avoid the difficulty with which he taxes Hume is, however, deeply problematic.

Kant first argues for what he calls the "transcendental ideality" of space and time in the "Transcendental Aesthetic" by arguing that our synthetic a priori knowledge of both certain very general truths about space and time (the topics of what he calls in the second edition of the *Critique* the "metaphysical expositions" of the concepts of space and time) as well as the more particular truths about space and time contained in specific branches of mathematics (the topics of the "transcendental expositions") can only be explained by the thesis that space and time are nothing but the pure forms of intuition we impose upon the appearances of objects that are not in themselves spatial and/or temporal—for if they were, then agreement between our own forms of experience and the forms that objects have in themselves would be contingent, not necessary and hence not knowable a priori (see especially *Pure Reason*, A 26–28/B 42–44, A 47–49/B 64–66, and *Prolegomena*, §13, Note 1, 4: 287–88).[15]

---

[15] I have defended this interpretation of Kant's argument for transcendental idealism at length in *Kant and the Claims of Knowledge* (Cambridge: Cambridge University Press, 1987), chap. 16. My interpretation has certainly not been universally accepted; for alternatives, see Henry E. Allison, *Kant's Transcendental Idealism: An Interpretation and Defense* (New Haven, CT: Yale University Press, 1983), chaps. 2 and 5, and his *Idealism and Freedom: Essays on Kant's Theoretical Philosophy* (Cambridge: Cambridge University Press, 1996), chap. 1 ("Transcendental Idealism: A Retrospective"), as well as Rae Langton, *Kantian Humility: Our Ignorance of Things in Themselves* (Oxford: Clarendon Press, 1998), especially chap. 4. However, my approach is supported by James Van Cleve, in *Problems from Kant* (New York: Oxford University Press, 1999), chap. 3. This issue was also discussed in chapter 1 of this volume.

Even if we accept this argument, we would still have to face a fundamental problem. Particularly in the *Prolegomena*, Kant makes it clear that transcendental idealism concerns only the spatial and temporal form of objects: it maintains that the spatial and temporal form of objects is only a feature of their appearance to us, not that their existence in any way depends upon us—for that reason, indeed, Kant suggests that he might have done better to call his position "formal idealism" rather than "transcendental idealism" (§13, Note III, 4: 293). But causal relations, Kant emphasizes, concern precisely the existence of objects (*Pure Reason*, A 160/B 199, A 178/B 220). Thus Kant's initial argument for transcendental idealism in the "Transcendental Aesthetic" cannot give rise to a general argument that we are ourselves responsible for all aspects of the order in the objects of nature, and would appear to leave entirely open the possibility that our success in discovering particular causal laws in nature, as contrasted to the laws of geometry and arithmetic, is contingent—for particular causal laws seem to depend upon the actual existence of objects that behave in an orderly fashion. But then it is not clear that there is anything in the general argument of the "Transcendental Deduction" and the "Schematism" that can remedy this gap. In these sections, Kant gives an account of how the mind can impose the pure concepts of the understanding and their schemata upon our experience by means of the process he calls "transcendental" and "figurative" synthesis, the interpretation of the pure concepts of the understanding in spatiotemporal terms and the application of the principles that thereby arise to experience. But this leaves unexplained how we come to know particular causal laws, as Kant insists. Thus his assurance in the *Prolegomena* that transcendental idealism makes our cognition of particular causal laws rather than the merely general principle of causality necessary and a priori rather than contingent is inconsistent with both the "Transcendental Deduction" and his most refined account of transcendental idealism itself, and is sheer bravado. The theory of the categories and their schematism seems to provide an answer to Hume's question about the origin of our *concept* of necessary connection and hence our *concept* of causation itself, but transcendental idealism is not capable of making our discovery of particular causal laws necessary rather than contingent, or improving upon Hume's supposition that our knowledge of particular causal laws is due to a fortunate preestablished harmony.[16]

Does Kant's argument in the second "Analogy of Experience" explain our cognition of particular causal laws in a way that can guarantee the necessity of such cognition rather than leaving it contingent? It is far from clear that it does, for while it addresses the concern that Hume raises in the *Treatise* but not in the *Enquiry* about the general principle of causation, by showing that every experience of an event—something that Hume took for granted—presupposes that we subsume that event under some causal law or other—the necessity that Hume doubted—it does not show how we come to have knowledge of particular causal laws and their necessity. On the contrary, the argument of the second "Analogy" seems to presuppose that particular causal laws are available to us for the general purpose of ordering states of affairs in time.

The argument of the second "Analogy of Experience" is no less controversial than that of the "Transcendental Aesthetic"—indeed, Peter Strawson, and before him Arthur Lovejoy, insisted that Kant's whole argument was a "*non sequitur* of numbing grossness."[17] Again, there is no room here for a detailed

---

[16] Eric Watkins has recently examined the question of whether Kant has any independent argument for transcendental idealism with respect to the categories rather than the forms of intuitions, and concludes that no such argument can be found in the "Transcendental Deduction"; see his "Transcendental Idealism and the Categories," *History of Philosophy Quarterly* 19 (2002): 191–215. But even if Kant had made such a general argument starting from the categories rather than the forms of intuition, there would still be a problem in allowing him the view, to which he seems to help himself in his claim that transcendental idealism provides the answer to Hume, that it guarantees the necessity of particular causal inferences.

[17] P. F. Strawson, *The Bounds of Sense: An Essay on Kant's Critique of Pure Reason* (London: Methuen, 1966), 137; Arthur Lovejoy, "On Kant's Reply to Hume," *Archiv für Geschichte der Philosophie* (1906): 380–407, reprinted in *Kant: Disputed*

discussion of the controversies surrounding the second "Analogy," but a simplified exposition of Kant's argument should suffice to show both how it answers Hume and what it leaves open. Here is Kant's most succinct statement of his argument:

> To all empirical cognition there belongs the synthesis of the manifold through imagination, which is always successive, i.e., the representations always follow each other in it. But the order of the sequence (what must precede and what must follow) is not determined in the imagination at all, and the series of successive representations can be taken backwards just as well as forwards. But if this synthesis is a synthesis of apprehension (of the manifold of a given appearance), then the order in the object is determined, or, to speak more precisely, there is therein an order of the successive synthesis that determines an object, in accordance with which something would necessarily have to precede and, if this is posited, the other would necessarily have to follow. If, therefore, my perception is to contain the cognition of an occurrence, namely that something actually happens, then it must be an empirical judgment in which one thinks that the sequence is determined, i.e., that it presupposes another appearance in time which it follows necessarily or in accordance with a rule. . . . Thus the relation of appearances (as possible perceptions) in accordance with which the existence of that which succeeds (what happens) is determined in time necessarily and in accordance with a rule by something that precedes it, consequently the relation of cause to effect is the condition of the objective validity of our empirical judgments with regard to the series of perceptions, thus of their empirical truth, and therefore of appearance. Hence the principle of the causal relation in the sequence of appearances is valid for all objects of experience (under the conditions of succession) . . . (*Pure Reason*, A 201–2/B 246–47)

Questions, ed. Moltke S. Gram (Chicago: Quadrangle Books, 1967), 284–308. I will comment on their charges in note 21 below.

The argument begins from the premises that we can distinguish between unchanging objects and changes in objects, that is, events, but that in either case, we experience the objects by means of a temporally extended sequence of representations of them. (Earlier in the "Analogy," Kant presents the second point as if it were a consequence of transcendental idealism's reduction of empirical objects to our own representations (A 189–91/ B 234–36), but it must hold for any representational theory of perception.) Thus, to use Kant's examples, whether we experience an unchanging house (a nonevent) or a ship changing its position by moving downstream (an event), we experience the object by means of a sequence of representations, for example, in the case of the house a representation of its roof followed by a representation of its first floor and in the case of the ship a representation of it at some particular point upstream followed by a representation of it at some point downstream (A 192–93/ B 237–38). If we assume that the house has not undergone any change, then we will also assume that we *could* have perceived the first floor before rather than after the roof (by changing the sequence of positions of our own body), thus that the order of our perceptions of it was reversible, while in the case of the moving ship, we assume that we *could not* have perceived it downstream before we perceived it upstream,[18] thus that the order of our perceptions was irreversible. So we might think that we could simply take the irreversibility rather than reversibility of a series of perceptions as an adequate criterion for the perception of an event. However, as Kant points out, since we can always imagine any sequence of perceptions occurring in an

---

[18] At least, that is, as long as we were not in a position to have changed the direction of the ship prior to the time of perception and as long as the mechanism of each perception is the same, i.e., that we are not perceiving the position of the ship at one moment by the unaided eye but its position at another moment only through a subsequently viewed tape, so that we could perceive its position upstream (on the tape) after we perceived it downstream (directly). For this condition, see Jonathan Bennett, *Kant's Analytic* (Cambridge: Cambridge University Press, 1966), 222–23. As Bennett suggests, however, since the technologies that could readily introduce this sort of time delay into some perceptions but not others are post-Kantian, there was no need for Kant to have stated this condition explicitly.

order other than it did, there is no way we can tell from the experience of any series of perceptions by itself that it *is* irreversible rather than reversible: as he says in the present passage, "the order of the sequence . . . is not determined in the imagination at all," or as he puts it elsewhere in the "Analogy," the imagination "can combine the two states in question in two different ways, so that either one or the other precedes in time; for time cannot be perceived in itself, nor can what precedes and what follows in objects be as it were empirically determined in relation to it" (B 233). Yet the irreversibility of a series of perceptions in the case of an event and its reversibility in the case of a nonevent, and thus the occurrence of a particular change or not, are not only not given immediately in perception; they also obviously cannot be inferred directly from the objects rather than from our representations of them, since we have premised precisely that objects, whether changing or not, are given only through our representations of them. So if the reversibility or irreversibility of series of perceptions is not directly given by representations and the absence or presence of change in objects cannot be inferred from that, how do we know whether or not an object has changed?

Kant's answer is that it is only if the sequence of states of the object is itself subject to a rule in accordance with which one of those states must follow rather than precede the other—in which case (subject to the condition mentioned in note 18) the perception of one of those states will also have to follow rather than precede the perception of the other—that we can determine that a particular change has occurred in the object rather than merely in our perception of it. As Kant puts it elsewhere in the "Analogy,"

> I must . . . derive the **subjective sequence** of apprehension from the **objective sequence** of appearances, for otherwise the former would be entirely undetermined and no appearance would be distinguished from any other. The former alone proves nothing about the connection of the manifold in the object, because it is entirely arbitrary. This connection must therefore consist in the order of the manifold of appearance in accordance with which the apprehension of one thing

(that which happens) follows that of the other (which precedes) **in accordance with a rule.** (A 193/B 238)

But a rule in accordance with which one state of affairs must follow another is nothing other than a causal law: "The schema of the cause and of the causality of a thing in general is the real upon which, whenever it is posited, something else always follows" (A 144/B 183). We can therefore determine that any particular event has occurred only by subsuming the objects involved under some causal law, and if we can always determine whether a particular event has occurred then we can always subsume the objects involved under some causal law. Hence the general principle that every event has some cause is nothing less than a principle of the possibility of experience, at least if experience includes the experience of events: "Thus the principle of sufficient reason is the ground of possible experience, namely the objective cognition of experiences with regard to their relation in the successive series of time" *(*A 200–201/B 246).

Many questions can be raised about this argument,[19] but here I want to make only two points about it. First, while the argu-

---

[19] Strawson's objection to the argument is that the transition from the *perception* of one state of affairs A to that of another B will be necessary (irreversible) as long as the state of affairs A precedes B, even if that order of the states of affairs themselves is not necessary and therefore not in accordance with a causal law (*The Bounds of Sense*, 137–38). This simply overlooks the epistemic character of Kant's argument, that is, its claim that we cannot know what the order of A and B is either directly from those states of affairs themselves or from our perception of them, but only from the subsumption of those states of affairs under causal laws. Lovejoy charged Kant with at least three different sins: first, he just took over the "Second Analogy" from Christian Wolff, and while Wolff correctly argued that we need to use the causal order of real events to distinguish them from dreams and delusions, Kant mistook this use for the use of causal order to distinguish between the representation of change and nonchange, whether veridical or not, which is in fact directly given to us and needs no special basis at all; second, Kant just illicitly infers from the necessity of the sequence of states of affairs in a particular event to the "necessary *uniformity*" of that sequence in "*repeated instances* of a given *kind* of phenomenon"; and third, the order of states of an object in the case of an event is determined by the *concept* of the object, so that laws for events are analytic, and not synthetic as Kant supposed ("On Kant's Reply to Hume," 289–92, 296–82, 300–301, and 306). But Lovejoy's objections are not convincing; first, while Kant may have connected his argument with Wolff's in passing (e.g., *Pure Reason*, B 278), his essential epistemic point can be put by saying that even the belief (whether or

ment presupposes that we can distinguish between the occurrence of change or not in the objects of our perception, or recognize objective events, and is therefore dependent upon an
empirical assumption, this does not mean that Kant is guilty of
the error with which he taxed such opponents of Hume as
"Reid, Oswald, Beattie, and finally **Priestly,"** the error, of "constantly taking for granted just what he doubted, and, conversely,
proving with vehemence and, more often than not, with great
insolence exactly what it had never entered his head to doubt"
(*Prolegomena*, Preface, 4: 258). Rather, as Lewis White Beck
pointed out,[20] Kant begins only with an empirical assumption,
namely that we do sometimes perceive events, which he assumes that Hume himself also accepts—and he assumes this
with some reason, since Hume says, "Suppose a person, though
endowed with the strongest faculties of reason and reflection,
to be brought on a sudden into this world; he would, indeed,
immediately observe a continual succession of objects, and one
event following another" (*Enquiry I*, Section 5, 36)[21]—but then

---

not it ultimately turns out to be veridical) that we have perceived a change cannot
be based on any direct perception of irreversibility in our perceptions, but can only
be inferred from the causal laws that (we believe to) apply to the objects of our
perceptions (although we can be wrong that those laws actually do apply, and therefore be wrong about whether any event or what event occurred); second, Kant never
supposes that we can infer causal laws from the experience of the irreversibility of
our perceptions, but precisely the opposite; and third, while that the concept of a
certain kind of event may analytically entail the occurrence of a certain sequence
of states of affairs, Kant's point could be put precisely by saying that we have no
basis for the application of such a concept in our experience in the first place except
our application of (synthetic) causal laws that entail that such a sequence of states
of affairs must have obtained and that *therefore* the relevant concept of an event
applies. Like Strawson, Lovejoy fails to fully appreciate the epistemic character of
Kant's argument.

[20] Beck, "A Prussian Hume and a Scottish Kant," 128–29.

[21] It is because Hume accepts the premise that we are conscious of a determinate
order of events and Kant then argues that he is not entitled to this on his other
premises that I believe, contrary to the view of Eric Watkins discussed in the Introduction to this volume, that it makes perfectly good sense to speak of Kant as
attempting to refute Hume. On the logic of Kant's reply to Hume, see also Lewis
White Beck, "Once More unto the Breach: Kant's Answer to Hume, Again," *Ratio*
9 (1967): 33–37, reprinted in his *Essays on Kant and Hume*, 130–36, especially 132.

shows that the ability that Hume takes for granted, that we can always observe "one event following another," rests precisely on the principle that Hume has thrown into doubt (in the *Treatise*, remember, if not in the *Enquiry*), that every event occurs as the consequence of some cause. Of course, if some skeptic wanted to question even whether we can ever reliably judge that an objective change has occurred, then Kant's argument would have no purchase—but that skeptic would not be Hume.

However, and this is my second point, Kant proves the general principle that Hume had doubted in the *Treatise*—that every event has some cause—without explicitly addressing the problem that Hume had raised in the *Enquiry*—namely, how do we come to know particular causal laws? Kant's proof in the "Second Analogy" of the general proposition that "All alterations occur in accordance with the law of the connection of cause and effect" works by assuming that we can always know whether some particular alteration has occurred and then arguing that we can do so only by inferring that such an alteration *must* have occurred in accordance with some particular causal law. For example, in spite of the fact that we can always alter the sequence of the representations of the position of a ship sailing downstream in imagination, we nevertheless know that it must have been sailing downstream because particular laws of nature tell us that under the prevailing conditions of wind, current, and so on, it could have done nothing else. So Kant's argument for the general principle of causality presupposes the availability of particular causal laws. But it does not tell us how we acquire knowledge of them,[22] and it certainly does not address Hume's concern that our confidence in particular causal laws depends upon a premise—that the future must resemble the past—which is itself demonstrable neither by reason nor from experience. So while Kant does not take for granted something that Hume had doubted in assuming that we do know the difference between objective events and nonevents, his proof of the general principle of causation from this premise nevertheless does presuppose the availability of knowledge that by

[22] For this point, see also Floyd, "The Fact of Judgment," 29.

Kant's own lights Hume had put into question, knowledge of particular causal laws, and does not itself offer any explanation of such knowledge.

Thus neither Kant's general theory of the categories and their schematism nor his argument in the "Second Analogy" offers a theory of how we come to know particular causal laws or an answer to Hume's problem about the underlying premise of the practice of induction. Does Kant ever offer such a theory and such an answer?

THE *CRITIQUE OF THE POWER OF JUDGMENT*

Several writers have recently argued that Kant's answer to Hume's problem about induction is not to be found in the *Critique of Pure Reason* but rather in the introduction to the *Critique of the Power of Judgment*.[23] There can be no doubt that in this passage Kant does take up the issue of how we can know particular laws of nature in a way that he does not in the sections of the *Critique of Pure Reason* that we have been discussing.[24] I will return to the third *Critique* in chapter 5, but for now I will suggest that even there Kant offers no direct response to Hume's question about the basis for induction.

[23] See Philip Kitcher, "Projecting the Order of Nature," in *Kant's Philosophy of Physical Science*, ed. Robert E. Butts (Dordrecht, the Netherlands: D. Reidel, 1986), 201–35, reprinted in *Kant's Critique of Pure Reason: Critical Essays*, ed. Patricia Kitcher (Lanham, MD: Rowman and Littlefield, 1998), 219–38, and Juliet Floyd, "Heautonomy: Kant on Reflective Judgment and Systematicity," in *Kant's Ästhetik—Kant's Aesthetics—L'esthétique de Kant*, ed. Herman Parret (Berlin: Walter de Gruyter, 1998), 192–218. In her more recent article cited previously, "The Fact of Judgment: The Kantian Response to the Humean Condition," Floyd argues not so much that Kant's theory of reflective judgment in the third *Critique* directly answers Hume as that it turns Hume on his head by showing that what he was seeking to find in nature can only be found in our own mind; see 32.

[24] Although there is some anticipation of the arguments of the third *Critique* in the Appendix to the "Transcendental Dialectic" of the first; see my articles "Reason and Reflective Judgment: Kant on the Significance of Systematicity," *Nous* 24 (1990): 17–43, and "Kant's Conception of Empirical Law," *Proceedings of the Aristotelian Society*, Supplementary Volume 64 (London: The Aristotelian Society, 1990): 221–42. These articles are reprinted as chapters 1 and 2 of my *Kant's System of Nature and Freedom* (Oxford: Clarendon Press, 2005).

Kant does not mention the name of Hume in either of the versions of the introduction to the third *Critique*,[25] and thus it is not clear that he explicitly intended the introduction or indeed any part of the work to resolve any issue in his response to Hume's treatment of causation that he recognized to have been left open by his arguments in the first *Critique*. Nevertheless, both versions of the introduction do address what we have seen to be at least one issue left open by Kant's earlier work: the source and nature of our cognition of the particular causal laws that are presupposed in Kant's proof of the general principle that every event has some cause but that cannot be directly derived from that general principle or from the pure concept of causation. Kant alludes to this gap in the first introduction when he writes that:

> We have seen in the critique of pure reason that the whole of nature as the totality of all objects of experience constitutes a system in accordance with transcendental laws, namely those

[25] Kant wrote one version of an introduction during the process of the composition of the third *Critique*, apparently early in 1789, which he then discarded in favor of a second version that he wrote in the final weeks before the publication of the book in April 1790. In 1793, he gave the first version to his disciple Jakob Sigismund Beck for the latter's use in compiling his *Erläuternder Auszug aus den critischen Schriften des Herrn Prof. Kant* (Riga, 1794), and Beck did include some extracts from it in his compilation. At the time, Kant told Beck that he had discarded this first version simply because of its greater length, which is what he had also earlier told his publisher, although there are differences other than length between the two versions: most obviously, the second version stresses the role of the faculty of judgment in bridging the gap between nature and freedom, or natural science and morality, far more than the first. The complete version of the first draft was not published until 1914, and was first translated into English in 1965. The two most recent English translations of the third *Critique*, that by Werner Pluhar (Indianapolis: Hackett, 1987) and that by Paul Guyer and Eric Matthews, viz., Immanuel Kant, *Critique of the Power of Judgment*, ed. Paul Guyer, trans. Paul Guyer and Eric Matthews (Cambridge: Cambridge University Press, 2000) (*CPJ*), both include both versions of the introduction, the early draft being referred to as the "first introduction" (*FI*) and the later version as the "published introduction" or simply "Introduction." The latter translation, which is used in what follows, gives a more detailed account of the circumstances surrounding the first introduction and its eventual publication at xliii–xliv.

that the understanding itself gives *a priori* (for appearances, namely, insofar as they, combined in one consciousness, are to constitute experience). For that very reason, experience, in accordance with general as well as particular laws, must also constitute (in the idea) a system of possible empirical cognitions. . . . But it does not follow from this that nature even in accordance with **empirical** laws is a system that **can be grasped** by the human faculty of cognition . . . (*First Introduction*, Section IV, 20: 208–9)

Here Kant takes the argument of the first *Critique* to assure us that a comprehensive set of empirical laws of nature—which, by the argument of the "Second Analogy," must include causal laws applicable to every event in nature—must exist, but not to guarantee that we can come to know all of these laws in a graspable system. It would thus seem as if his objective must then be to explain how we can come to know a system of particular laws of nature, certainly a problem left open by the first *Critique*'s theory of the categories and their schematism and by the "Second Analogy."

In the published introduction, Kant writes that:

The determining power of judgment under transcendental laws, given by the understanding, merely subsumes; the law is sketched out for it *a priori*, and it is therefore unnecessary for it to think of a law for itself in order to be able to subordinate the particular in nature to the universal.—But there is such a manifold of forms in nature, as it were so many modifications of the universal transcendental concepts of nature that are left undetermined by those laws that the pure understanding gives *a priori*, since these pertain only to the possibility of a nature (as object of the senses) in general, that there must nevertheless also be laws for it which, as empirical, may indeed be contingent in accordance with the insight of **our** understanding, but which, if they are to be called laws (as is also required by the concept of a nature), must be regarded as necessary on a principle of the unity of that manifold, even if that principle is unknown to us. (*Judgment*, Introduction, Section IV, 5: 179–80)

This passage makes two points: first, that the "universal transcendental concepts of nature" and "those laws that the pure understanding gives us *a priori*"—that is, the categories, and those general principles of empirical judgment, such as the general principle of causation, that can be derived from the categories by the schematism and the further arguments of the "System of Principles," such as that of the "Second Analogy"—are not sufficient to determine the content of the particular laws of nature; and second, that since the general concepts and laws of nature are not sufficient to determine by themselves the content of the particular laws of nature, they also cannot be sufficient to explain the necessity of those laws, which we apparently must assume in making use of those laws. While the argument of the "Second Analogy" maintained that the determinate sequences of states of affairs that constitute particular events must be seen as being *necessitated* by particular causal laws, it did not explicitly assert that those laws themselves must be *necessarily true* or explain in what sense they must be understood to be so. But here Kant assumes precisely that what is required for cognition of particular causal laws, and what remains to be explained, is knowledge of their necessity.

Kant thus seems to identify three different problems about particular laws of nature, including causal laws: the first introduction seems to assume that we can come to know at least some particular laws without further explanation, but cannot automatically grasp a complete system of them, while the published introduction claims that we can derive neither the content nor the necessity of any particular laws of nature directly from the general or "transcendental" concepts and laws of nature. But Kant proposes the same solution to these different problems in the two versions of the introduction: that we must simply "presuppose a system of nature which is also in accordance with empirical laws and [do] so *a priori*, consequently by means of a transcendental principle" (*First Introduction*, Section V, 20: 212, the principle

> that since universal laws of nature have their ground in our understanding, which prescribes them to nature (although

only in accordance with the universal concept of it as nature), the particular empirical laws, in regard to that in them which is left undetermined by the former, must be considered in terms of the sort of unity they would have if an understanding (even if not ours) had likewise given them for the sake of our faculty of cognition, in order to make possible a system of experience in accordance with particular laws of nature. (*Judgment*, Introduction, Section IV, 5: 180

Kant does not spell out how this presupposition that the particular laws of nature constitute a system given by an intelligence similar to our own (but presumably more powerful than it, since it reaches to a level of greater determinacy than ours can) will resolve the problems he has identified. In order for his solution to address his problems, however, we may assume that what he has in mind is that, first, a system designed by an intelligence that can take account of the limits of our understanding will be sufficiently compact, that is, consist of a sufficiently limited number of laws, for us to be able to grasp it; second, that the postulated membership of laws in a system will facilitate the discovery of particular laws, as we use the structure of such a system to move from laws that have been discovered to those that have not, thereby increasing the number of laws that we know not randomly but methodically, by filling in gaps in the system; and third, that individual laws that do not strike us as necessarily true when considered in isolation will gain a kind of necessity by being included in a system of laws, where they will seem to be entailed by laws above and around them in the system as well as to entail further laws beneath them.[26]

Even if we attribute such arguments to Kant, would they constitute an answer to the problem he found in Hume's willingness to leave the cognition of particular causal laws dependent upon the assumption of a preestablished harmony or to

[26] For a fuller account of these supposed benefits, see my "Reason and Reflective Judgment: Kant on the Significance of Systematicity" and "Kant's Conception of Empirical Law," as well as my "Two Puzzles about Kant on the Systematicity of Nature," *History of Philosophy Quarterly* 20 (2003): 277–95, reprinted in *Kant's System of Nature and Freedom* as chapter 3.

the problem in his answer to Hume's skeptical doubt that every event has some cause, namely that he has not explained our cognition of the particular laws of nature that his answer to Hume presupposes? If they provide any answers to Hume, they can provide only very limited ones. First of all, as Kant himself insists, the principle that nature is systematic that must be presupposed for the purposes of judgment, although it is "transcendental" in the sense of purporting to be about nature as the object of our judgment and not just about the structure of our judgments themselves (in which case it would be merely "logical"), is only a *regulative* principle that we use to guide our investigation of nature, but not a *constitutive* principle that literally structures nature itself. As he says of the understanding that we postulate as the source of such systematicity, "Not as if in this way such an understanding must really be assumed (for it is only the reflecting power of judgment for which this idea serves as a principle, for reflecting, not for determining); rather this faculty thereby gives a law only to itself, and not to nature" (*Judgment*, Introduction, Section IV, 5: 180). Or again:

> The power of judgment thus also has in itself an *a priori* principle for the possibility of nature, though only in a subjective respect, by means of which it prescribes a law, not to nature (as autonomy), but to itself (as heautonomy) for reflection on nature, which one could call the **law of the specification of nature** with regard to its empirical laws, which it does not cognize in nature *a priori* but rather assumes in behalf of an order of nature for our understanding in the division that it makes of its universal laws when it would subordinate a manifold of particular laws to these. (*Judgment*, Introduction, Section V, 5:185–86)

Far from using transcendental idealism to argue that we can impose the structure of our intellect on nature and thereby overcoming Hume's position that the correspondence between our way of thought and the course of nature is at most a preestablished harmony, Kant here, with the idea that the idea of the systematicity of the laws of nature is an idea that we prescribe only to ourselves and not to nature, an idea that we use to guide our investigation of nature but not to describe nature as it really is, seems instead to give up on the task of answering what he had identified as the most serious problem in Hume's account. While suggesting on the one hand that the idea of including particular laws of nature gives us both a method for the discovery of such laws and an account of their necessary truth, Kant seems to insist on the other that such an idea is a law only for our own intellect and not for nature. He may have gone well beyond Hume in his description of the resources and pattern of our reasoning, developing a model of judgment and reason that goes far beyond Hume's simple idea that rational demonstration depends on nothing but the recognition of identities and avoidance of contradictions, but he seems if anything even clearer than Hume that we cannot actually *impose* our manner of thought on the course of nature itself.[27]

There are also more particular problems in Kant's appeal to the idea of systematicity as an answer to Hume. For one, he does not argue that we have any reason to suppose that we can only organize the laws that we may know at any given time into a *single* system, and thus that we can always find only a unique new law for any particular phenomenon we may be investigating. If we could conceive of several different systematizations of whatever particular laws we already know, then we might also be able to generate alternative and competing hypotheses for new laws on any particular subject. Second, and perhaps even more obvious, even if all the laws that we currently know somehow do—now—seem to fit into only a single system, that fact by itself gives us no reason to assume that the system as a whole and thus any particular laws in it must continue to be or even seem true. That is, even if we can lend an appearance of

---

[27] As I noted, Juliet Floyd sees Kant as standing Hume on his head, and as anticipating subsequent thinkers such as Wittgenstein, Quine, and Goodman in seeing the principle of the systematicity of nature as standing on its own in our scientific practices, without the need for any further sort of grounding ("The Fact of Judgment," 29, 38–43). But Kant's explicit insistence that this principle is heautonomous, that is, applies only to our way of thinking and not to nature itself, seems uncharacteristic of these later thinkers, and more to concede Hume's point than to stand it on his head.

necessity to any particular law at any particular time by regarding it as a member of a system of laws, we have no obvious
reason to believe that the *whole system of laws* that has been
found to be true thus far must continue to be true in the future.
In other words, Kant's proposal that we ground the necessity
of particular laws of nature by embedding them in a system of
such laws simply does not address Hume's problem about the
indemonstrability of the underlying principle of induction that
the future must resemble the past. The issue that may seem to
us to be the deepest issue in Hume's examination of our idea
of and belief in causation does not even appear to be addressed
by Kant's theory that particular causal laws can be known only
as part of a system of such laws.[28]

[28] One argument I have not addressed is that of Michael Friedman, who in
numerous publications has argued that in the *Metaphysical Foundations of Natural
Science* (1786) Kant really develops his model of our knowledge of particular causal
laws, on which the particular laws of Newtonian phoronomy, dynamics, and mechanics are derived from the synthetic a priori principles of empirical thought deduced in the *Critique of Pure Reason* supplemented with considerations about the
spatial structure of matter necessitated by the a priori form of space. See Friedman,
Kant and the Exact Sciences (Cambridge, MA: Harvard University Press, 1992),
chaps. 3 and 4; "Causal Laws and the Foundations of Natural Science," in *The
Cambridge Companion to Kant*, ed. Paul Guyer (Cambridge: Cambridge University
Press, 1992), 161–99; and *The Dynamics of Reason* (Stanford, CA: CSLI Publications, 2001). Without denying the power of Friedman's reconstruction of Kant's
conception of the transition from the most general principles of the possibility of
experience to a specific system of physics including particular causal laws, I have
several reservations about whether we can look here for Kant's answer to Hume.
First, Kant insists that the concept of matter as the moveable in space, on which
the entire derivation of the system of natural law in the *Metaphysical Foundations*
is based, is itself an empirical concept, and to some degree the laws of nature that
result from the application of the general forms of intuition and laws of thought of
the first *Critique* to this concept must therefore remain empirical (as Kant's remarks
at A 127 and B 165 would suggest). Second, the reconstruction of Kant's system
of physics does not directly address the problem of induction, thus does not justify
the assumption that the system remains constant through time. Friedman writes,
"Kant has the upper hand in this eighteenth century philosophical debate with
Hume. For, in this context, there are simply no available alternatives to Euclidean
geometry and Newtonian mechanics. If one wants an empirical science of nature
at all in the eighteenth century then one simply has no options, as Kant incisively
argues, but to presuppose Euclidean geometry and the laws of mechanics as given

So where does this leave us? On Kant's behalf, we can say that he has shown us that we have far richer resources to draw on for our idea of necessary connection than Hume recognized, and that he has also shown us more precisely than Hume what role the cognition of particular causal laws must play in the most elementary form of empirical knowledge, the knowledge that one state of affairs has succeeded another. These are no mean feats of philosophical imagination. He has also suggested if not extensively demonstrated that knowledge of the content and necessity of particular causal laws depends upon the membership of those laws in a comprehensive system of such laws. This is a radical departure from any empiricist assumption that we could come to know a particular causal law just by sufficiently frequent observation of the particular type of phenomena to which it directly applies. But Kant has not given us any reason to believe that we can only formulate a single systematization of the particular laws of nature known at any given time, or that even if we do form only a unique systematization at any given time it and therefore all the particular causal "laws" it includes must always remain true in the future. Thus, his theory that particular causal laws can only be known (as necessarily true) as part of a system of such laws does not seem to address directly Hume's claim that we have no rational basis for the premise that the future must resemble the past. One might say on Kant's behalf that he has shown the psychological effort needed to doubt particular laws of nature is much greater than one might have thought: one cannot just doubt that the sun

---

. . ." (*Dynamics of Reason*, 26–27). In other words, Kant gave the best identification of the a priori conditions of the possibility of experience and its objects that was possible *relative to the actual scientific theories of the eighteenth century.* But those theories have changed, just as Hume's worry about whether the future must resemble the past allows, so neither Hume nor Kant would have seen Friedman's "relativized *a priori*" as solving the problem of induction and thus the problem of the necessity of particular causal laws, even if Kant's model of science does address the epistemological question of how we come to know particular laws. Of course, Friedman may be entirely right that the relativized a priori is the most we can hope for, but that is a different matter from whether Kant has answered Hume on the terms that both would have expected.

will rise tomorrow while continuing to have faith in everything else one knows about terrestrial and celestial mechanics; if one wants to doubt the former, one may have to doubt all of the latter. This may be enough to show that the question of whether the future will resemble the past cannot really gain any psychological grip on us. But then again, Hume made it clear both in the *Treatise* and even more so in the *Enquiry* that he did not expect any doubts that might arise from his explanation of our practice of causal inference to have any psychological grip on us; indeed, he took it to be a virtue of the psychological character of his explanation of our idea of necessary connection and our practice of causal inference that it would itself explain why doubts about causation cannot have a psychological grip on us. We may well think that Kant's theory of reflective judgment and his principle of systematicity provides a more adequate account of the psychology of causal reasoning than does Hume's model. But if we think that Hume has raised a logical problem about the rationality of induction, or that there is such a problem, then nothing that Kant has said will directly address it.

In this chapter, we have examined and evaluated the details of Kant's answers to Hume's problems about causation. In the next chapter, we will consider how the structure of his response to Hume on causation is paralleled in his response to problems about the self and objects, the kind of problems that Kant thought Hume should have but did not raise, although Hume did raise them in the *Treatise of Human Nature*.

3

CAUSE, OBJECT,
AND SELF

Kant's Generalization of Hume's Question about Causation

In the *Prolegomena to Any Future Metaphysics*, as we have seen, Kant asserted that "Hume started mainly from a single but important concept in metaphysics, namely that of the **connection of causes and effects**" (Preface, 4: 257), and claimed for himself the originality of having generalized Hume's doubts about causation to other metaphysical concepts, in order then to answer those doubts about causation as part of a more general defense of metaphysical concepts:

> So I tried first whether **Hume's** objections might not be presented in a general manner, and I soon found that the concept of cause and effect is far from being the only concept through which the understanding thinks connections of things *a priori*; rather, metaphysics consists wholly of such concepts. I sought to ascertain their number, and once I had successfully attained this in the way I wished, namely from a single principle, I proceeded to the deduction of these concepts, from which I henceforth became convinced that they were not, as **Hume** had feared, derived from experience, but had arisen from the pure understanding. (4: 260)

This statement is misleading in several ways. First, Hume did not *fear* that the concept of cause and effect is derived only from experience rather than from the pure understanding, but embraced this result proudly. Second, Kant did not derive concepts like that of cause and effect from pure understanding alone, but from the conjunction of the forms of pure understanding and pure intuition, through what he would call the "schematism of the concepts of the pure understanding." Finally, it was not Kant who first tried whether Hume's objections to causation could be "presented in a general manner," but Hume: in the *Treatise of Human Nature*, Hume himself raised objections about our conceptions of both external objects and our selves that are related, in at least some ways, to his questions about causation. Kant's ignorance of this fact is further evidence, should more be needed, that in spite of several sources available to him he knew little of Hume's positions on topics he had discussed in detail in the *Treatise* but not or hardly at all in the *Enquiry concerning Human Understanding*. But no matter, for although Kant was not aware that Hume had raised doubts about objects and the self that are in some ways analogous to his doubts about causation, Kant's accounts of our concepts and knowledge of objects and the self are in key ways both parallel to and interdependent with his account of our concept and knowledge of cause and effect—so Kant addressed the questions he did not know that Hume had raised in very much the same way as he addressed the question he did know that Hume had raised. Indeed, Kant's answers to Hume's worries about objects and the self are not merely parallel to his answers to Hume on causation; rather, Kant's defense of the concepts of both object and causation are ultimately part of a single larger argument about the conditions of the possibility of a kind of self-knowledge that Hume seems to have taken for granted.

Kant sometimes presents his response to Hume just as an account of our possession of *concepts* for which he thinks Hume cannot account. Thus he continues his claim that Hume started mainly from the "single but important concept . . . of the **connection of cause and effect**" by saying that Hume

> called upon reason, which pretends to have generated this concept in her womb, to give him an account of by what right she thinks that something could be so constituted that, if it is posited, something else must thereby be posited as well; for

that is what the concept of cause says. He indisputably proved
that it is wholly impossible for reason to think such a connection *a priori* and from concepts, because this connection contains necessity; and it is simply not to be seen how it could
be, that because something is, something else necessarily
must also be, and therefore how the concept of such a connection could be introduced *a priori*. From this he concluded that
reason completely and fully deceives herself with this concept,
falsely taking it for her own child, when it is really nothing
but a bastard of the imagination . . . (*Prolegomena*, Preface,
4: 257–58)

In a passage about Hume in the *Critique of Practical Reason*,
Kant similarly presents Hume's doubts as ones about the *concept*
of causation:

David Hume, who can be said to have really begun all the
assaults on the rights of pure reason which made a thorough
investigation of them necessary, concluded as follows. The
concept of **cause** is a concept that contains the **necessity** of
the existence of what is different just insofar as it is different,
so that if A is posited I cognize that something altogether
different from it, B, must necessarily also exist. But necessity
can be attributed to a connection only insofar as the connection is cognized *a priori*. . . . Now it is impossible, he says, to
cognize *a priori* and as necessary the connection between one
thing and **another**. . . . Therefore the concept of a cause is
itself fraudulent and deceptive and, to speak of it in the mild-
est way, an illusion to be excused insofar as the **custom** (a
subjective necessity) of perceiving certain things . . . as often
associated along with or after one another . . . is insensibly
taken for an **objective** necessity of putting such a connection
in the objects themselves; and thus the concept of a cause is
acquired surreptitiously and not rightfully. (*Practical Reason*,
5: 50–51)

These representations of Hume's doubts as solely about the *concept* of causation are again misleading, for as we saw in the previous chapter Hume raised doubts about both the legitimacy of

our common conception of the *contents* of this concept and about the legitimacy of our fundamental *belief* about causation, the belief that associations between antecedent and consequent events that have held in the past will continue to hold in the future, and thus truly count as relations between causes and effects. But again, no matter, for as we also saw, Kant's response to Hume's worries about causation takes the form of arguing *both* that we have a source for a genuinely a priori concept of causation and that we must believe in the universal validity of the *principle* that every event has a cause, where what it means for an event to have a cause is precisely for it to fall under a *rule* linking it to an antecedent event in a way that must hold in the future as well as the past (see *Pure Reason*, A 193–94/B 238–39, A 195/B 240, A 200–201/B 245–46)[1]—although, to keep the score straight, Kant did not directly respond to Hume's question about our knowledge of particular causal laws in the *Treatise* nor did he respond, at least very directly, to Hume's particular argument about the rationality of induction that is so prominent in the *Enquiry*. What I want to emphasize now is that Hume similarly raised doubts about both our ordinary *concepts* of object and self as well as our most fundamental *beliefs* about objects and the self, namely that we are entitled to believe in the distinct and continued existence of objects different from our perceptions of them and that we are entitled to believe in the existence of an identical self different from our individual perceptions. But again, in spite of his ignorance of the details of Hume's own work, Kant nevertheless attempted to show both that we have a genuine source for our concepts of objects and the self and also that we are entitled to believe in the continued existence of both objects and the self in contrast to the momentary existence of particular perceptions. Moreover, he argued that our beliefs in both the existence of external objects

---

[1] Jonathan Bennett ascribed "concept-empiricism" to Kant in *Kant's Dialectic* (Cambridge: Cambridge University Press, 1974), §9, 26–29. I differ from Bennett in claiming that Hume maintained and Kant attempted to overcome empiricism about the justification of our most fundamental beliefs, or "judgment-empiricism," *as well as* empiricism about the contents of our most fundamental concepts.

and causation are nothing less than the conditions of the possibility of a kind of knowledge of the self that Hume seems to have taken for granted.

In what follows, I will first analyze the structural similarities in Hume's doubts about both our concepts of and beliefs about causes, objects, and the self, and then show how Kant responds to Hume's two separable questions about each of these topics in what is ultimately an integrated account of the possibility of self-knowledge.

Hume's Questions

Subsection (1) of this section quickly reviews Hume's account of causation, discussed in the previous chapter. Subsections (2) and (3) draw the analogies between this account and his accounts of external objects and the self.

(1) Hume, as we have seen, raised several different concerns about causation. The first concerned the "idea of *causation*" (*Treatise*, I.iii.2, 53), or the contents of the *concept* of causation. The second concerned the "inference from the impression" of a cause "to the idea" of an effect (*Treatise*, I.iii.6, title, 61), but under this rubric Hume worried about both the justification for the *belief* in any particular causal connection and the possibility of justified belief in causation in general.

The problem of the content of the idea of causation arises because of Hume's principle "*that all our simple ideas in their first appearance are deriv'd from simple impressions, which are correspondent to them, and which they exactly represent*" (*Treatise*, I.i.1, 9), which implies that there can be no component of any complex idea that is not derived from some specific impression that it copies by itself. The problem for the idea of causation is then that analysis of it shows it to be a complex idea consisting of three simple ideas for only two of which, however, the correspondent impressions can be found. Our idea of cause and effect is the complex idea of two objects—thus Hume puts it, though we can talk about states of objects without modifying his analysis in any significant way—that are spatially *contiguous*, temporally *successive*, and stand in a *necessary connection* (*Treatise*, I.iii.2, 54–55). The last condition is indispensable, because "An object may be contiguous and prior to another, without being consider'd as its cause," as in the case of accidental juxtapositions. But although we can readily find impressions to be the basis of our simple ideas of contiguity and succession—that one thing is next to another and follows it are, Hume supposes, the sorts of things we can immediately perceive—we apparently have no impression of necessary connection. When "I turn the object on all sides, in order to discover the nature of this necessary connexion, and find the impression, or impressions, from which its idea may be deriv'd . . . I can find none but those of contiguity and succession; which I have already regarded as imperfect and unsatisfactory" (*Treatise*, I.iii.2, 55). We take ourselves to understand the difference between an accidental conjunction of states of affairs and a genuine causal relation between them, but we cannot provide a source for the key component in our conception of this difference.

Hume then leaves the "direct survey of this question" to take up "some other questions, the examination of which will perhaps afford a hint, that may serve to clear up the present difficulty." The two questions he then raises concern the justifiability of our belief in the general principle that every event has a cause and in particular causal laws, respectively; in his terms:

> *First*, For what reason we pronounce it *necessary*, that every thing whose existence has a beginning, shou'd also have a cause? [and]
> *Secondly*, Why we conclude, that such particular causes must *necessarily* have such particular effects; and what is the nature of the *inference* we draw from one to the other, and of the *belief* we repose in it? (*Treatise*, I.iii.2, 55)

These are serious questions, Hume goes on to argue, because the necessity of any event having any cause, let alone the same cause as prior instances of that event, cannot be demonstrated by "scientific reasoning" (I.iii.3, 58), for there is no absurdity, that is, self-contradiction, involved in denying these suppositions; but when we turn to "observation and experience," we also run into trouble. This trouble is that any inference from prior observations of conjunctions of events, no matter how numerous, cannot imply anything about future conjunctions except on the basis of the intermediate premise *"that instances, of which we have had no experience, must resemble those, of which we have had experience, and that the course of nature continues always uniformly the same"* (I.iii.6, 62), but that premise cannot itself be proven. It cannot be proven by *"demonstrative* arguments," because there is no contradiction in supposing that the future does not resemble the past in some regard, and it cannot be proven from experience, because experience never directly concerns anything "beyond those particular instances, which have fallen under our observation" (I.iii.6, 64). All that experience can ever tell us is that *in the past* or *as far as observed to date* the course of nature has always continued uniformly the same, but that observation cannot be projected into the future or the unobserved except by assuming the very premise that is supposed to be proved from experience. So no amount of past experience can logically license the projection of either the general principle of causation or specific causal laws into the future.

Hume takes these arguments to preclude only the justification of both the general principle of causality and particular causal beliefs by deductive reasoning from any mere concepts or from any particular amount of experience, no matter how extensive, and he introduces something else, the principles of the imagination, in order to explain if not to justify our practices of causal inference, which he does not for a moment think to revise. And his appeal to principles of imagination is ultimately supposed to answer his original question about the source of the idea of necessary connection in our complex idea of causation as well as his further questions about our confidence in causal inferences. His theory is that repeated experience of conjunctions of objects or their states creates strong associations in the mind, which themselves have two effects: first, when a current impression of one member of a pair of types of objects one has frequently experienced in the past occurs, association produces a vivid idea of a member of the other type, and belief is nothing other than "A LIVELY IDEA RELATED TO OR ASSOCIATED WITH A

PRESENT IMPRESSION" (*Treatise*, I.iii.7, 67); second, our internal feeling of the forcible transition of the mind from the impression to the lively idea is itself the impression from which our idea of necessary connection is derived (I.iii.14, 111), an idea the mind then "spreads" upon external objects because of its inherent "propensity" to do so (112) in a sort of mistake that, however, Hume apparently thinks is quite harmless, at least in the case of causation.

Hume, as we have seen, was perfectly happy with this solution to his problems about both the idea of causation and the justification of causal inferences; he did not express any qualms about it later in the *Treatise*, nor did he revise it in any essentials in the *Enquiry concerning Human Understanding*. Equally obviously, Kant was unhappy with it, although he makes only the general objection that no such explanation of either our concept or our belief in causation by appeal to principles of imagination—what Kant and we would call empirical psychology—can show them to be a priori and necessary. Kant does not offer any more detailed criticism of Hume's positive account of our concept and belief, but devotes his energy to his own demonstration that we do have both an a priori concept of causation and sound grounds for the synthetic a priori—and therefore general—principle that every event has a cause. Before returning to Kant's alternative account of our concept of and belief in causation, however, I want to show next that the general structure of Hume's discussion of external objects and the self is essentially the same as his discussion of causation. In each case, he first raises a problem about the *idea* and then raises a separate question about the basis for a key *belief* that we have about that idea. In these cases, however, Hume is left with a qualm about his account, although not one that ever leads him to question the basic premise of his empiricism, at least in part because his accounts of the belief-forming mechanisms involved do not yield the explanations for the problematic ideas in which we are supposed to believe that would be analogous to his discovery of a source for the idea of necessary connection in the explanation of our causal beliefs, and what he does ultimately use to explain how we can have ideas of both external objects and the self, his own bundle theory of the mind, may seem far more speculative and dubious even to him than his explanation of the idea of necessary connection does.

(2) First, then, Hume's problems with external objects. His problem about the idea of external objects is an immediate consequence of his principle that every idea must have its source in a correspondent and resembling impression, and is presented by him as such quite early in the *Treatise*. His chapter "Of the idea of existence, and of external existence" is included in the second part of Book One of the *Treatise*, and culminates in the claim that "since nothing is ever present to the mind but perceptions, and since all ideas are deriv'd from something antecedently present to the mind; it follows, that 'tis impossible for us so much as to conceive or form an idea of any thing specifically different from ideas and impressions" (*Treatise*, I.ii.6, 49). The same principle is at work in his later chapter "Of scepticism with regard to the senses," where he argues that "That our senses offer not their impressions as the images of something *distinct*, or *independent*, and *external*, is evident; because they convey to us nothing but a single perception, and never give us the least intimation of anything beyond," so that "If our senses, therefore, suggest any idea of distinct existences, they must convey the impressions as those very existences, by a kind of fallacy and illusion" (I.iv.2, 126). Hume then provides an intricate account of the mechanisms of the imagination that give rise to the belief in external objects, which must however remain fallacious and illusory because it never really generates a stable idea of external objects in which to believe.[2] Shorn of its detail, the

---

[2] Hume's problem with external objects is thus different from Descartes': Descartes took for granted the intelligibility of our idea of external objects, but raised doubts about the certainty of our inference to them from our internal representations of them (doubts he resolved to his own satisfaction but not that of Kant by his argument that a benevolent God would not give us any truly clear and distinct ideas that are false); Hume, conversely, had no problem with his psychological explanation of our grounds for believing in external objects, but found the very idea of them inexplicable on his empiricist premise. Kant's approach to an answer to Hume on external objects is thus part of his general response to Humean skepticism, while his answer to Cartesian skepticism is a separate argument, the "Refutation of Idealism," which is an afterthought in the design of the *Critique of Pure*

account is basically this. Our impressions are apparently fleeting and transitory, and rarely if ever exactly the same. But there are certainly strong resemblances among them, or "COHERENCE and CONSTANCY" (I.iv.2, 130), and the imagination has a strong imagination to substitute qualitative and numerical identity for mere coherence and constancy, thus to suppose the literally continued, numerically identical existence of one thing where there are in fact only intermittent but similar things. However, precisely since impressions are apparently fleeting and transitory, this continued existence must be imagined to be distinct from the existence of impressions, and therefore the "opinion of the *continu'd* existence of body" "produces" that "of its *distinct* existence" (I.iv.2, 132). Or at least it does so in philosophers: the vulgar may not focus on the apparently fleeting and transitory character of impressions in the first place, and so can rest content with their natural belief that "The very image, which is present to the senses," is also "the real body" (136); but philosophers will focus on that character of their impressions, and will thus attempt to produce the idea of a double existence, or of the distinctness of impression and object, even though there is no real basis for the idea of the latter. It has no "*primary recommendation either to reason or the imagination*" (140), because it certainly does not rest on any logically irresistible inference but neither is it generated by the imagination in the way that the idea of necessary connection is. The imagination therefore provides pressure to believe in continued existence, but it apparently cannot produce the idea of an object for this pressure to believe, that is, an idea of distinct existence that can be believed to be continued. And there is thus an instability in the account of belief in external objects that is not present in the belief in causation (but that could, although Hume never mentions this point, upset the prior explanation of our belief in causation insofar as that simply took for granted the intelligibility of the idea of external objects from the outset).

Reason. Hume's problem with external objects thus does not undercut the distinction between Humean and Cartesian skepticism made in chapter 1 or my assessment of Kant's greater interest in the former than in the latter.

(3) Finally, Hume's account of belief in an identical self is structurally similar. Hume proposes to examine the belief of "some philosophers, who imagine that we are every moment intimately conscious of what we call our SELF; that we feel its existence and its continuance in existence; and are certain, beyond the evidence of a demonstration, both of its perfect identity and simplicity" (*Treatise*, I.iv.6, 164). He first objects that we do not "have any idea of *self*, after the manner it is here explain'd [,] For from what impression cou'd this idea be deriv'd?" Initially, what he argues is that we do not have an impression of anything within us that is continued and simple, and could thus give us the idea of a continued and simple self, but then he goes even further and argues that we cannot have any idea of our self as contrasted to our particular perceptions, because "when I enter most intimately into what I call *myself*, I always stumble on some particular perception or other, of heat or cold, light or shade, love or hatred, pain or pleasure," and "can never catch *myself* at any time without a perception" (165).[3] Because I have perceptions of heat and cold and all the rest, I can also have ideas of such qualities; but because I do not have any impressions of anything internal other than those of such qualities, I cannot have the idea of a self that is in any way distinct from its several perceptions. A fortiori I cannot have the idea of a simple, numerically identical self.

Nevertheless, Hume continues, there are certainly strong relations of resemblance among our various particular perceptions—presumably they usually tend to change incrementally rather than drastically—and the same tendency of the imagination to feign identity where there is only coherence and constancy that explained our belief in external objects is at work here too; so "we feign the continu'd existence of the perceptions

---

[3] Hume can use the term "perception" as a generic term subsuming both impressions and perceptions, and in the theory that the mind is a bundle of perceptions that he is about to propose, he must mean the term in this generic sense, since the mind on any account has both impressions and ideas. But all of the perceptions of the mind, even though some of them are ideas that copy those that are impressions, can count as the impressions among which we will look, unsuccessfully, for the source of the idea of the self.

of the senses, to remove the interruption; and run into the notion of a *soul*, and *self*, and *substance*, to disguise the variation" (*Treatise*, I.iv.6, 166). That is, we are in some sense both aware of the noncontinuous existence of perceptions and yet pressured by the imagination to believe in their continued existence where there is merely strong resemblance; and in order to avoid outright contradiction we try to transfer that tendency to believe in continued existence from the perceptions that we know to be fleeting and transitory to the idea of a continuous self that has those noncontinuous perceptions, *even though we do not really have an impression that can be an adequate source of that idea.* So once again we have a strong tendency to believe in an idea we do not really have, and if we think about it too closely will find ourselves in a precarious intellectual position.

Hume does seem to suppose that our beliefs in both external objects and the self are intellectually precarious, the product of pressures of the imagination to *believe* in things we cannot quite *conceive*, and it is with regard to the problems with these ideas that concludes that we can be saved from the "doubt and ignorance" that should really be our conclusion only by the pleasurable distractions of nature and society, a walk by the river or dinner and backgammon with friends (*Treatise*, I.iv.7, 172). But at least in the case of the idea of the self, he does not seem to be able to keep his doubts at bay, and famously although opaquely expresses his doubts about the adequacy of his account in the Appendix to the *Treatise*.[4] One thing that makes Hume's afterthoughts puzzling is that he had offered a proposal that, if accepted, could provide an account of our ideas of *both* external objects and the self as distinct from the apparently fleeting and transitory perceptions that are inconsistent with a coherent idea of either, namely his bundle theory of the self. He first introduced this theory in order to explain how we can have ideas only if they are copies of impressions and yet still form the idea of something that is distinct from our current state of mind:

---

[4] *Treatise*, 398–400. For discussion of competing interpretations of the source of Hume's worry in the Appendix, see Don Garrett, "Hume's Self-Doubts about Personal Identity," *Philosophical Review* 90 (1981): 337–58.

As to the first question, we may observe, that what we call a *mind*, is nothing but a heap or collection of different perceptions, united together by certain relations, and suppos'd, tho' falsely, to be endow'd with a perfect simplicity and identity. Now as every perception is distinguishable from another and may be consider'd as separately existent; it evidently follows, that there is no absurdity in separating any particular perception from the mind; that is, in breaking off all its relations, with that connected mass of perceptions, which constitute a thinking being. (*Treatise*, I.iv.2, 137–38)

Hume's suggestion is that if we think of a perception as a continued existence of which we are not necessarily always conscious, then we can form an idea of the distinct existence of an object on the basis of our mere impressions of such perceptions by forming the idea of the existence of one perception or a combination of several as distinct from the whole bundle of which it is once or sometimes a part. Our tendency to imagine continued existence when we have experienced only resembling existences can then find a noncontradictory target: we can think of the perception that we imagine to be continuous as sometimes existing distinct (and therefore unperceived) from the bundle of which it is sometimes a part (when we are conscious of it). This theory requires that the perceptions we initially think are fleeting and transitory are not really so, which is why I have so repetitively used the qualifier "apparently" above, but that should not be a real problem: that we can only have simple ideas of actual impressions does not imply that every idea we have must veridically represent every aspect of the impression that ultimately grounds it, and the continued existence of perceptions outside of the temporary bundle of them that constitutes a mind or state of mind could be an aspect of them that is not reproduced in our ideas of them. And further, we might suppose, the bundle theory of the mind also explains how we can have an idea of the self that is distinct from our ideas of its several perceptions, although Hume does not quite spell this out (*Treatise*, I.iv.6, 165): the idea of the self is not the idea of something altogether different in nature from perceptions, which we therefore cannot explain, but rather precisely the idea of a bundle of perceptions, or more precisely a temporally extended bundle that various perceptions enter and leave, which is a complex idea that could be formed from our idea of perceptions themselves combined with our idea of a bundle, which can also be formed from an impression (or perhaps more precisely from our impressions of contiguity and succession, assumed to be genuine at the outset of the account of causation).

Why Hume was not satisfied with this account of the origin of our ideas of external objects and the self, if indeed he was not, is not clear. Perhaps he simply found it too speculative to be persuasive. Perhaps he had qualms about supposing that we could form ideas from impressions of perceptions without including a representation of the fleeting and transitory presence of particular perceptions in our bundles of them, or conversely wondered how we could get the idea of continued existence even of perceptions from impressions that present themselves to us only temporarily or intermittently, although his account in the Appendix does not make any such worries explicit. As we shall see, Kant was certainly inclined to take their appearance as fleeting and transitory as real characteristics of our perceptions or, as he calls them, representations (*Pure Reason*, B xli), and this plays a key role in his argument for why we must have genuinely a priori knowledge of something distinct from our mere perceptions altogether. But before we get ahead of ourselves, let us now consider the global structure of Kant's alternative to Hume's accounts of cause, object, and self.

Kant's Answers, Ultimately His Answer

The twofold character of Kant's answers to Hume's twofold doubts consists, first, in his appeal to the resources of both the logic of judgments and the pure forms of intuition for an a priori origin for the concepts that Hume could not derive from sensory impressions, and, second, in his analysis of the conditions of the possibility of empirical knowledge, ultimately empirical knowledge of the self, for his defense of the universal and necessary validity of the principles that Hume could ascribe only to imagination and custom.[5] More fully, Kant derives the concepts that Hume could not in his *transcendental* logic, which proceeds in three steps: first, it identifies fundamental aspects or "functions" of judgment in *general* logic; next, in the "meta-

---

[5] Wayne Waxman, in *Kant and the Empiricists: Understanding Understanding* (New York: Oxford University Press, 2005), argues that Kant should be seen as continuing the "psychologistic" project of Hume and the earlier empiricists, that is, the project of identifying the fundamental contents and principles of our knowledge by discovering the fundamental processes of human cognition, but as rejecting the "sensibilism" and "empiricism" of Hume, that is, his assumptions that the relevant processes of human cognition are all to be found within sense-perception and are all to be discovered empirically. Kant, by contrast, recognizes that among the key processes contributing to cognition there are intellectual ones, and that both sense-perception and intellection have key aspects that can be known a priori rather than intellectually. Specifically, Waxman argues that Kant's great addition to Hume was the idea of transcendental apperception, an act of the synthesis of all the data that we receive from sensibility that must precede and underlie the specific forms of spatiotemporal representation and intellectual conceptualization, including conceptualization in terms of causality. I agree with Waxman that Kant's objection to a psychological deduction of the principles of cognition (see especially *Pure Reason*, A 85–86/B 117–19 and B 127–28) is aimed at a strictly *empiricist* conception of psychology—see my essay "Psychology and the Transcendental Deduction," in *Kant's Transcendental Deductions: The Three "Critiques" and the "Opus Postumum,"* ed. Eckart Förster (Stanford: Stanford University Press, 1989), 47–68—and should not be confused with the neo–Kantian, Husserlian, and Fregean rejection of any kind of psychology as the basis for logic or epistemology. At the same time, the difference between the view of Locke and Hume that all the central concepts of our cognition can be derived from experience and have no genuine content beyond what can be explained by experience and Kant's view that the structure of our own minds furnishes synthetic a priori conditions of the possibility of experience is so profound that it seems misleading to suggest that the empiricists were the precursors of Kant in any sense but that of having turned the attention of philosophy toward the structure of the mind. The empiricists may have started the Copernican revolution by suggesting that we must determine the structure of thought before we can determine the structure of objects, but Kant's view that we have a priori resources for determining the structure of thought is profoundly alien to theirs. Further, although I will myself argue in this chapter that Kant's conception of transcendental apperception can certainly be read as part of his larger answer to Hume, that is, as his answer to the problems about the concept of the self and knowledge of personal identity that Hume had raised even though Kant did not know that, I think it may be a mistake to present Kant's theory of the transcendental unity of apperception as the foundation of his answer to Hume. This is for the simple reason that Kant's

physical deduction" of the pure concepts of the understanding, it associates the logical functions of judgment with the categories, that is, general forms for the concepts of objects, forms that concepts of objects must have if we are to be able to think about those objects by means of judgments, given the forms that judgments have; and finally, in the "schematism" of the pure concepts of the understanding, it assigns the categories spatiotemporal interpretations, reflecting the specifically spatiotemporal a priori structure of our intuitions of objects, so that the concepts of objects we form in accordance with the categories can be used to make judgments about the kinds of objects we actually experience. In transcendental logic, Kant thus appeals to the resources of both general logic and the forms of intuition ("transcendental aesthetic") to explain the origin of the key concepts that eluded Hume. Then Kant goes on to argue that it is only by the presupposition of the principles that in his view Hume doubted—that all change is alteration in the states of enduring substances, that such alterations must always be explainable by antecedent causes, and that the enduring self consists precisely in a sequence of representations that is distinct from but must be caused by alterations in the states of objects external to the self that are themselves causally governed—that we can explain our ability to cognize certain things that Hume, at least in Kant's view, took for granted that we could know, namely determinate changes in the objects of our experience or even in the sequence of our experiences as such. In terms of Kant's architectonic, we might say that the two stages of his

---

theory of the transcendental unity of apperception, especially if it is thought to include a theory of an a priori synthesis of all of our experience that somehow precedes that experience, is obscure and problematic. We may do much better to emphasize Kant's theory of the a priori forms of intuition and understanding, that is, of space, time, and the categories, and their role in *empirical* cognition, including *empirical* self–consciousness or apperception, as the heart of his reply to Hume, rather than placing too much weight on his idea of the *transcendental* unity of apperception. For my longstanding qualms about the idea of a transcendental synthesis on which Waxman relies, see my "Kant on Apperception and *A Priori* Synthesis," *American Philosophical Quarterly* 17 (1980): 205–12, and *Kant and the Claims of Knowledge* (Cambridge: Cambridge University Press, 1987), chap. 5.

response to Hume's twofold questions are reflected in his division between the "Schematism" and the "System of All Principles of Pure Understanding."[6]

(1) The two-staged structure of Kant's answers to Hume should be most evident in his response to Hume's treatment of causation, both because Hume most clearly separated his questions about idea and belief in this case and because Kant understood himself to be explicitly answering Hume only in this case. In the case of causation, then, Kant first accounts for our possession of the concept of causation by the threefold method described above, rather than by the simple appeal to impressions that Hume says must fail or by the displacement of an idea from within to without that Hume subsequently proposes. In the first of these three steps, Kant identifies the "hypothetical" form of judgments—the "if—, then—" structure—as a formal "function" of judgments, in this case one of the ways in which particular, simpler judgments can be linked to form more complex judgments (*Pure Reason*, A 70/B 95). Here Kant simply presupposes the availability of formal logic as a resource for the generation of concepts that Hume had overlooked in his insistence on deriving all concepts from impressions—for Kant, impressions are only the matter for conceptual thought, not the form. Next, Kant designates the relation between ground and consequence as the relation among objects, or their

[6] There have been a number of attempts recently at a "semantic" interpretation of Kant's project in the *Critique of Pure Reason*, that is, an interpretation of him as aiming simply to determine the conditions that make it possible for us to form judgments about objects, regardless of the truth of any particular judgments; see for example Robert Hanna, *Kant and the Foundations of Analytic Philosophy* (Oxford: Oxford University Press, 2001); Zeljko Loparic, *A Semântica Transcendental de Kant* (Campinas, Brazil: UNICAMP Centro de Lógica, Epistemologia e História da Ciência, 2002); and A. B. Dickerson, *Kant on Representation and Objectivity* (Cambridge: Cambridge University Press, 2004). It should be obvious from the present paragraph that I believe such an interpretation describes only the first stage of Kant's project, the second stage of which, aiming to justify certain fundamental principles as conditions for the possibility of empirical knowledge, is epistemological. See also my essay "Space, Time, and the Categories: The Project of the Transcendental Deduction," in *Idealismus als Theorie der Repräsentation?* ed. Ralph Schumacher (Paderborn, Germany: Mentis, 2001), 313–38.

properties or states, that makes it possible to formulate hypothetical judgments about them. Finally, Kant schematizes the general concept of ground and consequence into the specifically spatiotemporal concept of cause and effect, stating that, "The schema of the cause and of the causality of a thing in general is the real upon which, whenever it is posited, something else always follows. It therefore consists in the succession of the manifold insofar as it is subject to a rule" (A 144/B 183). Even this schema is still not a specific concept of a type of causality, such as impact or combustion or photosynthesis. It describes the general form of such concepts, although in spatiotemporal and not merely logical terms, but must itself be applied to our actual empirical intuition precisely through such concrete concepts of causation as those mentioned.

This account, I hasten to admit, simplifies and idealizes what Kant actually wrote. To take the lesser problem first, it will be noted that while I have said that a schematism is a *spatio*-temporal interpretation of a more purely logical form for the conception of objects, Kant characterizes a schema as a "transcendental product of the imagination, which concerns the determination of the inner sense in general, in accordance with conditions of its form (time) in regard to all representations" (A 142/B 180), in other words, as a purely *temporal* form or relation. But Kant will later argue that temporal relations ("time-determinations") can be made only on the basis of spatial relations, for example, we measure the passage of time by the rotation of bodies in space (see B 156 and 288–94), and we could revise his definition of the schema of causation, in a Humean direction, into something like "the succession of states of (spatially contiguous) objects in accordance with a rule" without harm to any of his arguments.[7] So there is not really a problem here.

[7] Adding Hume's requirement of spatial contiguity to Kant's criteria of temporal succession in accordance with a rule would not cause any problem for Kant's general account of the principles of empirical knowledge, but might cause a problem for his physics if he believed in action at a distance. However, his attempt to give an a priori argument for the existence of an all–pervasive ether for the transmission of causality suggests that he was not comfortable with the idea of action at a distance. For a discussion of Kant's attempt to prove the existence of the ether, see my "Kant's

What may seem like more of a problem is that Kant does not actually derive the abstract category of ground and consequence from the form of hypothetical judgments and introduce the more specific concept of cause and effect only as the schema of the category of ground and consequence; rather, he directly introduces the (mixed) relation "Of Causality and Dependence (cause and effect)" into his table of categories (A 80/B 106; I call this mixed because although "dependence" does not have a specifically temporal reference, "causality" does). This might just seem harmlessly overeager, but it has nasty consequences: it is later of great importance for Kant to be able to say that we can *conceive* of non-spatiotemporal objects such as God and our noumenal wills as *grounds* of *consequences* even though we cannot have *cognition* of such objects, which he can do if the general category of ground and consequence is distinct from the schematized category of cause and effect, but which he cannot do if they are identical. Further, even apart from this specific problem for Kantian morality and moral theology, it is patently false that all hypothetical judgments refer to causal relationships or that we must be able to conceive of causal relationships if we are to make any use of the hypothetical form of judgment. We can use the hypothetical form of judgment to express noncausal relationships, as in such claims as "If this is a plane triangle then its interior angles equal two right angles" or "If Kant was a bachelor then he was unmarried." But again this is not really a problem for Kant's larger argument against Hume, for he is not going to infer that there are causal relationships anywhere or everywhere in the world directly from the category of ground and consequence. In fact, if he were to do that he would have to prove not only that the concept of cause and effect is the *only* concept through which we can apply the hypothetical form of judgment but also that we not only *can* but also *must* use the hypothetical form of judgment in the first place, which he never

Ether Deduction and the Possibility of Experience," in *Akten des Siebenten Internationalen Kant Kongresses*, ed. Gerhard Funke (Bonn: Bouvier Verlag, 1991), vol. 2, part 1, 119–32, reprinted in my *Kant's System of Nature and Freedom: Selected Essays* (Oxford: Clarendon Press, 2005), chap. 4.

attempts to do directly. Rather, all that Kant needs to argue for the first stage of his response to Hume is that we *can* get the concept of causation from the schematization of the category of ground and consequence that is in turn the general condition for the application of the hypothetical form of judgment, and this he could argue even if the spatiotemporal concept of causation is not the only kind of relation of ground and consequence we can conceive. The proof that we *must* use the category of causation is separate.

This second part of Kant's answer to Hume, the argument that we not only can legitimately form the concept of causation but also must accept the universal principle of causation, comes in the "Second Analogy" in the "Systematic Representation of All Synthetic Principles of Pure Understanding" (A 189–II/B 232–56). This is the longest of all of Kant's proofs of the principles of knowledge, and is either very complicated or else very repetitive.[8] The fuller account given in the previous chapter will here be simplified in order to focus attention on the parallels with the cases of object and self to be discussed subsequently. The gist of Kant's argument is that a kind of empirical judgment that Hume (like the rest of us) assumes that we can always or at least often make without problem, the judgment that one state of affairs has succeeded another, can be made only on the basis of the principle that Hume questions, that every change has a cause from which it follows in accordance with a rule. Kant's key assumptions are these: although our perceptions or representations of successive states of affairs are successive, *so are all our other perceptions*, even when they are not perceptions of any change outside ourselves; and we cannot immediately tell which of our successions of representations represent changes in any objective states of affairs, even though we might think we can, because even though the sequence of our perceptions of an objective change would be irreversible, *we have no direct percep-*

---

[8] Robert Paul Wolff once identified no fewer than six separate arguments in the section; see his *Kant's Theory of Mental Activity: A Commentary on the Transcendental Analytic of the* Critique of Pure Reason (Cambridge, MA: Harvard University Press, 1963), 260–83.

tion of irreversibility and can rather imagine any sequence of representations as having occurred in a sequence opposite to that in which it did. As Kant puts it, the imagination can always "combine the two states in question in two different ways" (B 233). So, Kant concludes, the only way that I can judge that an objective change has occurred is if I can appeal to a rule that says that one of the states of affairs I have perceived must have preceded and the other must have followed, in which case I can infer that the sequence of my representations was also irreversible ("In our case I must therefore derive the **subjective sequence** of apprehension from the **objective sequence** of appearances"; A 193/B 238). And the only way in which I can infer that one state of affairs must have preceded and the other must have followed is if I can subsume them under a law that says that in the relevant sort of circumstances the one sort of state always precedes and the other always follows—in other words, a causal law. As Kant sums up:

> If therefore we experience that something happens, then we always presuppose that something else precedes it, which it follows in accordance with a rule. For without this I would not say of the object that it follows, since the mere sequence in my apprehension, if it is not, by means of a rule, determined in relation to something preceding, does not justify any sequence in the object. (A 195/B 240)

This argument presupposes that we do know "that something happens," that is, that we are aware of objective successions of states of affairs, and would have no purchase against a skeptic prepared to doubt that. But Hume does not seem to be a skeptic of such a sort: his question, how do we know that what has happened in the past will continue to happen in the future, presupposes that we do know what has happened—what sequences of states of affairs there have been in the past. After all, he takes our consciousness of the temporal succession of our ideas to be as fundamental as our recognition of spatial extension and relation: "As 'tis from the disposition of visible and tangible objects we receive the idea of space, so from the succession of ideas and impressions we form the idea of time" (*Trea-*

tise, I.ii.3, 28). So Kant's argument against Hume seems to be based on a premise that Hume accepts.

(2) I have considered some of the problems with Kant's response to Hume's account of causation in the previous chapter; here I want chiefly to display the two-staged structure of Kant's answer to Hume's concerns about causation so that we can see that he uses a similar structure in his unwitting responses to Hume on object and self. So having established the structure of Kant's response to Hume on causation, I now turn to his approach to the issue of external objects. It should be apparent that Kant's position on this issue has the same general structure as his position on causation, although in this case his presentation of the second stage of the argument suffers from brevity rather than excess, and its epistemological character may not be apparent. The first stage of Kant's response is again to find a basis for the concept of an external existence not in mere impressions but in the resources offered by the transition from logical function of judgment to category to schematized category. Under the rubric of "relation," Kant maintains that the structure of basic judgments, prior to the combination of such judgments in compound hypothetical and disjunctive judgments, is "categorical" (A 70/B 95), the relation "of the predicate to the subject" (A 73/B 98). He associates with this the category of "Inherence and Subsistence (*substantia et accidens*)" (A 80/B 106), assuming that a judgment that asserts a predicate of a subject can apply to an object only insofar as it ascribes an accident or property to a substance. This time he refrains from including any explicit spatiotemporal characteristics in the denomination of the pure category and saves that for the schematized version, thereby leaving open the possibility of non-spatiotemporal substance, as he desires for his subsequent practical purposes. The schema of the category of substance is then "the persistence of the real in time, i.e., the representation of the real as a substratum of empirical time-determination in general, which therefore endures while everything else changes" (A 144/B 183). Although Kant does not immediately say so, given his assumption that all representations as such are "variable and changeable" (B xli), the permanent existence of substance will

ultimately imply that it must be different from any mere representation. He is thus tacitly committed to Hume's view that we must infer distinct existence from continued existence (*Treatise*, I.iv.2, 132), but holds the idea of enduring existence to have a proper source in the combination of the resources of logic with the structure of intuition.

But what entitles Kant to the view that we must represent substance as the enduring substratum of changing states? Why cannot substance be as temporary as its states? Kant explains the categories as "concepts of an object in general, by means of which its intuition is regarded as **determined** with regard to one of the **logical functions** for judgments," by which he seems to mean that a category tells us how to apply the functions of judgment to our experience in a nonarbitrary way. So, he continues:

> The function of the **categorical** judgment was that of the relationship of the subject to the predicate, e.g., "All bodies are divisible." Yet in regard to the merely logical use of the understanding it would remain undetermined which of these two concepts will be given the function of the subject and which will be given that of the predicate. For one can also say: "Something divisible is a body." Through the category of substance, however, if I bring the concept of a body under it, it is determined that its empirical intuition in experience must always be considered as subject, never as mere predicate; and likewise with all the other categories. (B 128–29)

Somehow the category of substance is to tell us what sort of things in our experience is to be referred to by the subjects of our judgments and what sort by the predicates, so that it is not arbitrary whether we say "All bodies are divisible" or "Something divisible is a body." But why must this be nonarbitrary? And even if we suppose this cannot be arbitrary, why should we think that only something permanent can be the subject of predicates, as the schema of the category of substance implies?

Following Hume's precedent of "sinking" one question into another, it will be best to answer both of these questions at once, which will bring us to the second stage of Kant's anti-

Humean position on objects. The main point of Kant's epistemological argument in the first "Analogy of Experience," is that
we must posit the existence of enduring objects because the
only kind of change of which we can have empirical knowledge
is the alteration of the states of objects that do not themselves
go into or out of existence, which makes it natural for us to
make the ultimate subjects of our judgments those objects that
endure, and to use the predicate-place in our judgments to ascribe to those objects their various changing states. This would
mean that the transition from function of judgment to category
to schematized category gives us all the materials we need to
form the idea of enduring substances with changing states,
which because they endure must be distinct from any mere representations, but does not by itself establish the necessity of that
idea. Only the epistemological analysis of the conditions of the
possibility of our empirical knowledge of change establishes the
necessity of using that idea, in the principle that "All appearances contain that which persists (**substance**) as the object itself,
and that which can change as its mere determination, i.e., a way
in which the object exists" (A 182). In this regard Kant's overall
argument about substances exactly parallels the structure of his
argument about causation.

As I mentioned earlier, Kant's exposition of this principle is
brief, and it is far from clear what his argument for it really is.
First he says that the permanence of time itself, which cannot
be immediately perceived, has to be represented by something
(a "substratum") in what we do perceive (A 182–83/B 225–26),
but this does not seem compelling or even coherent. Kant offers
no argument for the general epistemological premise that we
can only represent a property in one thing (the permanence of
time) through the perception of the same property in another
thing (permanence in substance); indeed, this sounds danger-
ously like Hume's principle that we can only have an idea of that
of which we have had an impression, which Kant has clearly
rejected. Moreover, any suggestion that we can immediately perceive the permanence of substance would seem to conflict with
the premise of Kant's argument for the principle of causation
that our perceptions themselves are always successive, therefore

always changing. Next Kant points out that philosophers have always supposed that nothing comes from nothing, thus that anything new must be a changed state of something old but not something completely *ab novo* (A 185–86/B 228–29). But this is not an argument, just an assumption, as Kant makes clear (here Kant is in no mood simply to rely upon common sense).

The real argument for the permanence of substance seems to come when Kant writes:

> Alteration can therefore be perceived only in substances, and arising or perishing per se cannot be a possible perception unless it concerns merely a determination of that which persists that makes possible the representation of the transition from one state into another . . . which can therefore be empirically cognized only as a changing determination of that which lasts. If you assume that something simply began to be, then you would have to have a point in time in which it did not exist. But what would you attach this to, if not to that which already exists? (A 188/B 231)

The interpretation of this passage is not easy. Kant certainly assumes that you cannot perceive a change simply by perceiving a filled state of time following an empty state of time, for although he insists (in the "Transcendental Aesthetic") that we can *imagine* empty time (A 31/B 46), he explicitly says here that "an empty time that would precede is not an object of perception" (A 188/B 231). But even if that is so, why cannot we perceive that a change has taken place simply by observing a different state of affairs at one moment than we observed before, without the later state being an altered property of the same object that was in a different state in the earlier moment? Here it seems that we really have to supply an argument that Kant left out, so I have proposed[9] that his claim could be defended by an argument that says that if we do not conceive of a change that we perceive as a change in the state of a single, enduring

---

[9] Inspired, I hasten to add, by Arthur Melnick, *Kant's Analogies of Experience* (Chicago: University of Chicago Press, 1973), 71–77. For my fuller exposition of this proposal, see my *Kant and the Claims of Knowledge*, 224–30.

object, then we have no way of telling whether we are perceiving a change in anything at all rather than just changing what we are perceiving. For example, if I first perceive some black (I don't want to beg the question by saying "something black") and then perceive some red, I cannot judge that I am perceiving a change from a black state to a red state as opposed to a mere change in which state I am perceiving unless I conceive of what I am perceiving as the change of some one thing from black to red, say a piece of charcoal becoming red hot; otherwise I might just be changing which thing I am attending to, and not perceiving any objective change. But that is to say I can only have empirical cognition of a change when I perceive a substance undergoing an alteration from one state to another, and never simply perceive the creation or cessation of substances per se— which would make it natural to reserve the subject-place of my judgments for substances and to use the predicate-places to refer to their changing states. (It would also imply that the kinds of things we ordinarily think of as substances, such as divisible bodies, are not really substances, because they can surely go into and out of existence. The only things that can ultimately count as substances on Kant's criterion are whatever science tells us last through all changes of state, whether that turns out to be attractive and repulsive forces, atoms, quarks, strings, or whatever comes next.)[10]

One question about the argument here ascribed to Kant seems too obvious to pass up, namely, whether this argument could justify the inference from *continued* existence to *distinct* existence, that is, the existence of anything other than the that has a succession of different representations? Couldn't that self be conceived of as the enduring substance that has changing states?[11] (Although no doubt it is not a truly permanent sub-

[10] For this last point, and a defense of Kant's principle of the conservation of substance, see my *Kant and the Claims of Knowledge*, 230–36, and also Otfried Höffe, *Kants Kritik der reinen Vernunft: Die Grundlegung der modernen Philosophie* (Munich: C. H. Beck, 2003), 183–86.

[11] See Jonathan Vogel, "The Problem of Self–Knowledge in Kant's 'Refutation of Idealism': Two Recent Views," *Philosophy and Phenomenological Research* 53 (1993): 875–87, especially 885–86.

stance that never comes into or goes out of existence, and so must itself be a state of some other sort of substance that does endure!) The answer to this question can ultimately be found in Kant's "Refutation of Idealism," a key assumption of which is that our "empirical consciousness" of our selves is nothing but a determinate dating of our sequence of several representations, so the sequence of the latter cannot be determined by reference to the former, but must instead be determined by something other than the self altogether, therefore by objects that are not only continued but also distinct from the self. This at least is what I take Kant to be suggesting when he writes that "the inner intuition, in which alone my existence can be determined, is sensible, and is bound to a condition of time; however, this determination, and hence inner experience itself, depends on something permanent, which is not in me" (B xl). Fleshed out, this argument would have to be that I do not have immediate knowledge of the changing sequence of my own representations, because, as Kant pointed out in the second "Analogy," at any one time I can always imagine that the sequence of my representations is other than what I think it is, but I cannot have determinate knowledge of their sequence simply by ascribing them to my continuing self, because my representation of that is nothing but the representation of the determinate sequence of my representations; so to arrive at the latter I must go outside of the self altogether, and determine the sequence of my representations by interpreting them as representations of the changing states of some distinct substance.[12]

(3) In recounting Kant's arguments for both our idea and our knowledge of things distinct from ourselves, we have inevitably come to his analysis of the conditions of the possibility of self-knowledge itself. So let me know turn explicitly to Kant's thoughts about the self, and see whether we can find in Kant a response to Hume's concerns that we cannot form a genuine idea of the self in contrast to our ideas of its several impressions, and that even if we could we have no claim to real knowledge

---

[12] See my detailed account of this argument in *Kant and the Claims of Knowledge*, 305–17.

of its continued existence. What I want to argue here is that Kant suggests an account of the origin of an a priori idea of the self from the resources of logic, and that while he completely agrees with Hume that we have no knowledge of the continued existence of a simple, qualitatively identical substance that is the self (this is what he argues in the "Paralogisms of Pure Reason," A 341–405 and B 399–432), he does argue that we have genuine empirical knowledge of the continued existence of our *self-consciousness* with changing, qualitatively complex contents, and that this is based on a priori conditions of its possibility, in fact, the very same a priori principles about substance and causation already defended against Hume's doubts about those concepts.

Kant's treatment of the self is a large and vexed subject, and I need to limit my claims about it here severely.[13] First, I want to set aside any discussion of Kant's apparent suggestion that in "transcendental apperception" we have a priori but also synthetic knowledge of the numerical identity of our selves throughout the whole of our experiences (A 107, A 113, A 117n). I do this not because Kant does not assert such a thesis[14]—the passages just cited do make such a claim—but because it is not obvious how he could actually defend it. Second, I also want to set aside a recent proposal that by "apperception" Kant does not actually mean any form of self-consciousness or self-knowledge, but only, like Leibniz, one's non-self-referential awareness of the several representations that can comprise one's complex representation of an object.[15] While that proposal is certainly compatible with some of Kant's uses of the term (e.g., A 115, possibly B 139, B 142), it is equally obviously incompatible with many more of his other key uses (e.g., A 108, A 111, A 113, A 116, A 117n, A 122, A 123–24, B 132, B 140, B 157). Rather, what

---

[13] For an exhaustive (409–page) discussion, see Heiner F. Klemme, *Kants Philosophie des Subjekts: Systematische und entwicklungsgeschichtliche Untersuchungen zum Verhältnis von Selbstbewußtsein und Selbsterkenntnis*, Kant–Forschungen, Band 7 (Hamburg: Felix Meiner Verlag, 1996).

[14] As has been maintained by Henry Allison in "Apperception and Analyticity in the B–Deduction," in his *Idealism and Freedom: Essays on Kant's Theoretical and Practical Philosophy* (Cambridge: Cambridge University Press, 1996), 41–52.

[15] See Dickerson, *Kant on Representation and Objectivity*, 80–98.

I want to emphasize is only Kant's claim that we have an a priori formal concept of the self as a unity of diverse representations, which can yield empirical knowledge of the diverse contents of a continuing self only when filled in with particular representations, the order of which can in turn be determined only by connecting them to the changing states of external objects, whose alterations must be governed by causal laws and whose determination of the sequence of our own perceptions of them must also be determined by causal laws.

For present purposes, then, Kant's concept of apperception can be understood simply as the a priori concept of "the thoroughgoing identity of ourselves with regard to all representations that can ever belong to our cognition" (A 116), of the "**one consciousness**" that contains a synthesis of different representations (B 133), or of "the manifold representations of intuition . . . being **combined** in one consciousness, without any implication that our knowledge that any particular representations are related by means of this concept is synthetic a priori. Kant also sometimes uses the term "apperception" to refer to the faculty or power of combining representations into the representation of a self as well as to the product of that power, namely the combination itself (e.g., B 153). If Kant's account of the origin of this idea is to parallel his accounts of the origins of the ideas of cause and substance, it should begin with the logical functions of judgment and then combine a category derived from that with a pure form of intuition to yield a schematized category. But it is not immediately apparent that Kant can so derive the a priori idea of the unity of consciousness, for the simple reason that the concept of the self appears neither on the list of pure categories nor on the list of schematized categories (nor on a list of basic concepts in any contemporary logic textbook)—in this regard, Kant's treatment of the concept of the self is not exactly analogous to his treatments of the concepts of cause and substance. However, a flexible conception of the logical form of judgment may get around this problem. In the second-edition version of the "Transcendental Deduction," Kant famously says that "The **I think** must **be able** to accompany all my representations; for otherwise something would be represented in me that could not be thought at all. . . . Thus all manifold of intuition has a necessary relation to the I think in the same subject in which this manifold is to be encountered. But this representation is an act of spontaneity, i.e., it cannot be regarded as belonging to sensibility. I call it the pure apperception" (B 131–32). Our representations include not just individual impressions or empirical intuitions, but also judgments, which are complex representations of representations. So any time I can think some judgment , for example "S is P," Kant is claiming, I must also be able to think "I think that S is P." Take that as part of the full characterization of the form of judgment. Then the function "I think that . . ." would be one of the logical functions of judgment, even though not explicitly included on Kant's table—it would be an implicit part of the structure of any judgment. It would be the function by means of which a manifold of representations would be assigned to one's self, since any content of the form "S is P" is already a manifold of representations. And then the concept of the self would be the concept of that to which such a manifold of representations is ascribed, just as the concept of a substance is the concept of a subject to which predicates are ascribed, or the concept of a cause is the concept of the ground of a consequence. So if it is a part of logic and therefore a priori that we can formulate any judgment in the form "I think that," then the concept of the self to which the "I think that . . ." function refers must also be a priori, and, contrary to Hume, we do not need to seek for any distinctive impression of the self among the contents of our other impressions. The concept of the self would be given by logic rather than phenomenology.

But what about the schematism of this, thus far, merely logical conception of the self? That is, how do we get an a priori idea of the temporally extended self, analogous to the ideas of substance as the permanent in time or causation as succession in time in accordance with a rule? Here we simply have to recall the general remark on which, as Kant says at the outset of the first-edition deduction, "one must ground everything that follows," namely,

> Wherever our representations may arise, whether through the
> influence of external things or as the effect of inner causes,
> whether they have originated or empirically as appearances—
> as modifications of the mind they nevertheless belong to
> inner sense, and as such all of our cognitions are in the end
> subjected to the formal condition of inner sense, namely time,
> as that in which they must all be ordered, connected, and
> brought into relations. (A 98–99)

That is itself supposed to be an a priori claim: the "Transcendental Aesthetic" is supposed to have shown that we have a priori
knowledge that time is the form of all our representations. And
that means that any manifold to be united in a representation
of the unity of the consciousness of the self is a temporally extended manifold. So the unity of apperception must be the form
for the representation of a temporally extended manifold as the
manifold of representations of a single self. Further, as one continues to receive representations in the actual course of one's
experience, one's representation of their combination will continue to develop, and so the instantiation of the general idea of
the unity of apperception itself, that is, the representation of the
combination of one's representations, must also be conceived of
as temporally extended and developing. In this way the a priori
resources of logic on the one hand and the form of all intuition
on the other hand give rise to an a priori conception of the
temporally extended self that has representations.

We can take this as Kant's response to Hume's complaint
that he cannot find an *idea* of the self among his impressions.
What about Hume's concern that we have no genuine *knowledge* of the existence of a simple and identical self? As already
mentioned, Kant completely agrees that we have no knowledge,
hence no a priori knowledge, of the existence of a simple self,
and also suggests one line of thought on which we have no
synthetic a priori knowledge about the self except perhaps the
knowledge at any given time *that* I am.[16] But he will argue that

---

[16] I say that because of Kant's statement at B 157 that "In the transcendental
synthesis of the manifold of representations in general . . . hence in the synthetic
original unity of apperception, I am conscious of myself not as I appear to myself,

we justifiably employ the a priori idea of the self in genuine empirical knowledge of the temporally extended self with ever changing contents.

The first of these points is one of Kant's central claims in the "Paralogisms of Pure Reason," in which he gives his argument that the proposition that the "soul, or thinking I," is simple is "the Achilles of all the dialectical inferences of the pure doctrine of the soul" (A 351), that is, a thesis that seems invulnerable, but has an Achilles' heel, a vulnerable spot that must be found by careful diagnosis (and thus cannot be dismissed by a merely empirical claim that we cannot find a simple impression of the self). The key to Kant's diagnosis is his claim that even if the representation of the self, the representation "I," is simple, that does not imply that the itself is simple. As he puts it in the first edition, that "**I am simple** signifies no more than that this representation **I** encompasses not the least manifoldness within itself, and . . . it is an absolute (though merely logical) unity"; thus "the so famous psychological proof is grounded merely on the indivisible unity of a representation" (A 355). Or as he states about the error of all the paralogisms in the second edition, "The logical exposition of thinking in general is falsely held to be a metaphysical determination of the object" (B 409). To the specific claim of the first edition, one might object that it is not so clear that the representation "I" is really simple (although the English name for this representation is about as simple as can be!); after all, haven't we already analyzed it in describing the concept of the self as the concept of that to which the manifold of representations must be attributed? But even if this is a worry, the more general point of the second edition remains: we simply

---

nor as I am in myself, but only that I am." But I say "perhaps" because elsewhere Kant says that although "The 'I think' . . . contains within itself the proposition 'I exist,' " he also says that "I think" is itself "an empirical proposition" (B 422n). Kant believes that a proposition ultimately inherits its epistemic status from that from which it is derived—a mathematical proposition is synthetic a priori if it is derived from one that is synthetic a priori, even if the derivation proceeds solely in accordance with the law of noncontradiction (B 14); so if the proposition "I exist" is derived analytically from an empirical one it should still be empirical, and therefore not synthetic a priori.

cannot automatically assume that characteristics of representations are also characteristics of their objects. So even if the combination of general logic and transcendental aesthetic give us an a priori and (somehow) simple representation of the self, that does not give us a priori knowledge of the simplicity of the self. That conclusion could then be combined with Hume's empirical argument and indeed Kant's own argument in the "Antithesis" of the second "Antinomy of Pure Reason" (A 435–37/B 463–65) to establish that we have neither a priori nor a posteriori knowledge of the simplicity of the self.

So thus far Kant agrees with Hume. But then comes the positive part of his view of self-knowledge: we do have genuine although empirical knowledge of the self, not as something simple but as something enduring with complex contents with a determinate order among them. We might say that this is the culminating thesis of Kant's revisions to both the "Transcendental Deduction" and the "System of the Principles of the Pure Understanding" in the second edition of the *Critique*: §§24–25 of the second-edition deduction make the general point that neither pure apperception nor mere inner sense amount to determinate knowledge of the self, but that such knowledge requires determination of the manifold empirical intuitions in inner sense through the "synthetic influence of the understanding on the inner sense" (B 154), and will therefore be empirical knowledge; and the "Refutation of Idealism" attempts to spell out how this determination works.

I have discussed the "Refutation of Idealism" in detail elsewhere,[17] so I will just suggest its key moves here. The premise of Kant's argument is that the mere occurrence of representa-

[17] I have presented detailed accounts of the "Refutation of Idealism" and associated texts in "Kant's Intentions in the Refutation of Idealism," *The Philosophical Review* 92 (1983): 329–83, reprinted in *Immanuel Kant*, ed. Heiner F. Klemme and Manfred Kuehn, The International Library of Critical Essays in the History of Philosophy (Dartmouth, UK: Ashgate, 1999), 1: 277–332; *Kant and the Claims of Knowledge*, 279–329; and "The Postulates of Empirical Thinking in General and the Refutation of Idealism," in *Kant: Kritik der reinen Vernunft*, ed. Georg Mohr and Marcus Willaschek (Berlin: Akademie–Verlag, 1998), 297–324. For a response to my interpretation, see Vogel, "The Problem of Self–Knowledge in Kant's 'Refutation of Idealism.'"

tions in inner sense does not by itself amount to determinate knowledge of the sequence of those representations (something that everyone, even Hume, assumes we have). In his words, "inner sense . . . contains the mere **form** of intuition, but without combination of the manifold in it, which is possible only through the consciousness of the determination of the manifold through the transcendental action of the imagination (synthetic influence of the understanding on the inner sense)" (B 154). Kant does not spell out why the mere occurrence of representations in inner sense is not sufficient for determinate knowledge or, as he calls it, "empirical consciousness" (B 275) of their sequence, but we can assume that he has in mind two facts: first, that at the time of the occurrence of any later member in a sequence of representations one no longer has all the previous representations, but has to remember them; but, second, as he explicitly premised in the "Second Analogy," we can always imagine that any sequence of representations occurred in a different order from that in which we presently think it did.[18] From these assumptions we can infer that in order to have empirical knowledge of the sequence of our own representations, we have to constrain the imagination's ability to vary our recollection of their sequence by something other than the contents of those representations as such. This cannot be done by some straightforward appeal to the enduring empirical self, for that is what we need to construct; nor can it be done by any purely internal laws about representational sequences, for our representational faculties must be able to represent the sequence of changes in

---

[18] This addresses the question raised by Vogel (p. 585), namely, why couldn't qualitative differences between two states of mind considered merely as such, rather than as representations of some states of one or more external objects, suffice to make us aware that there is a succession in our own representations? The answer is that they could, but would not suffice to tell us *which* succession has occurred, that is, in which order we must have experienced these different mental states, or, more precisely, the original mental states represented by our current representations of them. The situation is the same as in the second Analogy: we can tell without further premises that the representations of a ship upstream and of a ship downstream are representations of two different states of affairs, but without a causal law we cannot tell which of these states must have preceded the other, thus which event transpired (the ship sailing downstream from upstream or vice versa).

the external world, assuming there is one, and that could not be done if our faculty of representations had its own internal laws dictating our sequences of representations.[19]

In the published text of the "Refutation of Idealism," Kant merely says that "All time-determination presupposes something **persistent** in perception," which must be outside me, "since my own existence in time can first be determined only through this persistent thing" (B 275). In some of the many further versions of the "Refutation" that he wrote between 1788 and 1790, however, that is, after the publication of the revised *Critique*, he spelled out what he had in mind in a little more detail:[20] his suggestion is that we must determine the sequence of our own representations by regarding them as representations of successive states of enduring objects, in accordance with the "First Analogy," other than ourselves, and where, further, in accordance with the "Second Analogy," the successive states of those objects must be governed by causal laws, but where we must also presuppose causal laws linking our representations to those external states of affairs, so that we can correlate the order of our representations to the order of those successive states. All of this I at least take to be implied by Kant's statement:

> I cannot know time as antecedently determined, in order to determine my own existence therein. (Therefore [I can determine it] only insofar as I connect my own alterations according to the law of causality.) Now in order to determine that empirically, something which endures must be given, in the apprehension of which I can cognize the succession of my own representations and through which alone . . . a series,

---

[19] Except on Leibniz's supposition that there is a preestablished harmony between the sequence of representations in a monad and all the other sequences of change in the world beyond that monad (e.g., *Discourse on Metaphysics*, §14), a supposition that Kant violently rejects at B 167–68, A 274–75/B 330–31, and A 390–91.

[20] These further drafts of the "Refutation of Idealism" are Reflections 6311–17, "Leningrad Fragment I," and 6319, translated in Kant, *Notes and Fragments*, ed. Paul Guyer, trans. Curtis Bowman, Paul Guyer, and Frederick Rauscher (Cambridge: Cambridge University Press, 2005), 355–74.

of which each part disappears when another comes into being, can become a whole. wherein I posit my existence. (Reflection 6313, 18: 615; *Notes and Fragments*, 359)[21]

The basic idea is that I can assign a determinate order to my own representations, most of which are now past, only by correlating them, by means of causal laws determining the relationship between states of objects and my representations of those objects, with successive states of enduring substances other than myself, which can in turn be assigned their determinate order only by causal laws governing the relation of their states to one another.[22] "Empirical consciousness," or determinate knowledge of the successive states of the empirical self, is therefore possible, but only by means of our a priori concepts of self, external, enduring objects, and causation and the a priori principles that substance endures through alterations of its state and that such alterations are governed by causal laws.

In the end, then, Kant presents not just parallel answers to Hume's doubts about cause, object, and self, but an integrated response. Where Hume fails to find impressions that could ground our ideas of cause, object, and self, Kant exploits the additional resources of logic and pure intuition to show that we can form such ideas independently of impressions, and thus a priori. And where Hume supposes that we can have determinate knowledge of the sequence of our own representations without already assuming external objects and causation, mere belief in which he supposes can be produced by the imagination from our prior impressions, Kant ultimately argues that the possibility

[21] In my elision, I have omitted the words "the simultaneity of." I think that what Kant means by this misleading term is that by the mechanism he is describing we transform a succession of representations at different times into a representation at one time of that succession; but establishing that would require a detailed examination of several passages in his notes besides the one quoted, so I simplify matters by leaving it out.

[22] I emphasize the need for both kinds of causal laws in order to save Kant from the famous charge that he has committed a "*non sequitur* of numbing grossness" in supposing that we need causal laws linking states of objects to one another when in fact all we need is causal laws linking our representations to objects. See P. F. Strawson, *The Bounds of Sense* (London: Methuen, 1966), 137.

of determinate knowledge of the history of our own representations that Hume takes for granted presupposes our commitment to the endurance of external objects through their alterations of states and to the causal governance of such alterations as well as the effect of those alterations on our own perceptions.

Is all of this a good answer to Hume? That is a vast question. Kant's complex model of self-consciousness would certainly be ludicrous if taken as a phenomenological description of consciousness in our ordinary moments as adults, let alone as small children. For this reason, Hume, who fancied himself an empirical scientist of the mind, who must "glean up our experiments in this science from a cautious observation of human life, and take them as they appear in the common course of the world" (*Treatise*, Introduction, 6), might well have rejected Kant's approach altogether; and for this same reason I have suggested that we should take Kant's views about the dependency of our concepts and knowledge of ourselves as an epistemological account of the conditions of the possibility of confirming our judgments rather than as anything like an empirical psychology of our beliefs or even a "transcendental psychology" of how the mind constitutes representations of both itself and other objects.[23] But Kant's identification of a priori sources of our ideas of self, objects, and causes in the forms of judgment and pure intuition certainly seems more promising than Hume's empiricist restriction of ideas to copies of impressions, and Kant's account of the interrelations among our judgments about self, objects, and causes at the very least suggests that Hume could hardly throw up his hands about the first two while maintaining his confidence in the latter.

---

[23] For criticism of my "epistemic" approach to Kant, see Béatrice Longuenesse, *Kant and the Capacity to Judge*, trans. Charles T. Wolfe (Princeton, NJ: Princeton University Press, 1998), 337–38. But I remain convinced that a traditional interpretation of Kant, according to which a "transcendental," timeless self literally constitutes both a temporal, "empirical" self and the world of empirical objects, is subject to insuperable difficulties, and that the only way to continue to make use of Kant is to interpret him as offering a theory of the origin of our concepts and of the conditions of the possibility of confirming our judgments, but not as insisting upon a theory of our constitution of the objects of our judgments.

4

REASON, DESIRE,

AND ACTION

IT SEEMS as if there could hardly be two more opposed positions on the relations between reason, desire, and action than those of Hume and Kant. Hume famously holds that reason is incapable of furnishing a motive and end for action, and is strictly limited to determining suitable means for the realization of ends that are set by desire alone. Thus, "Reason is, and ought to be only the slave of the passions, and can never pretend to any other office than to serve and obey them" (*Treatise*, II.iii.3, 266), and "'Tis not contrary to reason to prefer the destruction of the whole world to the scratching of my finger. 'Tis not contrary to reason for me to choose my total ruin, to prevent the least uneasiness of an *Indian* or a person wholly unknown to me." A desire or affection, Hume claims, can be called "unreasonable" or contrary to reason only if it "is founded on the supposition of the existence of objects, which really do not exist," and/or if "we choose means insufficient for the design'd end, and deceive ourselves in our judgment of causes and effects" (267). And since reason is incapable of providing any motive and end for action, and morality concerns the motives and ends of action, reason is incapable of providing any motive and end for morality. Kant, however, holds that pure reason must and can provide the end, the principle, and a sufficient motive for morality. The moral law must originate within pure reason alone: "Everyone must grant that a law, if it is to hold morally, that is, as a ground of obligation, must carry with it absolute necessity . . . that, therefore, the ground of obligation must not be sought in the nature of the human being or in the circumstances of the world in which he is placed, but *a priori* simply in concepts of pure reason" (*Groundwork*, Preface, 4: 389); and pure reason alone must determine the end for the moral will, apparently nothing other than the production of a *good* will itself:

> Since reason is . . . given to us as a practical faculty, that is, one that is to influence the **will**; then, where nature has everywhere else gone to work purposively in distributing its capacities, the true vocation of reason must be to produce a will that is good, not perhaps **as a means** to other purposes, but **good in itself**, for which reason was absolutely necessary. This will need not, because of this, be the sole and complete good, but it must still be the highest good and the condition of every other, even of all demands for happiness. (*Groundwork*, I, 4: 396)

It is hard not to read Kant's claim that reason's role is not merely to produce a will that is good as a means to some other purpose that is not itself determined by reason as anything other than diametrically opposed to Hume's thesis that reason's role is only to discover actions that would be sufficient means to ends set by desire entirely independently from reason.

Surprisingly, Kant does not directly engage Hume's view that reason can recommend actions only as means to ends that are given independently of it anywhere in his writings on moral philosophy, although Hume at least briefly recapitulates the detailed arguments for this conclusion that he had offered in the *Treatise* in the first section of the *Enquiry concerning the Principles of Morals* (*Enquiry II*, Section 1), nor does he directly engage Francis Hutcheson on this point (from whom Hume adopted his purely instrumental conception of practical reason lock, stock, and barrel),[1] although he often cites Hutcheson as a chief representative of the "moral sense" theory that moral principles

---

[1] See Francis Hutcheson, *An Essay on the Nature and Conduct of the Passions, with Illustrations on the Moral Sense*, Treatise II, Sections I–III; in the edition by Aaron Garrett (Indianapolis: Liberty Fund, 2002), 137–73.

are based on feeling rather than reason.[2] Rather, Kant's most extensive discussion of Hume in the *Critique of Practical Reason* excoriates Hume for having advocated a general "skepticism with respect to inferences rising from effects to causes" rather than having recognized, as did Kant, that causal laws of nature can hold for all objects of experience while not holding for things as they are in themselves, or more precisely, while the moral law of pure practical reason rather than any law of nature holds for the free will as a "*causa noumenon*" (*Practical Reason*, 5: 52, 55)—in other words, for not having arrived at Kant's solution to the problem of free will.[3]

---

[2] For example, *Practical Reason*, 5: 40, where Hutcheson is the example of a philosopher who holds that the "practical material determining grounds in the principle of morality" lie in "internal" and "subjective" "moral feeling." In the 1760s, when Kant insisted that the "immediate supreme rule of all obligation must be absolutely indemonstrable," he held that "Hutcheson and others have, under the name of moral feeling, provided us with a starting point to develop some excellent observations" about the "indispensable" but "indemonstrable" "postulates" that "contain the foundations of all other practical principles"; see *Inquiry concerning the Distinctness of the Principles of Natural Theology and Morality*, Fourth Reflection, §2, 2: 300, as well as *M. Immanuel Kant's Announcement of the Programme of His Lectures for the Winter Semester, 1765–1766*, 2: 311, where he does mention Hume along with Hutcheson. (Both of these texts are translated in Immanuel Kant, *Theoretical Philosophy, 1755–1770*, ed. David E. Walford in collaboration with Ralf Meerbote [Cambridge: Cambridge University Press, 1992].) Obviously Kant's later attitude toward the moral sense school was less favorable than his earlier attitude; this change of view was explicit in Kant's lectures on moral philosophy by the late 1770s, by which time he was arguing that any foundation of the supreme principle of morality on a feeling, even a moral feeling, would grant it mere "private validity" and give rise to no obligation, because there is "no obligation to act in accordance with feeling"; see Immanuel Kant, *Vorlesung über Moralphilosophie*, ed. Werner Stark (Berlin: Walter de Gruyter, 2004), 58. This is an edition of the Kaehler transcription of Kant's course from the summer semester of 1777; the passage is repeated verbatim in the Collins transcription from the winter semester of 1784–85, which is translated in Immanuel Kant, *Lectures on Ethics*, ed. Peter Heath and J. B. Schneewind (Cambridge: Cambridge University Press, 1997), see 66.

[3] Kant also describes Hume in the Preface to the second *Critique* as having been "quite content with [his] system of universal empiricism of principles" (5: 13), without explicitly saying that this committed Hume to empiricism or skepticism about moral principles.

Perhaps Kant shied away from a direct engagement with Hume on the question of whether reason can set ends or merely discover means, because in spite of the profound contrast between their views on this issue, there are also some deep affinities between their conceptions of the relations between reason, desire, and action—some clearly intended and other perhaps not—and it is these that shall be the topic of this chapter.[4] First, both Hume and Kant share the "internalist" principle that any genuine moral principle must be a motive for action:[5] that principle is the premise for Hume's argument that reason *cannot* be the source of genuine moral principles, because he does not see

[4] I have discussed Kant's attempt to show that pure reason sets the necessary end for moral action—by setting itself as that end—in a number of publications, beginning with "The Possibility of the Categorical Imperative," *Philosophical Review* 104 (1995): 353–85, reprinted in my *Kant on Freedom, Law, and Happiness* (Cambridge: Cambridge University Press, 2000), chap. 5; and also including "The Form and Matter of the Categorical Imperative," in *Kant und die Berliner Aufklärung: Akten des IX. Internationalen Kant-Kongresses*, ed. Volker Gerhardt, Rolf-Peter Horstmann, and Ralph Schumacher (Berlin: Walter de Gruyter, 2001), 1: 131–50, and "Ends of Reason and Ends of Nature: The Place of Teleology in Kant's Ethics," *Journal of Value Inquiry* 36 (2002): 161–86, both reprinted in my *Kant's System of Nature and Freedom* (Oxford: Clarendon Press, 2005), chaps. 7 and 8; my *Kant* (London: Routledge, 2006), chap. 5; and my *Kant's Groundwork for the Metaphysics of Morals: A Reader's Guide* (London: Continuum Books, 2007), chap. 5, sections 2–3.

[5] "Internalism" is a term that neither Hume nor Kant use, but it has many meanings in contemporary moral philosophy. It is fairly easy to say what kind of internalism Kant holds: in the first instance, Kant is a *normative* internalist, for he holds that respect for the moral law ought to be our motive for acting in accordance with the law; we might then say he is also a *metaphysical* internalist, because, using the "ought implies can" principle, he infers from his normative internalism that a respect for the moral always *can* be our motive for complying with the moral law (although he famously gets himself into trouble when he sometimes infers that respect for the moral law ensures that we will comply with the moral law). Hume's position is less obvious: he clearly does not infer that morality must be motivating from some antecedent moral concept or principle like Kant's concept of the good will, nor would he seem to be able to infer it a priori from any other sort of concept; so it would seem that he could only infer it from a common conception of morality that he formulates on the basis of observation. For discussion of this issue, see Charlotte Brown, "Is Hume an Internalist?" *Journal of the History of Philosophy* 26 (1988): 69–87, and Elizabeth S. Radcliffe, "How Does the Humean Sense of Duty Motivate?" *Journal of the History of Philosophy* 34 (1996): 383–407.

how reason can be motivating, but it is equally the basis for Kant's conviction that reason must be capable of producing a distinctive moral feeling, because he also assumes that some sort of what Hume would call an "affection" must be the proximate phenomenal or empirical cause of any action, and therefore infers that pure reason must produce a moral feeling that can in turn cause the action that reason requires. Second, both Hume and Kant assume that at the phenomenal level—which is all there is for Hume, although not for Kant—we can and ought to modify those of our natural desires and inclinations that might lead to actions that would be unwelcome—for Kant, unwelcome to pure practical reason, for Hume, unwelcome in the light of some moral principle grounded in some other, welcome sentiment—by various natural techniques for reweighting individual desires and thereby producing an altered constellation of desires and in turn actions. Finally, while in presenting his general thesis that moral principles are grounded in sentiment rather than reason Hume insists so dramatically that all actions are equally good in the eye of reason, he does not really think that it would be either natural or reasonable to prefer the destruction of the whole world to the scratching of one's finger, but instead supposes that we can set ourselves the goal of a life that would satisfy a coherent set of desires in which the desire for calm and tranquility is primus inter pares, a goal that, if not set by reason per se, is set by a part of us that is capable of playing a similarly supervisory role over our other desires; and while Kant, especially the mature Kant of the 1780s, is certainly convinced that he can derive the validity of the moral law from some entirely a priori conception of our rationality, in fact his original argument in behalf of adherence to the moral law furnished by pure practical reason was that it is the only means to a life in which we are dominated neither by our own mere impulses nor by the mere impulses of others—a goal that may not be all that different from Hume's goal of a life in service of a calm and coherent set of desires, affections, or passions—and this thought, although supposedly entirely removed from empirical psychology or what Kant called "anthropology," may well underlie the conception of dignity that is the foundation for the entire edifice of Kant's mature moral philosophy.

I will first defend the three claims I have just made about Hume, and then defend my claims about Kant.

Hume

Here I want to establish, first, that Hume's argument that reason cannot be the source of the principles of morality is based on the assumption that any genuine principle of morality must be motivating, which Kant shares; second, that Hume holds that we can modify our choices of actions by modifying our desires by means of various behavioral practices rather than by some sheer act of will, a model that Kant also shares; and third, that Hume has a conception of the desirability of a life of calm passions that is not all that different from the conception of the goal of a life not ruled by impulse to which the use of pure reason is the necessary means that, I suggest, underlies Kant's entire moral philosophy.

(1) The following passage from the first Part and Section of the *Treatise*'s Book III, "Of Morals," shows that the assumption that moral principles must be motivating is the central premise in Hume's argument that reason is not the source of moral principles:

> If morality had naturally no influence on human passions and actions, 'twere in vain to take such pains to inculcate it; and nothing wou'd be more fruitless than that multitude of rules and precepts, with which all moralists abound. . . .
>
> Since morals, therefore, have an influence on the actions and affections, it follows, that they cannot be deriv'd from reason; and that because reason alone, as we have already prov'd, can never have any such influence. Morals excite passions, and produce or prevent actions. Reason of itself is utterly impotent in this particular. The rules of morality, therefore, are not conclusions of our reason. (*Treatise*, III.i.i., 294)

Why is Hume so confident that reason "can never have any such influence" and "is utterly impotent in this particular"?

For an answer to this question, Hume refers us back to the section of Book II from which the opening citations of this chapter have been drawn. What this section shows is that Hume thinks that reason is incapable of having any influence on action other than that of determining suitable means for the realization of ends set by desire or passion because he conceives of reason in a particular way. In this section, Hume sets out to "prove *first*, that reason alone can never be a motive to any action of the will; and *secondly*, that it can never oppose passion in the direction of the will." He then bases his proof on the premise that "The understanding"—here obviously equated with reason—"exerts itself after two different ways, as it judges from demonstration or probability," that is, "as it regards the abstract relations of our ideas, or those relations of objects, of which experience only gives us information." In Kantian language, reason or understanding either analyzes the contents of our concepts a priori or establishes causal relations among objects a posteriori. Hume scornfully insists that "it scarce will be asserted, that the first species of reasoning alone is ever the cause of any action," for it deals only with ideas, while the will "always place[s] us in [the world] of realities." So he initially focuses on the possibility that empirical causal reasoning could be the source of morality. His argument is then just that causal reasoning, which as Book I of the *Treatise* has shown is always based on experience rather than anything a priori, comes into the determination of action only to find means once ends have been set by desire.

Here is the heart of his argument:

> 'Tis obvious, that when we have the prospect of pain or pleasure from any object, we feel a consequent emotion of aversion or propensity, and are carry'd to avoid or embrace what will give us this uneasiness or satisfaction. 'Tis also obvious, that this emotion rests not here, but making us cast our view on every side, comprehends whatever objects are connected with its original one by the relation of cause and effect. Here

then reasoning takes place to discover this relation; and according as our reasoning varies, our actions receive a subsequent variation. But 'tis evident in this case, that the impulse arises not from reason, but is only directed by it. (*Treatise*, II.iii.3, 266)

Discovering that one thing is the cause of another could not by itself give us a motive to do anything. Having a desire to do some thing or an aversion to having it happen, however, gives us a motive to find out what would bring it about or prevent it, and so gives us a motive to engage in the causal reasoning that will then tell us what needs to be done in order to realize our preference. It is in this sense that reason "is and ought to be only the slave of the passions," that is, it is the instrument for the discovery of the means to the ends set by passion. And it is from this picture of the limited role of reason that Hume then derives his famous conclusion that as far as reason alone is concerned a preference for the destruction of the world is as good as a preference to avoid scratching one's finger. Reason can only tell us what we need to do in order to bring about or avert the destruction of the world or the scratching of a finger, whichever we independently desire.[6]

While his focus in Book II is on the place of causal reasoning in morality, however, Hume does make one argument against the idea that a priori reasoning about concepts could be the source of any moral motive or principle, and then returns to this topic in the first section of Book III. His argument in Book II is that since "A passion is an original existence, or, if you will, modification of existence, and contains not any representative quality, which renders it a copy of any other existence or modification," it is therefore impossible "that this passion can be oppos'd by, or be contradictory to truth and reason; since this contradiction consists in the disagreement of ideas, consider'd as copies, with those objects, which they represent" (*Treatise*,

---

[6] For the two-stage structure in which Hume first eliminates a priori reasoning and then eliminates a posteriori, causal reasoning as possible original sources of motivation, see also Brown, "Is Hume an Internalist?" 71–72, and Elijah Milgram, "Was Hume a Humean?" *Hume Studies* 21 (1995): 75–93, at 77–78.

II.iii.3, 266–67). This argument is not compelling for two reasons: first, it does not so much prove that reasoning cannot produce passions, which would be motivating, as rather that passions do not provide premises for reasoning; and second, Hume has tacitly changed his definition of the first form of reasoning, now treating it as concerning not "abstract relations" among concepts or their components but rather relations between representations and the external objects they represent, in particular already extant external objects.[7]

Perhaps Hume recognized the weakness of this argument; in any case, in his defense of the claim that moral distinctions are not derived from reason in the opening section of Book III, Hume does not just rely upon an appeal back to the arguments of Book II, but offers further support for his claim that reason in its first form, that is, the capacity to analyze relations among ideas rather than to discover causal relations founded in experience, cannot be the source of moral motivations and principles. He now refines his definition of reason, equating it with "the discovery of truth or falshood," which in turn can consist in agreement or disagreement either within the "*real* relations of ideas" or between ideas and "*real* existence or matter of fact." This obviates my charge against the earlier argument that he is departing from his own conception of reason when he argues that because passions are not representations of real existence they cannot be unreasonable. Next, Hume refines his argument from the premise that passions are original existences, not ideas:

---

[7] Milgram appeals to this argument to demonstrate that Hume is not even an instrumentalist about practical reasoning, on the ground that reason produces only representations and the passions that are the motives for action are never motivations. He does not notice the flaws in Hume's argument I just mentioned. Elizabeth S. Radcliffe argues persuasively that Milgram's argument is based on the non-Humean assumption that reason can be practical only if it issues in "ought" statements or imperatives, but that Hume's assumption that reasoning can play a causal role in the origination of desire, namely by discovering causal connections by means of which our desire for an end can be transmitted to what reason tells us is the means for it, is sufficient to consider Hume an instrumentalist about practical reason. See Radcliffe, "Kantian Tunes on a Humean Instrument: Why Hume Is Not *Really* a Skeptic about Practical Reasoning," *Canadian Journal of Philosophy* 27 (1997): 247–70.

he says that "our passions, volitions, and actions, are not susceptible of any such agreement or disagreement," because, "being original facts and realities, compleat in themselves, and *implying no reference to other* passions, volitions, and actions," it is therefore impossible "that they can be pronounc'd either true or false, and be either contrary or conformable to reason" (*Treatise*, III.i.1, 195, emphasis added). What Hume is now claiming, then, is that neither passions nor the actions they motivate are subject to reason because they cannot agree or disagree with each other.

Hume next attacks the idea that morality concerns the truth-relation between ideas and external objects by deriding the theory of William Wollaston that all immoral actions are a form of lie and derive their immorality from their offense against truth.[8] He does not insist, as one might, that any such theory would be question-begging, presupposing a moral imperative to tell the truth; he rather argues that it misplaces the moral problem, because even in many immoral actions that "may give rise to false conclusions in others," the immorality lies not in giving rise to a false belief, but in the action itself: "when a person, who thro' a window sees any lewd behaviour of mine with my neighbour's wife, may be so simple as to imagine she is certainly my own," my offense is not that I perform "the action with any intention of giving rise to a false judgment in another," but simply in the fact that I "satisfy my lust and passion" in a way that is not prohibited by considerations about truth but is offensive to some other primary human passion (*Treatise*, III.i.1, 296).

Finally, Hume attacks the theory, hinted at by Locke and developed by Samuel Clarke, that in order to be matters of demonstrative reasoning, "vice and virtue must consist in some relations; since 'tis allow'd on all hands, that no matter of fact is capable of being demonstrated" (*Treatise*, III.i.1, 298). He then argues that any relation that might be thought to be intrinsically immoral and discoverable to be so by demonstra-

---

[8] It is this argument against Wollaston and the following argument against Samuel Clarke that Hume so clearly takes over from Hutcheson.

tion is objectionable only when it obtains among human beings. Thus, when an oak or elm sapling "at last overtops and destroys the parent tree," although the relation between "child" and "parent" here is formally the same as in a case of human parricide, we do not think anything immoral has transpired; likewise, although "incest in the human species is criminal . . . the very same action, and the same relations in animals have not the smallest moral turpitude and deformity" (300–301). Hume's conclusion is that there is no general relation among ideas of the type that reason can discover that is the source of the immorality of parricide or incest among human beings, since those very same relations carry no moral stigma when they occur among other beings; their immorality must therefore be grounded only in the "sentiment of [dis]approbation, which arises in you, toward this action."

As previously noted, Kant does not explicitly address these arguments from Hume's *Treatise*. We could nevertheless see him as offering a response to them by his argument that immorality arises from contradictions within our maxims, more precisely between our intentions and the universalization of our maxims; among our various maxims; or between our maxims and our wills. Whatever these contradictions amount to, they are relations that obtain only for human or other rational beings capable of forming intentions and maxims—the same relations do not after all obtain among trees or animals—but yet are discernible by pure reason. Kant also makes room for the idea of contradictions among actions, which Hume treats as nonreferential original existences, by linking actions to maxims, which are the kinds of things that can contradict or agree with one another. Thus, Kant suggests grounds for questioning Hume's argument. Whether Kant can prove that we are motivated to approve or disapprove of these relations among human intentions, maxims, and/or actions by reason alone is another matter. I will return to that question in the final part of the chapter. All I want to have established for now is that Hume's arguments for the thesis that moral distinctions are derived from a moral sense rather than from reason depends upon the premise that moral distinctions must be motivating, a premise that as we will see Kant shares and will try to accommodate by showing that and how reason itself is motivating, while Hume's claim that reason cannot be motivating depends upon a restriction of the proper scope of reason that Kant did not share even if he did concede that in a general way reason does concern itself with relations.

(2) The next part of Hume's position that I want to illustrate is his view that since it is only passions, not reason, that motivate us to act in certain ways, or as we might say in accordance with certain principles, changes in the manner of our action or in our principles are effected by modifications of our passions brought about by various methods, but not simply by the adoption of new principles by reason in a sheer act of will. Hume states his view in general terms in his initial discussion of reason and action in Book II:

> Since reason alone can never produce any action, or give rise to volition, I infer, that the same faculty is as incapable of preventing volition, or of disputing the preference with any passion or emotion. This consequence is necessary. 'Tis impossible reason cou'd have the latter effect of preventing volition, but by giving an impulse in a contrary direction to our passion; and that impulse, had it operated alone, wou'd have been able to produce volition. Nothing can oppose or retard the impulse of passion, but a contrary impulse; and if this contrary impulse ever arises from reason, that latter faculty must have an original influence on the will, and must be able to cause, as well as hinder any act of volition. But if reason has no original influence, 'tis impossible it can withstand any principle, which has such an efficacy, or ever keep the mind in suspence a moment. Thus it appears, that the principle, which opposes our passion, cannot be the same with reason . . . (*Treatise*, II.iii.3, 266)

Hume's argument is that since action that follows from a passion can only be averted by means of a contrary impulse or passion, and since no passion, whether the original or the contrary one, can be generated by reason alone, something else must be the source of the contrary impulse that would counteract the initial one. But he does recognize various mechanisms for the modification of passions, and his general position is thus that changes in human behavior are always effected by mechanisms for changing the constellation of passions that agents antecedently have.

While Hume does not offer a catalogue of mechanisms for changing passions, he does give a variety of examples. In the next section of Book II, he says that "when we wou'd govern a man, and push him to any action, 'twill commonly be better policy to work upon the violent than the calm passions, and rather take him by his inclination, than what is vulgarly call'd his *reason*." He then says that we can do this by placing the object to which we want to direct him "in such particular situations as are proper to encrease the violence of his passions . . . all depends upon the situation of the object, and . . . a variation in this particular will be able to change the calm and the violent passions into each other" (*Treatise*, II.iii.4, 269). That is, since reason is not motivating, we cannot change anyone's motivations (our own or anyone else's) simply by appealing to reason; but we can change people's passions by changing their relation to relevant objects, which will naturally cause such a change although not give a reason for any change of passions. Further, Hume observes that "nothing has a greater effect both to encrease and diminish our passions, to convert pleasure into pain, and pain into pleasure, than custom and repetition" (II.iii.5, 271); these are again natural mechanisms that can cause changes in our constellations of impulses and passions and thereby effect changes in our behavior that mere appeals to reason cannot. And in his discussion of justice in Book III, Hume argues that conventions that are not original to us in the state of nature, and are in this particular way "artificial," but which do naturally arise from our often tacit recognition of what is in our own interest in various circumstances, as when we just naturally realize that we will move more quickly if we row in rhythm with our boatmates than if we do not (III.ii.2, 315), gain and maintain our allegiance not by some formal appeal to our reason, but by generating new passions or, more likely, altering the "direction" of our "interested affection" (316). The redirection of our passions need not always be a natural response to the unintended but natural emergence of new conventions; Hume also refers to the "artifice of politicians, who in order to govern men more easily, and preserve peace in human society, have endeavour'd to produce an esteem for justice, and an abhorrence of injustice." But the "utmost politicians can perform, is, to extend the natural sentiments beyond their original bounds; but still nature must furnish the materials, and give us some notion of moral distinctions" (III.ii.2, 321). The point is that politicians cannot gain allegiance for their programs and thus change the conduct of their public simply by appealing to reason, but they can use rhetoric to cause the modification, redirection, or counterbalancing of naturally occurring passions and desires, and thereby modify the actions of their public. All of these are illustrations of Hume's point that actions are never changed by a mere appeal to reason, but by the creation of new or the reorientation of existing passions that then motivate the change in conduct.

(3) Further, Hume holds that happiness or a good life as a whole is founded on transforming whatever constellations of desires and passions one might naturally have, including violent and unruly ones, into a harmonious set of calm passions in which the love of tranquility is foremost, and that there are techniques available to us that make it possible for this to be accomplished, within limits. To illustrate this point I will first turn from the *Treatise* to the *Essays Moral, Political, and Literary*. In the second volume of these essays, published in 1742 just two years after the second volume of the *Treatise*, Hume included the four essays in philosophical styles called "The Epicurean," "The Stoic," "The Platonist," and "The Sceptic." Although there is material in several of these that is relevant to the present point, I will concentrate on "The Sceptic," which certainly most consistently expresses Hume's own philosophical point of view. The essay begins with an argument for the genuinely Humean thesis of the ontological subjectivity of value, that is, for the position that the values of objects lie in their effects upon our sentiments, and not elsewhere.

(This does not imply that value is subjective in the everyday sense of being idiosyncratic.) It then turns to a discussion of happiness. Here Hume first describes what in his view makes for a happy life:

> All the difference, therefore, between one man and another, with regard to life, consists either in the *passion*, or in the *enjoyment*: And these differences are sufficient to produce the wide extremes of happiness and misery.
>
> To be happy, the *passion* must be neither too violent nor too remiss. In the first case, the mind is in a perpetual hurry and tumult; in the second, it sinks into a disagreeable indolence and lethargy.
>
> To be happy, the passions must be benign and social; not rough or fierce. The affections of the latter kind are not near so agreeable to the feeling, as those of the former. . . .
>
> To be happy, the passion must be chearful and gay, not gloomy and melancholy. A propensity to hope and joy is real riches: One to fear and sorrow, real poverty.
>
> Some passions or inclinations, in the *enjoyment* of their object, are not so steady or constant as others, nor convey such durable pleasure and satisfaction. (*Essays*, 167)

Hume next raises the possibility that, desirable as it might be for anyone to modify his or her passions in the direction that this ideal of happiness directs, a person's set of desires is pretty much determined by nature, and thus that one is not free to modify one's passions, however much they might depart from this ideal, to better conform to it. "No man would ever be unhappy, could he alter his feelings. . . . But of this resource nature has, in great measure, deprived us. The fabric and constitution of our mind no more depends on our choice, than that of our body. The generality of men have not even the smallest notion, that any alteration in this respect can ever be desirable" (168). However, this radically skeptical conclusion is more pessimistic than is warranted. Hume's own position is that, while the mere pronouncement of "general maxims" rarely has much influence on people (169), there is a variety of other techniques by which people may indeed modify their naturally given con-

stellation of passions in the desired direction. First, he maintains that "a serious attention to the sciences and liberal arts
softens and humanizes the temper, and cherishes those fine
emotions in which true virtue and honour consists" (170; see
also the essay "On the Delicacy of Taste and Passion," 3–8);
that "study and application" and "education" will not merely
"convince us, that the mind is not altogether stubborn and in-
flexible, but will admit of many alterations from its original
make and structure" (170), but also help us to make such
changes; and that "Habit is another powerful means of re-
forming the mind, and implanting in it good dispositions and
inclinations" (170–71), so that desirable feelings that are initially
hard to maintain can in time become, as it were, second nature.
Second, Hume argues that, again, while it usually does little
good just to tell people what general maxims they should follow,
philosophical discourse can put things in a new light for people,
and lead to a natural modification of their passions: "Here
therefore a philosopher may step in, and suggest particular
views, and considerations, and circumstances, which otherwise
would have escaped us; and by that means, he may either moderate or excite any particular passion" (172)—in the direction, if
the philosopher is a wise one, that is necessary in order to realize
the ideal of happiness.

Hume does not claim that it is easy to modify one's desires
by such methods and considerations, or that the modification
can ever be complete. Nor does he ask whether a person is simply free to choose to undertake the various measures by which
such modification can be effected—free to choose to devote
himself to study if he has not previously been inclined to do so,
or to choose to seek out the company of philosophers if she has
not been so lucky as already to enjoy it—regardless of his or
her previous dispositions. In other words, he does not raise the
question of whether the availability of such methods presupposes a kind of freedom of the will to which he ought not to be
hospitable given his own empirical confidence in determinism.
Leave it to Kant to raise such a question. All I have wanted to
establish here is that Hume assumes that happiness consists in
having a certain kind of constellation of desires or passions that

may well differ from the one that anyone initially has, and that there are various naturally effective means by which one's initial constellation of desires might be modified in this direction. Part of my argument will now be that there is a considerable extent to which Kant agrees with Hume about this point.

Before turning to Kant, we may observe that in the *Enquiry concerning the Principles of Morals*, published in 1751 a decade after the *Essays Moral, Political, and Literary*, Hume adopts a position that is in some ways even closer to that which Kant subsequently develops. In the second *Enquiry*, Hume argues that the qualities of persons that we regard as morally meritorious are those that are either useful or agreeable either to oneself or others, which is to say those that are either mediately or immediately agreeable to oneself or others. He clearly does not suppose that all of those qualities that are immediately agreeable can be reduced to any single property or that there is any metric in light of which they are all commensurable; thus he rejects any ancient conception that there is a single highest good and perhaps also, in spite of his idea that all goods are either mediately or immediately agreeable to oneself or others, the idea that such goods can be aggregated into a single sum as would be required for the application of the utilitarian formula of the greatest good for the greatest number in actual decision making. Nevertheless, Hume does suppose that among the diverse qualities and goods that are immediately agreeable, that of "tranquillity" stands very high:

> Conscious of his own virtues, say the philosophers, the sage elevates himself above every accident of life; and securely placed in the temple of wisdom, looks down on inferior mortals, engaged in pursuit of honours, riches, reputation, and every frivolous enjoyment. . . . And the nearer we can approach in practice, to this sublime tranquillity and indifference (for we must distinguish it from a stupid insensibility) the more secure enjoyment shall we attain within ourselves, and the more greatness of mind shall we discover to the world. (*Enquiry II*, Section 7, 63)

Hume clearly prizes very highly the capacity not to extirpate one's natural desires and emotions—that would be "stupid insensibility"—but to gain mastery over them rather than letting oneself be at their mercy. We will see that for Kant the idea of not being pushed around by mere impulses but of gaining mastery over them is central to his ethical ideal. Hume gives no special role to reason in gaining this mastery, while Kant insists that pure reason is the source of such mastery, but even so, we will see, the difference between the practices they recommend are not so great as the differences in their theory.

We might also note that Hume, like Kant, utterly rejects any idea that the principles of morality can be derived from enlightened self-love alone, and instead maintains that quite apart from self-love "every man, or most men," has "some sentiment, so universal and comprehensive as to extend to all mankind," thus that "While the human heart is compounded of the same elements as at present, it will never be wholly indifferent to public good, nor entirely unaffected with the tendency of characters and actions" (*Enquiry II*, Section 9, 75). In recognizing benevolence as well as self-love as a fundamental sentiment of the human heart, Hume firmly aligns himself with the views of Hutcheson and Joseph Butler (in spite of Hutcheson's famous qualm that Hume wanted "a certain Warmth in the Cause of Virtue").[9] Moreover, Hume claims, "the immediate feeling of benevolence and friendship, humanity and kindness, is sweet, smooth, tender, and agreeable, independent of all fortune and accidents" (81)—in other words, this sentiment is tranquil, and shares in the very high standing of tranquility among the immediately agreeable goods. So Hume does not argue that the concern for humanity, whether in one's own person or that of any other, as Kant will put it (*Groundwork*, 4: 429), can be derived from reason, but it is recommended as a great source of tranquility, which we might think of as Hume's analogue of reasonableness.

[9] See Hume's letter to Hutcheson of September 17, 1739, in *The Letters of David Hume*, ed. J. Y. T. Greig (Oxford: Clarendon Press, 1932), 1: 32.

Kant

So let us now turn to Kant. Here I want to argue three main points. First, although Kant's metaphysics could have allowed him to argue that pure practical reason sets moral ends and principles and determines us to act in accordance with them entirely independently of any feelings or desires, he does not do so, but instead supposes that pure practical reason motivates us to act precisely by creating a feeling, namely, moral feeling or the feeling of respect for the moral law, which can then move us to act. Second, while it also could have been open to Kant to hold that the feeling of respect motivates us to act entirely by itself, by simply striking down or outweighing feelings or desires that would lead us to act contrary to morality, he does not always do this either, but instead argues that the feeling of respect at least often moves us to act in accordance with morality by recruiting other, more specific feelings to which we have some natural disposition, such as feelings of sympathy toward other humans or aesthetic feelings toward nonhuman nature, to its own cause. Further, in his practical ethics Kant prescribes a variety of techniques available to us by means of which naturally occurring feelings that would be helpful to the cause of morality can be strengthened and others that would not be so helpful can be weakened. Finally, I will suggest that although the mature Kant obviously wanted to maintain that pure practical reason is the source of the principle of morality and of the motivating feeling of respect entirely by itself, his original derivation of the fundamental principle of morality began with a natural desire for freedom and then argued that adherence to universalizable principles of pure reason is the best or only means for realizing the end of autonomy we so desire—thus making reason instrumental to a goal set by a natural feeling in behalf of freedom. While Kant does not offer such an empirical, psychological account of the value of freedom and such an instrumental account of the role of reason in his mature writings, his conception of the incomparable dignity of autonomy as the condition in which we are not governed by any mere law of nature but only by a law of our own making (*Groundwork*, 4: 434–35) is an echo of this original argument that we have a natural love of freedom that is greater than our love of anything else. Kant's deepest foundation for the principle of morality in the ideal of being in control of our inclinations rather than controlled by them may thus not be entirely unrelated to Hume's idea of the special agreeableness of tranquility.

(1) Everyone will concede that the mature Kant supposes that pure practical reason alone gives the moral law, and that it is also in some sense sufficient to motivate our conformity to the moral law. Kant often makes it sound as if pure practical reason can, if necessary, move us to morally requisite action independent of any feelings or desires we may have, either in favor of the action morality commands or against it. For example, in the lectures on moral philosophy transcribed by C. C. Mrongovius in the winter semester of 1785, after the publication of the *Groundwork*, Kant states that "The imperative of morality abstracts from all inclinations. The motivating ground is not drawn from sense, or from happiness, but given solely from pure reason. The motivating grounds and the law itself must be *a priori*" (*LE*, 27: 598). And in the version of the lectures on ethics that Kant had been giving in the years preceding the publication of the *Groundwork*, he is recorded as saying that "There is in man a certain rabble element which must be subject to control, and which a vigilant government must keep under regulation, and where there must even be force to compel this rabble under the rule." Prudence alone will not suffice to keep this rabble, that is, our desires, under control, but "we have to have another discipline, namely that of morality. By this we must seek to master and compel all our sensory actions, not by prudence, but in accordance with the moral laws. It is in this authority that moral discipline consists" ("Collins," *LE*, 27: 360). In such passages, it may sound as if reason is supposed to determine our actions directly and entirely on its own without any assistance from feelings and desires, overpowering any that might stand in the way of doing what morality demands while ignoring those that might be neutral or that one might have thought even helpful to the cause of morality.

But Kant's view is more complicated than this. Kant actually supposes that pure practical reason moves us to action through suitable feelings, which are the immediate causes of our actions (indeed, as we will see, sometimes, perhaps often through two layers of feelings); and it is in this sense that Kant's theory of action resembles Hume's, at least at the phenomenal level. Kant suggests this a few moments after the passage just cited from the Collins lectures. Speaking of self-mastery, because he is here in the midst of his discussion of duties to oneself, he says that "self-mastery rests on the strength of the moral feeling." The "moral feeling" must "be cultivated, and then morality will have strength and motivation; by these motives, sensibility will be weakened and overcome, and in this way self-command will be achieved. Without disciplining his inclinations, man can attain to nothing" (*LE*, 27: 361). That is, reason cannot attain its own moral goal by simply ignoring or overriding our desires, but must modify them, strengthening morally helpful ones and weakening morally harmful ones or alternatively learning how to work around them.

Kant makes the premise of this position explicit in his last major work, the *Metaphysics of Morals*. In his discussion of "moral feeling" in the Introduction to the "Doctrine of Virtue," he says that,

> This is the susceptibility to feel pleasure or displeasure merely from being aware that our actions are consistent with or contrary to the law of duty. Every determination of choice proceeds **from the representation of a possible action** to the deed *through the feeling of pleasure or displeasure*, taking an interest in the action or its effect. The state of **feeling** here (the way in which inner sense is affected) is either **pathological** or **moral**. (*MM*, DV, 6: 399; italics added)

Here Kant says that the representation of a possible action, which may be held up to the moral law for a test of its permissibility or necessity, produces an effect upon the feeling of pleasure or displeasure, and that in turn is the immediate cause of the action—presumably a positive effect, a feeling of pleasure, moving us to perform an action, and a negative effect, a feeling of pain, moving us to avoid the action.

Indeed, Kant describes various sorts of feelings that may be involved in the etiology of moral conduct, both very general ones such as the moral feeling that he is discussing here as well as the feeling of respect that he discusses a few pages later, as well as in the earlier *Groundwork* and *Critique of Practical Reason*, but also more specific feelings such as the feeling of sympathy that he discusses later in the "Doctrine of Virtue." But before we can sort out what relation among these two sorts of morally relevant feelings Kant might have in mind, we must first ask why Kant supposes that the influence of practical reason upon our actions must always proceed through an effect of reason upon the faculty for feeling pleasure and displeasure. Kant's basic conception of the relations among reason, the free will, and action does not require this premise. Rather, this assumption would seem to be a piece of empirical psychology, part of his picture of the phenomenal world that he shares with Hume, even though for Kant the phenomenal story is not the whole story of human action.

The point I have in mind here is this. On the basis of arguments that I will not here expound or evaluate, Kant holds that we must suppose that we have freedom of the will at the noumenal level, where the causal determinism that holds throughout the phenomenal world and that might there seem sometimes to stand in the way of our being free to do as morality requires does not obtain. He also holds that the noumenally free will is actually identical with pure practical reason, thus that the law that pure practical reason would give itself is the law governing the operation of the free will (e.g., *Groundwork*, 4: 446–47).[10] He does not, however, hold that the noumenally free will miraculously interrupts the rule of causal law in the phenomenal world, just as he does not hold that we should

---

[10] I have examined Kant's argument in *Groundwork* III that the moral law must be the causal law of the noumenally free will in my *Kant's Groundwork for the Metaphysics of Morals*, chap. 6.

believe that God achieves his ends by miracles rather than through uniform laws of nature;[11] rather, he holds that even though we might not initially realize this, and therefore might not initially realize what we are capable of doing when morality places its stern demands upon us, our noumenal choice will be effective by being the underlying ground of our whole phenomenal character, which operates in accordance with the empirical laws of psychology. As he says in the *Critique of Practical Reason*, the subject who "views his existence **insofar as it does not stand under conditions of time** and himself as determinable only through laws that he gives himself by reason" will realize that his "every action—and in general every determination of his existence changing conformably with inner sense, even the whole sequence of his existence as a sensible being—is to be regarded in the consciousness of his intelligible existence as nothing but the consequence and never as the determining ground of his causality as a *noumenon*" (*Practical Reason*, 5: 97–98). This claims that the effect of one's noumenally free and rational choice can be manifest *everywhere* or *anywhere* in one's phenomenal inclinations, dispositions, and character, and thus leaves entirely open where this influence occurs or what form it takes. One might suppose that there is a phenomenal faculty of reason that is empirically distinct from all feeling and desire, and that in a person who has chosen to be rational and moral this faculty of reason will be empirically manifest in his empirical psychology in his having a reason that is capable of ignoring or overpowering all of his feelings of desire. But Kant does not suppose this; instead, we have seen, he supposes that even when pure practical reason is efficacious, it works by modifying our feelings and desires and by determining our actions only through them. Since this is not a conclusion that is entailed by

---

[11] This was a constant theme in Kant's thought about a divine design of nature, whether he held that idea to be a constitutive idea of metaphysical speculation, as in the early work *The Only Possible Basis for a Demonstration of the Existence of God* (1763), or only a regulative idea for the conduct of our own investigation of nature, as in the *Critique of the Power of Judgment* (1790).

Kant's metaphysics of the free will, it can only be a piece of empirical psychology that he shares with his contemporaries, including Hume.[12]

(2) Thus, although his fundamental conviction that the noumenally free and rational will is capable of determining our actions is metaphysical, the supposition that it does so by producing moral feelings as well as all of the details of Kant's theory of moral feelings must be regarded as part of his empirical psychology. That said, let us now turn back to the relation between general moral feelings and more particular ones, such as the feeling of sympathy. Kant addresses the most general sort of moral feeling three times in his published works. In the *Groundwork*, he says simply that it is "a feeling **self-wrought** by means of a rational concept and therefore specifically different from all feelings . . . which can be reduced to inclination or fear"; it "signifies merely consciousness of the **subordination** of my will to a law without the mediation of other influences on my sense" (*Groundwork*, 4: 401n). Here the feeling of respect seems to be merely epiphenomenal with regard to the will's determination of action, not part of the process by which that determination takes place.

In the *Critique of Practical Reason*, Kant provides a phenomenologically fuller characterization of the feeling of respect and suggests a more positive account of its role in the etiology of action. That is, here Kant describes the feeling of respect as both a painful feeling of the way in which pure practical reason "strikes down self-conceit" and "humiliates it" but also as a "positive," presumably pleasurable, feeling that it is nothing but our own pure practical reason that does this (*Practical Reason*, 5: 73); and he also suggests that modifying our feelings, in the

---

[12] I have previously developed this argument in "Duty and Inclination," in my *Kant and the Experience of Freedom* (Cambridge: Cambridge University Press, 1993), 335–93, at 361–68. However, there I did not suggest that it leads Kant to a model of the etiology of action at the phenomenal level that is similar to Hume's, nor did I so clearly develop the two-staged model of moral feeling to which I will shortly turn.

form of weakening self-conceit, is a necessary step in the production of morally appropriate action. He says that "As the
effect of consciousness of the moral law . . . this feeling of a
rational subject affected by inclinations is indeed called humili-
ation (intellectual contempt); but in relation to its positive
ground, the law, it is at the same time called respect for the law;
there is indeed no feeling for this law, but inasmuch as it moves
resistance out of the way, in the judgment of reason this removal
of a hindrance is esteemed equivalent to a positive furthering
of its causality" (5: 75). Kant is still somewhat cautious about
ascribing too much of a causal role to the feeling of respect in
the production of an action from the determination of the will
to act in accordance with the moral law, but he is clear that not
merely overriding but modifying self-interested desires (self-
conceit) is part of the causal process of acting as morality requires, and that there is some way in which the positive feeling
of respect furthers the causality of reason.

Finally, in the "Doctrine of Virtue" of the *Metaphysics of Morals*, Kant claims that a general capacity for "being affected by
concepts of duty, antecedent predispositions on the side of **feeling**," is a necessary condition of being moved by the concept of
duty, to have which cannot be thought to be a duty but is rather
that "by virtue of which [one] can be put under obligation"
(*MM*, 6: 399). He then describes the general "moral feeling" as
the feeling of pleasure through which reason determines us to
action, and says that although we must have a predisposition to
this feeling and cannot create it out of whole cloth, we have an
obligation "to **cultivate** it and to strengthen it through wonder
at its inscrutable source" (6: 399–400). In line with his general
division of ethical duties in the "Doctrine of Virtue" into duties
to promote one's own perfection and the happiness of others,
Kant then describes two more specific forms of moral feeling,
"**love** of one's neighbor" (6: 399) or "love of human beings" (6:
402), and "respect (*reverentia*)" for one's "own being" as a moral
agent, a "feeling" that "is of a special kind" and "is the basis of
certain duties, that is, of certain actions that are consistent with
[one's] duty to himself" (6: 402–3). Subsequently, he will also

introduce specific categories of duties of respect toward others, such as the duties not to defame or ridicule them (*MM*, Doctrine of Virtue, §§37–44). In both of the last two contexts, "respect" is being used more narrowly than in the previous works, as respect for persons,[13] and what Kant has here called "moral feeling" is the heir to the more general idea of a feeling of respect for the moral law that he used earlier.

Kant never makes explicit precisely what relation is supposed to obtain between this general moral feeling and the more specific feelings of love and respect, that is, benevolence toward others and self-esteem. I suggest, however, that he understands such more particular feelings as naturally occurring sorts of feelings, with their particular objects, which will typically be the most immediate springs to action, and which we can be moved to cultivate through the strength of the more general moral feeling or feeling of respect for the moral law, which can thus be regarded as the more remote cause of moral actions at the phenomenal level, and which as Kant has said can and should be cultivated. I will set aside for the moment the question of exactly how any of these feelings can be cultivated or strengthened—Kant says nothing about that in the present context—and turn next to further and in some ways even more specific moral feelings that Kant also says we can have and cultivate.

I say that these more specific sorts of moral feelings are "often" or "typically" the most immediate causes of moral actions because in the Introduction to the "Doctrine of Virtue" in the *Metaphysics of Morals* Kant says that "pathological" love, that is, love as a felt emotion, will *follow* "practical" love, that is, the determination to be beneficent out of principle (see *MM*, Doctrine of Virtue, Introduction, Section XII, 6: 402). But in the main body of the text, Kant specifically says that feelings of

---

[13] The duties of respect toward others are not, however, duties to feel a certain way toward them, but duties to avoid certain kinds of actions toward them, namely what Allen Wood has characterized as actions that are expressive of certain attitudes toward them. See Wood, *Kant's Ethical Thought* (Cambridge: Cambridge University Press, 1999), 141–42.

sympathy toward which we have a natural disposition should be preserved and strengthened because they are the means to the fulfillment of our duty of beneficence toward others. In this part of the work, under the general rubric of duties of love toward others—positive, imperfect duties to promote their good—Kant discusses beneficence, gratitude, and sympathy. The first is a form of action rather than feeling, and Kant also construes the duty of gratitude as one that requires a form of action—honoring—although one that is connected with a feeling of "respect for the benefactor" (§31.B, 6: 454), thereby blurring his line between duties of love and duties of respect toward others. The duty of sympathy, however, is "an indirect duty to cultivate the compassionate natural (aesthetic) feelings in us, and to make use of them as so many means to sympathy based on moral feelings and the feeling appropriate to them" (§35, 6: 457). He also says "Nature has already implanted in human beings receptivity to these feelings. But to use this as a means to promoting active and rational benevolence is still a particular, though only a conditional duty" (§34, 6: 456). The best way to understand Kant's confusing classification here would be that our direct and positive duty of love toward others is to perform acts of beneficence toward them under appropriate circumstances, but that the feelings of sympathy toward which we have a natural disposition ("receptivity") are the means that nature affords us to move us to such acts, or their immediate causes, and thus that we have an indirect but positive duty to preserve and cultivate such feelings. Just as acts of beneficence themselves must be performed only in appropriate circumstances—the duty of beneficence is an imperfect duty, so its performance must be subordinated at least to the fulfillment of one's perfect duties—so too feelings of benevolence must be acted upon only in appropriate circumstances; this is why Kant says that using these feelings as a means to acts of beneficence is only a conditional duty. The moral law will determine what these appropriate circumstances or conditions are. Next, Kant mentions various steps that can be taken to strengthen the compassionate natural feelings in us so that they will be available as effective means to the beneficent acts we are to perform: visiting "sickrooms or debtors' prisons and so forth," acts that we might prefer to avoid but must perform in order to strengthen these valuable feelings. This is a gesture toward the way in which these feelings can and must be cultivated.

Now we can ask, what would move us to undertake these steps? At one level it can only be our commitment to the moral law itself; but if Kant's present analysis is to be reconciled with his earlier model of how the moral law actually motivates at the phenomenal level, then his picture can only be that the *general* moral feeling that is the phenomenal manifestation of the noumenal respect for the moral law will move us to cultivate the *particular* moral feelings that are the means implanted in us by nature to the performance of particular morally mandated acts. Far from being stop-gap measures that might allow us to act in outward compliance with the demands of morality in circumstances in which our respect for the moral law might seem insufficient to motivate us directly, these feelings of sympathy (or other feelings at that level) would be the means through which our respect for the moral law is ordinarily made effective in the phenomenal world, and our cultivation of them would be triggered by our more general moral feeling that is the immediate expression and consequence in the phenomenal world of our purely volitional respect for the moral law at the noumenal level, that is, the determination of the will at the noumenal level always to act in accordance with the moral law for its own sake (see *Groundwork*, 4: 400–401).

The analysis would presumably apply to another natural disposition to feeling that Kant says "greatly promotes morality or at least prepares the way for it," namely the aesthetic "disposition to love something (e.g., beautiful crystal formations, the indescribable beauty of plants) even apart from any intention to use it" (*MM*, Doctrine of Virtue, §17, 6: 443), although the model here would have to be even a little more complicated, since such feelings, unlike feelings of sympathy, would not directly prompt morally requisite actions, but would do so in some less direct way. Kant does not describe the further links between morally valuable feelings and morally requisite actions that would be necessary here. However, elsewhere he does offer some further suggestions about the techniques that we can use to cultivate valuable feelings and weaken or get around morally dysfunctional ones. This is in his discussion of "self-mastery" in his lectures on ethics, which was earlier mentioned. Here Kant says that we must learn to control our imagination, whose images might otherwise inflame feelings or desires we should not act upon; we must learn to pay careful attention to our own actions, so that we can learn better what sort of temptations we really have; we must learn to put off judgments and decisions long enough not only to consider all the relevant reasons but even more importantly to allow initial feelings of anger or other inappropriate feelings to settle down or dissipate; and finally, we must learn to keep our minds "active and effective under the burden of work," so as to cultivate feelings of contentment with and confidence in what we are doing rather than to succumb to feelings of discouragement and distress ("Collins," *LE*, 27: 364–66). Such specific stratagems for suppressing morally undesirable feelings and strengthening morally beneficial ones do not differ in spirit from the techniques that Hume prescribes for the same purposes. On Kant's model, however, it will be the general moral feeling of respect for the moral law that will in turn move us to cultivate these particular stratagems for moral success, and Hume would not have characterized our most general sentiments of moral approbation in this way.[14]

(3) So even though the ultimate goal in being moral is assumed by Kant to be supplied by pure practical reason, while for Hume reason supposedly plays no role in determining our ultimate ends, at what for Kant is the phenomenal level their models of how our deepest moral commitments actually move us to action are in many ways quite similar. I now suggest that Kant's original strategy for explaining the motivating force of the moral law was also not so different from Hume as his later writings suggest, and that some form of this original view lies

---

[14] See his famous argument that it cannot ordinarily be a "regard to virtue" that is the motive for virtuous action at *Treatise*, III.ii.1. For a good discussion of what Hume really means by this, see Radcliffe, "How Does the Humean Sense of Duty Motivate?" 394–403.

at the basis of Kant's mature view even if it is then supposed to be purified of any tinge of empirical psychology. What I say here will be only a sketch of arguments that must be worked out much more fully.[15]

How Kant intended to deduce the binding force of the moral law is a vexed subject, and it is well known that in the *Critique of Practical Reason* he gave up on the very idea of doing so, settling instead for a derivation of the specific content of the categorical imperative from our self-evident antecedent recognition of the binding force of moral law in general and then for a derivation of the fact of our freedom from that same antecedent recognition—the two claims subsumed under the name of the "fact of reason" (*Practical Reason*, 5: 31–32).[16] But in the *Groundwork* he did attempt to follow his analysis of the content of the moral law (Sections I and II) with a proof that this law is binding for us (Section III). Kant's first move in *Groundwork* III is to argue that the moral law must be the causal law of a will that is noumenally free, a move that caused a problem as soon as Karl Leonhard Reinhold, a century before Henry Sidgwick, observed that the converse of this premise is that a will that does not observe the moral law must not really be free, and thus cannot be responsible for its breach of morality.[17] But Kant did not immediately recognize this problem, and instead attempted to prove that we really are free, from which it would

[15] See also my "Kant on the Theory and Practice of Autonomy," in *Autonomy*, ed. Ellen Frankel Paul, Fred D, Miller Jr., and Jeffrey Paul (Cambridge: Cambridge University Press, 2003), 70–98, reprinted in my *Kant's System of Nature and Freedom*, and *Kant's Groundwork for the Metaphysics of Morals*, chap. 2.

[16] For the classical discussion of the "fact of reason," see Lewis White Beck, *A Commentary to Kant's Critique of Practical Reason* (Chicago: University of Chicago Press, 1960), 166–70.

[17] Reinhold's version of the objection, in the second volume of his *Letters on the Kantian Philosophy*, is excerpted in Rüdiger Bittner and Konrad Cramer, eds., *Materialen zu Kants "Kritik der praktischen Vernunft"* (Frankfurt: Suhrkamp, 1975), 310–24, and is discussed by Henry Allison in *Kant's Theory of Freedom* (Cambridge: Cambridge University Press, 1990), 133–35. Sidgwick's more famous version of the charge was originally presented in "The Kantian Conception of Free Will," *Mind* 13 (1888), reprinted as an appendix (511–16) to the seventh edition of *The Methods of Ethics* (London: Macmillan, 1907).

follow that the moral law is actually the *causal* law of our will, which would obviate the need for a normative argument that it is binding for us—if it is the law for our will at the deepest level, then, Kant seems to have supposed, the question of whether it ought to be does not have to be separately addressed. Kant then offered a two-staged proof that we really are free, although the two steps of his attempted proof have often been interpreted as if they were intended to be two alternative strategies.

The first step of his proof is the attempt to show that any being that even thinks of itself as acting must think of itself as subject to the moral law, because in order to think of itself as acting it must think of itself as free, thus "all the laws that are inseparably bound up with freedom hold for him just as if his will had been validly free also in itself and in theoretical philosophy" (*Groundwork*, 4: 448). Kant's second step then depends on what is a step into theoretical philosophy: the argument that the distinction between one's own phenomenal and noumenal self, which is forced upon one by the general distinction between the phenomenal and the noumenal, entails, in virtue of the initial equation between a noumenally free will and a will subject to the moral law, the conclusion that one really is subject to the moral law (4: 451–52).[18] However, this argument falls be-

[18] In contemporary literature, the first of these steps is often treated as if it were supposed to be a complete argument that the mere concept of oneself as an agent entails the necessity of acknowledging the binding force of the moral law, although a few interpreters defend Kant's second claim that metaphysical insight into our real identity as agents entails our obligation under the moral law. Thomas E. Hill Jr.'s approach in "Kant's Argument for the Rationality of Moral Conduct," *Pacific Philosophical Quarterly* 66 (1985): 3–23, reprinted in his *Dignity and Practical Reason in Kant's Moral Theory* (Ithaca, NY: Cornell University Press, 1992), 97–122, exemplifies the former strategy, while Christine M. Korsgaard's argument that the metaphysical necessity of stopping an infinite regress of conditional values by the supposition of a genuinely free conferrer of values in such writings as "Kant's Formula of Humanity," *Kant-Studien* 77 (1986): 183–202, reprinted in her *Creating the Kingdom of Ends* (Cambridge: Cambridge University Press, 1996), 106–32, exemplifies the second. However, Kant's famous worry about a "circle," after he has stated that acting under the concept of oneself as an agent entails the validity of the moral law, shows that he regards this conceptual connection as merely analytic, and that it remains to be proven that this concept really applies to us, that is, that

fore Kant's own recognition, in *Religion within the Boundaries of Mere Reason*, that true freedom entails the possibility of choosing to act for the sake of self-love when that is *contrary* to the moral law, as well as the possibility of choosing to act *in accordance with* the moral law even when that is contrary to self-love, and is thus incompatible with the supposition that the moral law is the causal and therefore exceptionless law of the noumenally free will. In other words, the "ought" of the moral law cannot be derived from the "is" of the noumenally free will after all, even if the latter can be proved. (Kant's characterization of the radical freedom to choose for or against the moral law, which is what makes evil radical when it is chosen, as the freedom to choose between subordinating self-love to the moral law or the moral law to self-love, is his way of retaining from his original analysis of common moral cognition in *Groundwork* I the idea that every human being at least recognizes the claim of the moral law upon her actions, which is itself the premise for the second *Critique*'s proof of freedom, which is in turn necessary for the proof of freedom on which the argument of the *Religion* depends—a tight but not a vicious circle.)

Does this mean that Kant had no plausible strategy for proving the binding force of the moral law? That conclusion would be too quick. In many texts prior to the *Groundwork*, Kant had suggested a very different way of explaining the force of the moral law on us, although it is a way whose fundamental step is not a priori and is more akin to the recognition of the value of a calm and orderly life in Hume's moral psychology. In his earliest notes on moral philosophy, written not under the immediate influence of Hume but of Hume's quondam friend Rousseau, Kant wrote of an abhorrence of domination and a love of making our own choices as the most fundamental facts of human nature. "Nothing can be more appalling than that the actions of one human stand under the will of another. Hence no abhorrence can be more natural than that which a person

we really are agents; see *Groundwork*, 4: 450, and my discussion in *Kant's Groundwork for the Metaphysics of Morals*, chap. 6.

has against servitude."[19] Conversely, "We have gratification in certain of our perfections, but far more if we are the cause. We have the most if we are the freely acting cause. To subordinate everything to the free capacity for choice is the greatest perfection."[20] The first of these remarks might suggest that we dislike only being under the thumb of the impulses of *another* person, but the latter suggests that our deepest satisfaction lies in making our own choices, whatever satisfaction lies in their particular realization, freely, thus, being under the thumb neither of *our own* impulses nor those of anyone else.

Several years later, Kant then suggested that action in accordance with a rule of consistency is what is necessary in order to realize and maintain freedom of choice. Thus, in his anthropology lectures from the mid-1770s, he observed that "Freedom is the greatest life of the human being, whereby he exercises his activity without hindrance," but that this cannot mean activity without any rule whatever, since in that case actions could cancel one another out and reduce one's overall sphere of free activity; thus "no freedom can please us except that which stands under the rule of the understanding."[21] In some reflections from around the same time, he writes, "The formal condition of freedom as a use that is in complete concordance with life is regularity,"[22] and "Freedom is the original life and in its connection [*Zusammenhang*] the condition of the coherence [*Übereinstimmung*] of all life. . . . The universality makes all our feelings agree with one another."[23] It would take some argument to show this, but I believe that what Kant is pointing toward is that the only way to avoid simply being pushed around by whatever inclinations either oneself or someone else has at any particular

[19] From Kant's notes in his copy of his 1764 work, *Observations on the Feeling of the Beautiful and Sublime*; in *Notes and Fragments*, 11.

[20] *Notes and Fragments*, 16.

[21] *Anthropologie Friedländer*, 25: 560; quoted from my "Kant on the Theory and Practice of Autonomy," reprinted in my *Kant's System of Nature and Freedom*, 130.

[22] Reflection 6870, 19: 187; translated in my *Kant's System of Nature and Freedom*, 130.

[23] Reflection 6862, 19: 183; *Notes and Fragments*, 443; also in my *Kant's System of Nature and Freedom*, 131.

moment, and thus to preserve one's freedom, is to act in accordance with a principle that allows actions only if they satisfy a condition of intra- and interpersonal consistency among the inclinations that will be allowed to be acted upon. If such a principle is observed, then impulses will not randomly obstruct or cancel one another: each person will be allowed free choice to act upon inclinations, but only when so doing is consistent with her own continued free choice and that of all others who could possibly be affected by her choices. In that sense, our impulses can be said not to be in control of us, and we will instead be in control of them. And on such a principle it is not only one's own freedom that will be preserved, but the freedom of all will be preserved to an equal degree, since all will have both the obligation but also the benefit of seeking to act only on a consistent set of impulses.

This line of Kant's early reasoning is premised on the undeniably empirical assumption that human beings do love their freedom from domination by either their own impulses or anyone else's more than anything else, and for that reason seems to have been suppressed by the mature Kant. It also represents the value of the freedom of others as instrumental to the preservation of one's own freedom, rather than as intrinsically valuable in its own right and as not to be abridged for that reason; this is certainly inconsistent with Kant's claim in the *Groundwork* that each human being values his own humanity "from the representation of what is necessarily an end for everyone because it is an end in itself" that holds "subjectively" *because* it holds "objectively" (4: 428–29). Nevertheless, in writings from the 1780s Kant would retain at least the general strategy of arguing that freedom from determination by mere impulse can only be achieved through submitting one's actions to rules of intra- and interpersonal consistency. The moral law is thus introduced as "the limitation of freedom by the condition under which our own freedom may co-exist with the general freedom" ("Mrongovius," *LE*, 29: 618). This law, which Kant describes as a law of reason rather than as a mere rule for satisfying a psychological desire for tranquility, is the *means* to the realization of freedom as an *end*. As Kant says in his 1784 lectures on natural right, "If only rational beings can be ends in themselves, this could not be because they have reason, but because they have freedom. Reason is merely a means."[24] But the relation between the rule as a means to the preservation of freedom as an end is retained, even if the ultimate value of freedom for all is supposed to have a source different from the mere desire for the preservation of one's own freedom.

To be sure, it is not always easy to see how this line of thought manifests itself in the *Groundwork*. It is not too hard to see that in demanding that we treat humanity, whether in our own person or that of any other, as an end and never as a means, Kant is requiring that the end of maintaining the possibility for the self-determination of ends in both oneself and others is the "supreme limiting condition" on the choice to pursue all more particular ends (*Groundwork*, 4: 431), and thus making the preservation of freedom of choice in all persons rather than its self-destruction our ultimate end. What is harder to see is just how he means to motivate our acceptance of the moral ideal of the fundamental and unconditional value of freedom in all persons. Given all the emphasis he places on the need for a pure and a priori principle of morality in the Preface to the *Groundwork* (4: 389–90) and the opening of its Section II (4: 411–12), he cannot have meant simply to appeal to a psychological love of freedom, analogous to Hume's happily psychological love of tranquility—like any other psychological feeling, it would be contingent that any one person had that, let alone recognized its value in all persons. However, it is a fundamental normative premise of Kant's analysis of the common concept of duty in *Groundwork* I that people do not deserve esteem for anything that merely *happens* to them, including under this description whatever inclinations they happen to have, but only for what they freely do, for what is not merely an "effect" *on* the will but an activity *of* the will. This makes freedom of choice at least a *necessary* condition of moral merit, not a *suffi-*

[24] *Naturrecht Feyerabend*, 27: 1321.

cient condition or ultimate source of moral value. Nevertheless, perhaps in the absence of any other candidate for a source of unconditional value, Kant may have adopted the normative premise that freedom of choice is not only a necessary condition for moral merit but also the ultimate source of moral value, and attributed this recognition or determination of value to pure practical reason.[25]

Hume's argument that reason can never determine ends but only means was clearly based on a narrow conception of reason as a faculty restricted to deductive or inductive inference (although even allowing reason the capacity for the latter actually broadened the conception of reason that Hume had employed in his doubts about causation). Kant's claim that pure practical reason makes freedom into our sole unconditional end as well as discerning what principles we need to observe in order to realize this end is clearly based on a generous conception of reason. I have not attempted to determine here which is the more plausible conception of reason—although since Hume's conception of reason is ordinary enough, there is a burden of proof on Kant to justify his broader conception of reason, a burden of proof the continuing debate about the real basis of

---

[25] Christine Korsgaard has attributed to Kant the argument that the unconditional value of one's own freedom of choice is the condition of the possibility of the conditional value of any particular object of choice, for without it there would be the risk of an infinite regress of conditional values, in which the value of any object of choice would be conditional on the value of some other object of choice that is itself merely conditional, and so on; see her "Kant's Formula of Humanity," especially 119–24 as reprinted in her *Creating the Kingdom of Ends*, as well as Wood, *Kant's Ethical Thought*, 124–32. The problem with this argument is that although it would take something of unconditional value to stop an infinite regress of conditional values, it would seem as if it should be a separate question whether there is in fact anything of unconditional value, thus that the existence of something of unconditional value should be established independently of a mere analysis showing the need for such a value. That is, it seems as if Kant should have an independent reason for his thesis that humanity, understood as freedom of choice, should always be treated as an end and never as a means, whether in oneself or others, or if he does not, then it should be admitted that this is, in the language of the 1764 *Inquiry into the Distinctness of the Principles of Natural Theology and Morality*, an indemonstrable material first principle of morality.

Kant's argument in the *Groundwork* and his sudden appeal to a "fact of reason" in the second *Critique* suggests he may not have met. But if I have succeeded in suggesting that in spite of the self-described differences in their metaethics there are nevertheless strong substantive similarities between the normative ethics and empirical theories of moral motivation of Hume and Kant, then I will have accomplished what I set out to do in this chapter.

SYSTEMATICITY, TASTE,
AND PURPOSE

KANT'S AMBITIONS in the *Critique of the Power of Judgment* are vast. The Introduction to the book, while setting the stage for the issues to be addressed in its two main parts, not only returns to an issue first broached in the Appendix to the "Transcendental Dialectic" of the *Critique of Pure Reason*, the idea of a system of empirical laws of nature, but also suggests for the first time that their *systematicity* can ground the necessity of such laws, a clear addition to the theory of experience of the first *Critique*. The first main part of the book, the "Critique of the Aesthetic Power of Judgment," takes up a wide range of the topics debated in eighteenth-century aesthetics, including the ontological status of beauty, the universal validity of judgments of taste and the possibility of aesthetic criticism, the contrast between the beautiful and the sublime, the nature of genius, and the moral significance of aesthetic experience, and attempts to show that the whole variety of our aesthetic judgments and practices have a rational foundation even though they cannot be grounded on determinate principles. The second main part of the work, the "Critique of the Teleological Power of Judgment," takes up specific debates in contemporary biology, such as the controversy between epigenetic and preformationist theories of reproduction and the emerging debate over the possibility of speciation by evolution, while also tackling broader philosophical problems such as the possibility of comprehending organisms in general and the moral significance of nature as a whole. Above all, the third *Critique* argues that our pleasures in the beautiful and the sublime and our sense of the purposiveness of nature stemming from our experience of organisms can help bridge the "incalculable gulf fixed between the domain of the concept of nature, as the sensible, and the domain of the concept of freedom, as the supersensible" (*Judgment*, Introduction II, 5: 175–76), and thereby unify Kant's theoretical and practical philosophy into a single theory of human experience and thought. In all of this, although he does not drop many names in the book, Kant also expressly or tacitly responds to a wide array of contemporary authors, learning from but also criticizing the empiricist theories of taste of Francis Hutcheson, David Hume, and Henry Home, Lord Kames; the psychological analyses of our feelings of beauty and sublimity by Edmund Burke; the cognitivist aesthetics of Alexander Gottlieb Baumgarten and Georg Friedrich Meier; Alexander Gerard's argument that genius is manifest in both fine art and natural science; the preformationism of Albrecht von Haller and Charles Bonnet; the epigenesis of the Comte de Buffon; the *Bildungstrieb* of Johann Friedrich Blumenbach; and especially Leibniz's version of the preestablished harmony between the principles of nature and grace and Hume's critique of the argument from design in the *Dialogues concerning Natural Religion*.

So it would be impossible to discuss even just the major topics or the highlights of the historical context of the *Critique of the Power of Judgment* in a single essay, let alone both. At the same time, it would be profoundly misleading to attempt to reduce the topics of the book to a single idea (even though Kant himself attempts to do this with his new conception of "reflecting judgment) or to a response to a single author.[1] Nevertheless, just as it can be immensely helpful to interpret and evaluate the *Critique of Pure Reason* as a response to Hume's doubts about our ordinary conceptions of causation, external objects, and the self, so I want to suggest here too that it can be illuminating to read much in the third *Critique* as a protracted

---

[1] As one commentator has done in seeing the whole work as an argument between Kant and his one-time student Johann Herder; see John Zammito, *The Genesis of Kant's* Critique of Judgment (Chicago: University of Chicago Press, 1992).

argument with Hume in which Kant accepts certain of Hume's conclusions but goes beyond them in distinctive ways. In this chapter I will discuss three of the main topics in the work, the necessary truth of particular laws of nature, the universal validity of judgments of taste, and the moral significance of a teleological conception of nature, as Kant's attempts to provide a priori foundations for what Hume thought were matters of mere imagination and custom without relapsing into the rationalist metaphysics, aesthetics, and teleology of Leibniz, Christian Wolff, and Alexander Baumgarten. Hume gave a strictly empiricist explanation of our belief in the necessity of particular causal laws, of our confidence in the existence of a standard of taste, and of our belief in an intelligent designer and creator of nature. In the third *Critique*, Kant wanted to show that an a priori and transcendental although regulative rather than constitutive principle of the systematicity of nature underlies our belief in the necessity of particular causal laws; that an a priori principle underlies our claims of universal validity for our judgments of taste although it cannot yield a standard of taste in the sense of rules for making those judgments; and that our experience of nature leads us to an a priori conception of its designer and his purposes, although that conception can be made determinate only by moral conceptions and can be put to use only for moral purposes.

Hume on Necessity, Taste, and Design

I will begin with a recapitulation of Hume's empiricist theory of our belief in the necessity of particular causal laws, and then present brief accounts of his empiricist conception of the standard of taste and his empiricist critique of our belief in the intelligent design and creation of nature.

THE NECESSITY OF CAUSALITY

As we saw in chapters 1 and 2, Hume raised three major questions about our belief in causation: what is the source of the idea of necessary connection that we include alongside of our ideas of spatial contiguity and temporal succession in our complex idea of causation (*Treatise*, I.iii..2, 53–55); why we believe the general principle "that *whatever begins to exist, must have a cause of existence*" (I.iii.3, 56); and "*Why we conclude that such particular causes must necessarily have such particular effects, and why we form an inference from one to another?*" (58). In the *Treatise of Human Nature*, where all three of these questions are explicitly raised, Hume says that it would be "more convenient to sink" the second of these questions into the third, and in the end much more clearly answers the first and third of his questions than the second. Kant did not know the *Treatise* in any detail, however, only the abbreviated *Enquiry concerning Human Understanding*, where Hume does not raise the second of these questions at all (*Enquiry II*, Section 4, Part I, 25–28), and so, it would seem, he would have attempted to answer only the first and third of these questions. Thus one might think that in the *Critique of Pure Reason* Kant would have focused exclusively on the source of our idea of the necessity of causal connections and the basis for our belief in particular causal laws. However, as we saw in chapter 2, in the first *Critique* Kant offered an elaborate theory of the origins of the category of causation and justification of our belief in the universal principle that "Everything that happens (begins to be) presupposes something which it follows in accordance with a rule" (*Pure Reason*, A 188), thus answering Hume's first and second questions, while he apparently ignored Hume's third question. In the Introduction to the *Critique of the Power of Judgment* Kant address some issues about our knowledge of particular laws of nature, and has been interpreted by at least some commentators as there giving his answer to Hume's question about our belief in particular causal laws. So I will begin by reviewing the first and third of Hume's questions.

Hume's problem about the source of the simple idea of necessary connection that is an essential part of our complex idea of causation arose from the fundamental principle of his empiricism, "*that all our simple ideas in their first appearance are deriv'd from simple impressions, which are correspondent to them, and which they exactly represent*" (*Treatise*, I.i.1, 9). His argument was then that in any case of causation we can readily find the impressions of spatial contiguity and temporal succession that give rise to our ideas of those relations, but we can find no impression from which we might get the idea of necessary connection by means of which are supposed to be able to distinguish a causal relation from a merely accidental juxtaposition of two objects or states of affairs—necessary connection is just not the sort of thing we can see or touch (I.iii.2, 55). Hume's problem about our belief in particular causal laws, or in his terms particular causal inferences, was developed in two stages. First, causal inferences are not what he calls truths of reason, or what Kant would call analytical truths, that is, the concept of the effect is not contained in the concept of the cause and cannot be inferred from it by purely logical methods, and we cannot infer the supposed effect from the supposed cause through the idea of necessary connection itself, because we do not yet have a source for that idea. But, second, if we turn to the only alternative to reason, namely experience, more precisely our prior experience of the "constant conjunction" of pairs of objects or events, then we could only infer that a new experience of a token of the type that we think of as the cause must be followed by a token of the type of effect we expect if we could proceed upon the principle "*that instances, of which we have had no experience, must resemble those, of which we have had experience, and that the course of nature continues always uniformly the same*" (I.iii.6, 62)—yet that principle is not a truth of logic nor could it be inferred from prior experience without presupposing its own truth. Thus we apparently have no adequate basis in either reason or experience for our particular causal inferences, or belief in particular causal laws.

Hume did not conclude with skepticism about causation, which he believed is the basis for all our knowledge of the external world, but instead offered a naturalistic explanation of both our idea of necessary connection and our belief in particular causal laws, indeed a single explanation of both of these: "'twill appear in the end, that the necessary connection depends on the inference, instead of the inference's depending on the necessary connexion" (I.iii.6, 62). His theory is that because of the way the imagination works, repeated experience of pairs of objects or events of a certain type creates both a tendency to have a vivid idea of the second member of the pair when presented with an impression of the first, an idea so vivid that it is as good as belief (I.iii.8, 69–74), as well as a feeling of the transition of the mind from the impression to that vivid idea, "an internal impression of the mind, or a determination to carry our thoughts from one object to another," which is then transformed into an idea of necessity in the *object* because "the mind has a great propensity to spread itself on external objects, and to conjoin with them any internal impressions, which they occasion, and which always make their appearance at the same time that these objects discover themselves to the senses" (I.iii.14, 111–12). Repeated experience of constant conjunction thus gives rise to both causal inferences and our idea of necessary connection.

Hume recognized the empirical character of this answer to his first and third questions, that is, that it depends upon *observation*[2] of how the mind itself *has* worked rather than upon any reasoning about how it *must* work; at least that is what his designation of this account as a "Sceptical Solution" of his "Sceptical Doubts concerning the Operations of the Understanding" suggests (*Enquiry II*, Section 5). Kant clearly found Hume's empirical account inadequate, and tried to supply an a priori origin of our concept of causation in his theory of the categories and his derivation of the "synthetic principles of pure understanding" in the *Critique of Pure Reason*. As we saw, Kant holds that we can transform the purely logical concept of ground and consequence into the "schematized" category of cause and effect by interpreting it in light of our equally pure and a priori intuitions of space and time, and that we can justify the synthetic a priori principle that every event has a cause by demonstrating that knowledge of particular causal laws is the condition of the very possibility of our knowledge of succession in objective states of affairs, a kind of knowledge that Hume never thought to doubt. But in the first *Critique*, Kant offers no account of how we can

[2] He says that " 'Tis a common observation, that the mind has a great propensity to spread itself . . ." (*Treatise*, I.iii.14, 112).

come to know particular causal laws even though he explains the role they play in our knowledge of change; indeed, he seems to hold that we can know particular causal laws only a posteriori (*Pure Reason*, A 127, B 165), which would suggest that we cannot actually know them to be necessary. But he returns to the question of particular causal laws in the Introduction to the third *Critique*, so we can look there to see whether he ever answers Hume's second question about causation.

A STANDARD OF TASTE

In the Introduction to the *Treatise*, Hume claimed that the "four sciences of *Logic, Morals, Criticism,* and *Politics*" need to be based on a "science of man," the "only solid foundation" for which "itself must be laid on experience and observation" (4). Thus both the theory of beauty dispersed throughout the *Treatise* and first *Enquiry* and the solution to the problem "Of a Standard of Taste" that Hume offered in his famous 1757 essay of that name and which rests upon his theory of beauty are intended to be empirical in method. Hume's theory of beauty is that in a certain number of cases our pleasure in an object is just an inexplicable response to certain features of its appearance or "*species*," while in a larger number of cases it is a response to the perception of its actual or apparent utility, which we enjoy either directly or else because of the imagination's tendency to sympathy with the pleasure of others or its tendency to carry our response from actual utility over to merely apparent or imagined utility (*Treatise*, II.ii.5, 235, and III.iii.6, 393). In all cases, "beauty is nothing but a form, which produces pleasure, as deformity is a structure of parts, which conveys pain; and since the power of producing pain and pleasure makes in this manner the essence of beauty and deformity, all the effects of these qualities must be deriv'd from the sensation." The beauty of mere appearance "is such an order and construction of parts, as . . . is fitted to give a pleasure and satisfaction to the soul" "by the *primary constitution* of our nature," while the beauty of actual or apparent utility, which is "a great part of the beauty, which we admire either in animals, is deriv'd from the idea of convenience and utility," either our own, which we enjoy directly, that of another, which we enjoy by sympathy, or merely apparent utility, which we enjoy through the associative mechanisms of the imagination (II.i.8, 195).[3] Kant will incorporate Hume's distinction between the two varieties of beauty in his own distinction between "free" and "adherent" beauty (*Judgment*, §16), but what he will attempt to reject is Hume's strictly empirical observation that beauty and all of its effects are derived solely from sensations that are due to nothing more than the constitutions of our physiology and imagination.

Hume's theory of beauty is expounded only episodically in the *Treatise*, chiefly to illustrate points in his theory of the passions and moral philosophy, and is not accompanied with an explicit statement about its epistemological status beyond what was implied in the Introduction. But the strictly empiricist character of Hume's methodology is explicit in "Of the Standard of Taste," his contribution to the eighteenth-century debate about the intersubjective validity of aesthetic judgments. Hume uses empiricist language when he states that

> It appears then, that amidst all the variety and caprice of taste, there are certain general principles of approbation or blame, whose influence a careful eye may trace in all operations of the mind. Some particular forms or qualities, from the original structure of the internal fabric, are calculated to please, and others to displease . . . (*Essays*, 233)

People do not always agree in their pleasure in and approbation of particular objects, but Hume does not take that to imply that the "general principles of approbation" are merely statistical or probabilistic; rather, if these principles "fail of their effect in any particular instance, it is from some apparent defect or imperfection in the organ." Or as he puts it,

---

[3] I have given a detailed analysis of Hume's theory of beauty in "The Standard of Taste and the 'Most Ardent Desire of Society,' " in *Pursuits of Reason: Essays in Honor of Stanley Cavell*, ed. Ted Cohen, Paul Guyer, and Hilary Putnam (Lubbock: Texas Tech University Press, 1993), 37–66; reprinted in my *Values of Beauty: Historical Essays in Aesthetics* (Cambridge: Cambridge University Press, 2005), chap. 2.

But though all the general rules of art are founded only on experience and the observation of the common sentiments of human nature, we must not imagine, that, on every occasion, the feelings of men will be conformable to these rules. Those finer emotions of the mind are of a very tender and delicate nature, and require the concurrence of many favourable circumstances to make them play with facility and exactness, according to their general and established principles. (232)

The project of the essay is then to determine the "favourable circumstances" that allow some people, the best qualified critics, to discern most reliably the pleasures that objects have to offer us and therefore to make judgments of taste that should be paradigmatic for the rest of us.[4] These "favourable circumstances" obtain when critics have "a perfect serenity of mind, a recollection of thought, a due attention to the object" (232), or, more fully, delicacy of taste, practice, opportunity for frequent comparisons among objects, and the freedom and good sense to "check" inappropriate prejudices and adopt appropriate prejudices for the enjoyment of particular objects (234–41). But we need not worry about the details of these conditions here; the chief point for us is simply that Hume is confident that the general principles of taste, the mechanisms of physiology and imagination that make them "tender and delicate,"[5] and the conditions for their optimal operation are all "founded only on experience and on the observation of the common sentiments of human nature." This will be Kant's target in the "Analytic

---

[4] This is a simplification of Hume's strategy, since it omits his recognition of the value we place in the fact of consensus with others in addition to the pleasures we may derive directly from objects. See again "The Standard of Taste and the 'Most Ardent Desire of Society.' "

[5] A long debate on the adequacy of Hume's conditions for qualified critical judgment goes back to Harold Osborne, "Hume's Standard and the Diversity of Taste," *British Journal of Aesthetics* 7 (1967): 50–56, and Peter Kivy, "Hume's Standard of Taste: Breaking the Circle," *British Journal of Aesthetics* 7 (1967): 57–66. For review of the debate and discussion, see Astrid von der Lühe, *David Humes ästhetische Kritik* (Hamburg: Felix Meiner, 1996), 207–35, and Dabney Townsend, *Hume's Aesthetic Theory: Taste and Sentiment* (London: Routledge, 2001), chap. 6, 180–216.

of the Beautiful" and the "Deduction of Judgments of Taste" in the third *Critique*.

DESIGN AND PURPOSE IN NATURE

Hume criticized the traditional argument from the apparent design of the natural world to an omniscient, omnipotent, and benevolent God in Section 11, "Of a Particular Providence and of a Future State," in the *Enquiry concerning Human Understanding*, which Kant knew after they were translated into German by the middle of the 1750s, and in the *Dialogues concerning Natural Religion*, which were translated into German in 1781, very quickly after their posthumous publication in English in 1779. It is easy to read Hume as completely rejecting the argument from design, which was advocated by moderate and enlightened divines from the end of the seventeenth century until the end of the eighteenth, well after Hume's own book.[6] In both the *Enquiry* and the *Dialogues*, Hume certainly argues that it is not rational to infer to a perfectly intelligent and purposive creator from a nature that is imperfect and often contrapurposive, at least as far as we can see. For example, in the *Enquiry* the "friend" who seems to speak for Hume (unlike the rest of the *Enquiry*, this section is written in dialogue form) says that,

> The Deity is known to us only by his productions, and is a single being in the universe, not comprehended under any species or genus, from whose experienced attributes or qualities we can, by analogy, infer any attribute or quality in him. As the universe shows wisdom and goodness, we infer wis-

---

[6] William Paley published his *Natural Theology, or Evidences of the Existence and Attributes of the Deity Collected from the Appearances of Nature*, as late as 1802. A list of both British and German works on the argument from design that would have been known to Kant is given in Johann August Eberhard, *Vorbereitung zur natürlichen Theologie* (Halle, Germany: Im Waisenhause, 1781), §1; reprinted in the *Akademie* edition at 18: 513–14. Kant's lecture notes on Eberhard's textbook are reproduced at 18: 491–606. Eberhard does not mention Hume's *Dialogues*, which were translated into German only in the same year in which his own book was published.

dom and goodness. As it shows a particular degree of these perfections, we infer a particular degree of them, precisely adapted to the effect which we examine. But farther attributes or farther degrees of the same attributes, we can never be authorized to infer or suppose, by any rules of just reasoning. ... Every supposed addition to the works of nature makes an addition to the attributes of the Author of nature; and consequently, being entirely unsupported by any reason or argument, can never be admitted but as mere conjecture and hypothesis. (*Enquiry I*, Section II, 108–9)

And in the *Dialogues*, Hume's apparent spokesman Philo makes much sport with the argument, proposing that if we examine the world around us closely—that is, commence an argument from design with honest empirical observation of what sort of design we actually find in nature—we might have to infer that it has just grown like a vegetable, or perhaps was designed by an immature god or a superannuated god or an ill-managed committee of gods. But it is important to note that throughout all of the fun Hume's apparent spokesmen deny the rationality of arguing for the existence of God by analogy with other forms of creation that we know, not the naturalness of the belief in an intelligent and purposive design and designer of the universe.

In fact, Hume's spokesman Philo seems to allow that belief in the purposive design of the universe and the intelligence of its author is not only natural but also useful:

A Purpose, an Intention, a Design strikes every where the most careless, the most stupid Thinker; and no man can be so harden'd in absurd Systems, as at all times to reject it. *That Nature does nothing in vain*, is a Maxim establish'd in all the Schools, merely from the Contemplation of the Works of Nature, without any religious Purpose; and, from a firm Conviction of its Truth, an Anatomist, who had observ'd a new Organ or Canal, wou'd never be satisfy'd, till he had also discover'd its Use and Intention. One great Foundation of the *Copernican* System is the Maxim, *that Nature acts by the simplest Methods, and chooses the most proper Means to any End*; and Astronomers often, without thinking of it, lay this strong

Foundation of Piety and Religion. The same thing is observ-
able in other Parts of Philosophy: And thus all the Sciences
almost lead us insensibly to acknowledge a first intelligent
Author . . . (*Dialogues*, Part 12, 245)

As with causation in general, Hume seems to think that our
belief in God as the author of nature cannot be logically derived
from reason or experience but is still a natural, irresistible, and
useful product of the real source of our most fundamental beliefs, the imagination. Kant will clearly agree with Hume that
the conception of God is the source of useful strategies for the
investigation of nature—indeed, Hume's use of the term
"maxim" in this passage may make it a direct source for Kant's
discussion of the maxims of scientific inquiry in the Introduction to the third *Critique* (Section V, 5: 182). But he will equally
clearly reject Hume's merely empirical recognition that the idea
of an intelligent designer of nature comes to us through the
ordinary mechanisms of the imagination. Kant will insist that
the idea of God has an a priori origin in pure reason, although
it has only heuristic value for the conduct of scientific inquiry
and can be made *determinate* only from a moral point of view,
indeed only in order to support our own efforts to comply fully
with the demands of morality.

This will have to suffice for a sketch of Humean positions to
which Kant will respond in the *Critique of the Power of Judgment*. Let us now turn to Kant's responses.

Kant on the Necessity of the Laws of Nature

Kant presents the whole *Critique of the Power of Judgment* as
a theory of "reflecting" rather than "determining" judgment,
although this distinction seems to have come to him quite late
in the development of his thought.[7] Judgment is "determining"
when "the universal (the rule, the principle, the law) is given,"

---

[7] There is no hint of it even in the second edition of the *Critique of Pure Reason*,
published in 1787.

and the power of judgment only "subsumes the particular under it." Judgment is "reflecting," however, when "only the particular is given, for which the universal is to be found" (*Judgment*, Introduction IV, 5: 179). In other words, determining judgment seeks to apply a given universal to a particular, while reflecting judgment seeks to find an appropriate universal for a particular that is already given. Whether this conception of reflecting judgment fits all the cases of judgment that Kant discusses in the third *Critique*, especially the judgment of the beautiful, which Kant says "pleases universally without a concept" at all (*Judgment*, §9, 5: 219), is debatable.[8] But it certainly fits the first use of the power of judgment that Kant describes in the Introduction to the third *Critique*, namely the search for determinate empirical laws of nature by means of which the a priori but completely abstract principles established in the first *Critique*—such as the principle that "All alterations occur in accordance with the law of the connection of cause and effect" (B 232)—can be applied to particular objects of experience. There is an issue here because the concepts contained in such general principles are not specific enough to be applied directly to our empirical intuitions—the concept of causation, for example, is only the abstract idea of "the succession of the manifold insofar as it is subject to a rule," or what Kant calls a "schema" for an empirical concept (A 144/B 183)—and there are in practice always a variety of conceivable ways in which such a general idea could be applied to particular sensory data, that is, a variety of hypotheses about causation that are equally consistent with the empirical data. Changes in the temperature of substances, for example, could be explained as the regular outcome of transfers

---

[8] In my *Kant and the Claims of Taste*, originally published in 1979 (2nd ed., Cambridge: Cambridge University Press, 1997), I argued that the case of aesthetic judgment does not fit with Kant's general account of reflecting judgment (chap. 2, especially 47–59). However, in "Kant's Principles of Reflecting Judgment," in *Kant's Critique of the Power of Judgment: Critical Essays*, ed. Paul Guyer (Lanham, MD: Rowman and Littlefield, 2003), 1–61, I argue that aesthetic judgment could be counted as a case of reflecting judgment after all, as long as the conception of the universal that is to be sought is broad enough to include the intersubjective agreement that we seek to realize in a successful aesthetic judgment.

of some substance distinct from that the temperature of which has changed (phlogiston) or as the regular outcomes of changes in the velocity of the particles of the same substance whose temperature has changed. We assume that grounds for preferring one causal explanation over another can be found in due course, sooner or later—and in this case the molecular theory of heat won out over the phlogiston theory. But neither the concept of heat by itself, as Hume observed, nor the general concept of causation by itself nor the general principle that every alteration has a cause, as Kant recognized, tells us which of these more concrete hypotheses about causation to adopt.

This is at least the most obvious interpretation of the problem that Kant has in mind in the initial discussion of reflecting judgment in the first draft of the Introduction to the third *Critique*, which was apparently written in early 1789, about half-way through his composition of the book.[9] Here Kant writes thus:

> With regard to the general concepts of nature, under which a concept of experience (without specific empirical determination) is first possible at all, reflection already has its directions in the concept of a nature in general, i.e., in the understanding. . . . But for those concepts which must first of all be found for given empirical intuitions, and which presuppose a particular law of nature, in accordance with which alone **particular** experience is possible, the power of judgment requires a special and at the same time transcendental principle for its reflection, and one cannot refer it in turn to already

[9] Kant set this draft aside and wrote a new version in March of 1790, as the rest of the book was already being set in type. Several years later, he gave it to his disciple Jakob Sigismund Beck, who was preparing several volumes of excerpts from Kant's philosophical works, telling him that he had decided not to use it in the published *Critique* only because of its length. Beck published some excerpts from the manuscript under the title of "Philosophical Encyclopedia," and it was not recognized for what it was and published as the first draft of the Introduction to the third *Critique* until 1914. Since then it has been known as the "First Introduction" (*FI*) to the *Critique of the Power of Judgment*. For details, see my Editor's Introduction to the *Critique of the Power of Judgment*, xli–xliii.

known empirical concepts and transform reflection into a mere comparison with empirical forms for which one already has concepts. For it is open to question how one could hope to arrive at empirical concepts of that which is common to the different natural forms through the comparison of perceptions, if, on account of the great diversity of its empirical laws, nature (as it is quite possible to think) has imposed on these natural forms such a great diversity that all or at least most comparison would be useless for producing consensus . . . (*FI*, Section V, 20: 212–13)

In other words, the problem is that on the basis of only the abstract laws of nature established in the first *Critique*, "we could not hope to find our way in a labyrinth of the multiplicity of possible empirical laws" (20: 214).

Kant's response to this problem is that we must simply "presuppose that even with regard to its empirical laws nature has observed a certain economy suitable to our power of judgment and a uniformity that we can grasp, and this presupposition, as an *a priori* principle of the power of judgment, must precede all comparison" (20: 213). In fact, we must not merely presuppose that the number of possible empirical concepts of nature is sufficiently small to be manageable by creatures with limited cognitive resources like ourselves; we must also presuppose the "general but at the same time indeterminate principle of a purposive arrangement of nature in a system, as it were for the benefit of our power of judgment, in the suitability of its particular laws (about which understanding has nothing to say) for the possibility of experience as a system" (20: 214). By a system, Kant means "a hierarchical order of species and genera" (20: 213). Such a system could be a system of concepts of natural *forms*, such as the Linnean taxonomy of plants and animals, which divides them into species, genera, families, orders, and so forth on the basis of morphological similarities of parts such as reproductive organs, teeth, and the like, or a system of natural *laws*, or laws about natural *forces*, which subsumes more particular laws, such as the laws of chemistry, under more general laws, such as the laws of physics.[10] Kant spells out this conception of a system in some detail (20: 214–15), but does not actually explain in equal detail how presupposing that our concepts of forms and laws can be organized into systems will address the problem of the underdetermination of particular laws by the general laws of nature. But his idea seems to be that seeking to find "in the immeasurable multiplicity of things in accordance with possible empirical laws sufficient kinship among them to enable them to be brought under empirical concepts (classes) and these in turn under more general laws (higher genera) and thus for an empirical system of nature to be reached" (20: 215) will help us by directing us to prefer among possible empirical concepts for some given data those that fit into a system with other empirical concepts we already have over those that do not, or those that fit better into a system over those that fit worse. With a guideline such as this, our search for empirical concepts to mediate between empirical intuitions and the general concepts of nature—the task of reflecting judgment—would not be "arbitrary and blind" (20: 212).

Kant insists that we should not merely strive to find empirical concepts of nature that fit into a system, but that we must presuppose the "transcendental" principle

> that nature in its boundless multiplicity has hit upon a division of itself into genera and species that makes it possible for our power of judgment to find consensus in the comparison of natural forms and to arrive at empirical concepts, and their interconnection with each other, through ascent to more general but still empirical concepts; i.e., the power of judgment presupposes a system of nature which is also in accordance with empirical laws and does so *a priori*, consequently by means of a transcendental principle. (20: 212)

[10] The contemporary approach to cladistics, which attempts to classify organisms according to their actual descent and divergence from precursors rather than on the basis of morphological similarities that might have arisen independently from a common descent, might be thought of as attempting to bridge any gap between classification based on forms and classification based on causal forces.

The principle of reflecting judgment is not merely the "logical" or methodological prescription that we should prefer systematic over nonsystematic empirical concepts, but the "transcendental" principle "of regarding nature *a priori* as qualified for a logical system of its multiplicity under empirical laws" (20: 214), the principle that "Nature specifies its general laws into empirical ones, in accordance with the form of a logical system, in behalf of the power of judgment" (20: 216). Contrary to Hume, Kant maintains that we must make the a priori presupposition that nature itself is systematic, and that we can only seek particular laws of nature, thus particular causal laws, on this presupposition.

But why must we not just seek to introduce systematicity into our own concepts, and instead presuppose that nature itself is systematic? Several assumptions might account for such a claim. One would be the assumption of a correspondence theory of truth, on which a systematic set of concepts of nature could be true only if the forms or laws of nature are themselves systematic. Another would be an assumption about practical rationality, on which it is rational to seek to realize a goal only if we have some sort of guarantee that such a goal can actually be achieved—so that it would be rational to seek systematicity among our concepts of nature only if we have the guarantee that nature itself is systematic. Kant holds a correspondence theory for empirical truths (see *Pure Reason*, A 59–60/B 84–85), and his doctrine of the postulates of pure practical reason is based on the principle that it is rational to seek a goal only if we have a guarantee that the accomplishment of that goal is possible (although at least once he recognizes that if a goal is sufficiently important, as the goal of durable international peace certainly is, then it is entirely rational to pursue it as long as we just have sufficient reason to believe that its necessary conditions are *not impossible*).[11] So both of these could certainly be among Kant's motives for insisting that the principle of the systematicity of

---

[11] See "On the common saying: That may be correct in theory but it is of no use in practice," 8: 312.

nature itself is not merely logical but transcendental, that is, an a priori principle about the object of our investigation.

In the published version of the Introduction, however, Kant makes a new point, missing from the first draft, which makes it clear that his conception of the systematicity of the forms and laws of nature is meant as a direct answer to Hume's problem about the necessity of causal laws—that is, not just the necessity that we know causal laws, but the necessary truth of those laws themselves. Here the way that Kant presents the fundamental problem for reflecting judgment is thus:

> The determining power of judgment under universal transcendental laws, given by the understanding, merely subsumes; the law is sketched out for it *a priori*, and it is therefore unnecessary for it to think of a law for itself in order to be able to subordinate the particular in nature to the universal.— But there is such a manifold of forms of the universal transcendental concepts of nature that are left undetermined by those laws that the pure understanding gives *a priori* . . . that there must nevertheless also be laws for it which, as empirical, may indeed be contingent in accordance with the insight of our understanding, but which, if they are to be called laws (as is also required by the concept of a nature) must be regarded as necessary on a principle of the unity of the manifold, even if that principle is unknown to us. (*Judgment*, Introduction IV, 5: 179–80)

Or as he formulates it a second time:

> The understanding is of course in possession *a priori* of universal laws of nature, without which nature could not be an object of experience at all; but it still requires in addition a certain order of nature in its particular rules, which can only be known to it empirically and which from its point of view are contingent. These rules, without which there would be no progress from the general analogy of a possible experience in general to the particular, it must think as laws (i.e., as necessary), because otherwise they would not constitute an order of nature, even though it does not and never can cognize

their necessity. Thus although it cannot determine anything *a priori* with regard to those (objects), it must yet, in order to investigate these empirical so-called laws, ground all reflection on nature on an *a priori* principle, namely, that in accordance with these laws a cognizable order of nature is possible—the sort of principle that is expressed in the following propositions: that there is in nature a subordination of genera and species that we can grasp; that the latter in turn converge in accordance with a common principle . . . ; that since it seems initially unavoidable for our understanding to have to assume as many different kinds of causality as there are specific differences of natural effects, they may nevertheless stand under a small number of principles with the discovery of which we have to occupy ourselves, etc. (*Judgment*, Introduction V, 5: 184–85)

In response to this formulation of the problem, Kant then reformulates the transcendental principle of reflecting judgment thus:

Now this principle can be nothing other than this: that since universal laws of nature have their ground in our understanding, which prescribes them to nature (although only in accordance with the universal concept of it as nature), the particular empirical laws, in regard to that which is left undetermined in them by the former, must be considered in terms of the sort of unity they would have if an understanding (even if not ours) had likewise given them for the sake of our faculty of cognition, in order to make possible a system of experience in accordance with particular laws of nature. (*Judgment*, Introduction IV, 5: 180)

This obviously differs from the formulation of the principle in the first draft in making explicit Kant's assumption that all laws must originate in mind—what we might think of as a profoundly Neoplatonic assumption underlying Kant's entire philosophy—so if some laws do not originate in our mind, they must be thought of as if they originate in a mind more capacious than our own. But in context, it also makes it clear that laws must be thought of as part of a system in order to give them the necessity they need in order to be laws but cannot otherwise possess.

What is Kant's idea here? Once again, he does not explain himself, but the most obvious interpretation of his idea would seem to be that a generalization that seems contingent when considered on its own can seem to be necessary when it is part of a system in which it is entailed by the higher-order generalizations under which it is subsumed and is the only candidate to entail the lower-order generalizations that are subsumed under it. If so, then looking for laws that are a part of a system is not just a heuristic for choosing among alternative hypotheses when our search would otherwise be blind and arbitrary, but a heuristic that has nothing to do with the modal status of the generalizations so found; rather, its position within a system would be precisely what gives a generalization the modal status of a law. Thus we could not leave acknowledgment of their position in a system behind once we have found our generalizations, as we could do with a mere heuristic; membership in a system would remain a condition of our recognition of our generalizations as laws. And since in Kant's way of thought the idea of the imposition of laws by a mind is necessary to explain the necessity of those laws, it would be precisely by imposing upon nature a system of laws that the understanding more capacious than our own that we imagine in the principle of reflecting judgment would impose the necessity upon those particular laws that the categories of our own understanding are not sufficient to impose.

Now we can come back to the question of Kant's motivation for making the principle of reflecting judgment a transcendental rather than merely logical principle. It is just that there must be a source of the necessity of particular laws of nature when that source obviously cannot be our own minds, which can impose only the necessity of the general principles of the understanding upon our experience of nature. In the first instance, we can think of that additional source of necessity as the systematicity of nature itself, although we might also go on to think, as Kant does in the published Introduction, that this systematicity must be imposed upon nature by an understanding greater than our own. And the idea that we must presuppose the systematicity of nature in order to lend necessity to particular laws of nature can also explain what might seem another puzzle about Kant's account, namely what good it could do us to suppose that these laws are "necessary on a principle of the unity of the manifold, even if that principle is unknown to us" (*Judgment*, Introduction IV, 5: 180). The answer to this question is simply that we must be able to regard particular laws of nature as necessarily true even before we have discovered the whole system of them—which indeed we may never do—and we can only do that if we assume that the whole system of laws that makes the particular ones we know necessary exists even if we do not know it. Thus we must suppose that the system of laws, beyond the bits of it that we happen to know, exists in nature itself (put there, if we want to follow the rest of Kant's thought, by an understanding greater than our own).

Thus Kant's thought is that the transcendental principle of the systematicity of nature provides an a priori basis for the objective necessity of causal laws instead of the subjective basis in the merely empirically known workings of the imagination, which was all that Hume could offer for the origin of the idea of necessary connection. Now we must ask whether all of this furnishes Kant with a persuasive response to Hume's question about the rationality of our belief in particular causal inferences.[12]

One question that arises is how we could think that placing a particular law of nature within a hierarchical system of such laws could lend that law even an appearance of necessary truth when we might well be able to imagine whole other systems of

---

[12] Sympathetic accounts of Kant's conception of systematicity as an answer to Hume's worries about inductions have been offered by Philip Kitcher, "Projecting the Order of Nature," in *Kant's Philosophy of Physical Science*, ed. Robert E. Butts (Dordrecht, the Netherlands: D. Reidel, 1986), 201–35; reprinted in *Kant's Critique of Pure Reason: Critical Essays*, ed. Patricia Kitcher (Lanham, MD: Rowman and Littlefield, 1998), 219–38, and Juliet Floyd, "Heautonomy: Kant on Reflective Judgment and Systematicity," in *Kants Ästhetik—Kant's Aesthetics—L'esthétique de Kant*, ed. Herman Parret (Berlin: Walter de Gruyter, 1998), 192–218.

laws consistent with other laws we take ourselves to know and the empirical observations we have made? Presumably Kant's assumption that nature itself is systematic is supposed to take care of this: if it is nature itself that is systematic, not merely our representation of nature through concepts and laws, then there must be some *one* way in which it is systematic (or some *one* system of organization that has been imposed upon it by the understanding greater than our own). If we do not know what that whole system is, as Kant reasonably presupposes, then we can have no way of being certain that some particular law we are considering is actually a part of it, and thus no way of being certain that this law is necessarily true. But that is not an objection if what Kant is offering is not an *epistemology* for necessary truth but more like a *metaphysics* for necessary truth, that is, a theory that explains how there can be necessary truth for particular laws of nature, not a method that guarantees that we can discover it. We can take Kant to be offering an account of how we can think that the particular laws we claim to know are necessarily true *if* they are true at all. As our knowledge of the whole system improves, we may then have to revise our beliefs about which particular laws of nature are necessarily true because we will have to revise our beliefs about which of such laws are true.

However, Hume did not ask how we can claim that one causal law rather than another is true, but rather asked how we can rationally believe that any generalization is necessarily true when we cannot believe that on the basis of the finite number of cases we have sampled and any premise we could rationally add to those cases. So we must ask whether Kant's claim that we must make the a priori supposition that nature itself is systematic could possibly be a compelling answer to Hume's question. This seems dubious, for Kant seems to do the very thing he accused earlier respondents to Hume of doing: taking for granted precisely what Hume doubted (*Prolegomena*, Preface, 4: 258). Kant begins with the assumption that we must have a basis for regarding particular laws of nature as necessarily true, something we cannot do merely on the basis of our own pure understanding (and pure intuition), and then presupposes an a priori idea of the systematicity of nature to ground that initial assumption. It is not clear that Hume would have been much impressed with this move. Further, as we saw in chapter 2, Hume raises his famous question about whether we have a rational, noncircular reason for assuming that the future must resemble the past, or more generally whether unobserved cases must resemble observed cases, specifically in connection with his question about the rational basis for our belief in particular causal connections. But Kant's thesis that we can only impute necessity to particular causal laws by conceiving of them as part of a system of laws in which they would be entailed by more fundamental laws does not address the problem of induction, for there is no obvious reason why the whole system of laws that holds or is believed to hold at one time must continue to hold at every other time. Or to put it more gently, unless the presupposition that nature is constant is included in the very idea of the systematicity of nature, Kant's conception that our search for particular causal laws depends on our assumption that they are part of a system and our imputation of necessity to them depends upon their actually being part of a system, Kant's principle of systematicity does not address Hume's worry about induction—but if it is, then it begs the question against Hume's worry.

Does this mean that Kant's response to Hume's doubts about the necessity of causal laws is in vain? That would be too hasty a conclusion. There are two ways in which Kant clearly improves upon Hume. First, by recognizing that we think of particular laws of nature as necessary only within the context of a whole system of laws, Kant changes what we might call the Humean psychology of doubt. Hume gets us to doubt the rationality of particular causal inferences by considering them in isolation: for example, he imagines us being incapable of explaining why bread should nourish us rather than lions or tigers, thus appearing to make it reasonable to doubt whether we can know that the bread that has nourished us in the past will continue to do so in the future, by considering our claim to know that bread is nourishing for us in isolation from anything else we might know. But Kant makes it clear that we do not claim to know that such generalizations are necessarily true in isolation, but only as part of a whole system of natural laws, including more general ones that entail the particular one at issue. In order to doubt one causal law we would therefore have to doubt much else that we take ourselves to know, perhaps even the whole of the rest of our knowledge of nature. This may make doubting particular causal inferences psychologically more difficult than Hume supposes. Or to put this point another way, while it must always be remembered that Hume did not think his philosophical questions about the rationality of causal belief either should or could put our actual practices into doubt, or lead us to psychologically genuine doubt about the reliability of our particular causal beliefs—this is what Kant was alluding to when he said that Reid and his followers responded only to what Hume never thought to doubt, namely, the usefulness, indeed indispensability of causal beliefs in practice—Hume has nothing to say about why his arguments do not change our practices except for his general confidence that nature is stronger than argument. Kant's model shows in more detail why we cannot psychologically doubt particular causal laws unless we are psychologically prepared to doubt our entire edifice of causal beliefs.

Kant's a priori idea that natural laws are always part of a system of such laws also offers a much richer heuristic for the conduct of scientific inquiry than Hume's. As we saw in an earlier quotation from the *Dialogues concerning Natural Religion*, Hume introduced the idea of a "maxim" for the conduct of inquiry, and in so doing may well have influenced Kant. But he only offered one such maxim, that nature always takes the shortest way. Kant's idea of a hierarchically ordered system of concepts or laws gives much more concrete guidance in searching for particular concepts or laws: a system is a well-ordered structure in which we can seek to fill particular gaps either by dropping specific predicates from our concepts in order to move upward or by adding predicates in order to move downward—a structure within which, in Kant's terms, we can seek both greater homogeneity and greater specificity for our concepts (see *FI*, Section V, 20: 214–15 and *Pure Reason*, A 657–58/B 685–

86). Kant's conception of systematicity gives rise not just to the *lex parsimoniae*, "Nature takes the shortest way," but also to the *lex continui in natura*, that is, nature "makes no leaps, either in the sequence of its changes or in the juxtaposition of specifically different forms," and the *principia praeter necessitatem non sunt multiplicanda*, "the great multiplicity of its empirical laws is nevertheless unity under a few principles" (*Judgment*, Introduction V, 5: 182). We may think of these as strictly heuristic or methodological principles, useful for the regulation of our inquiry but open to at least provisional refutation by the actual results of our inquiry; we may not be tempted by Kant's attempt to assign "transcendental" although not quite "constitutive" validity to these maxims. Nevertheless, Kant's a priori idea of systematicity leads to a richer philosophy of science than Hume ever contemplated.

Kant on the A Priori Principle of Taste

In the first half of the *Critique of the Power of Judgment*, the "Critique of the Aesthetic Power of Judgment," Kant touched upon nearly every major issue discussed in eighteenth-century aesthetics. In the whole of his works, essays as well as treatises, Hume also managed to touch on a wide range of contemporary issues in aesthetics, but unlike most other philosophers in mid-century Britain (that is to say, chiefly Scotland) and Germany, he never wrote a systematic work on aesthetics, and his signature work in the field, the essay "Of the Standard of Taste," is focused on the single issue of the conditions in which we may reasonably expect and secure agreement in judgments of taste. This was not a major issue among German aestheticians preceding Kant, so Kant is responding to the British debate when he makes this issue the focal point of the "Analytic of the Beautiful" (§§1–22),[13] the first book of the "Critique of the Aesthetic

---

[13] Leading British aestheticians other than Hume who also made the problem of taste central to their work include Edmund Burke, who added an "Introduction on Taste" to the second edition of his *Philosophical Enquiry into the Origin of our*

Power of Judgment," and the subsequent "Deduction of Judgments of Taste" (§§30–40). Kant mentions Hume often enough throughout the *Critique of the Power of Judgment* to suggest that the Scot was never entirely absent from his mind. His most direct reference to Hume's views in aesthetics comes in a section arguing for the thesis that "No objective principle of taste is possible," in which he says that "Although critics, as Hume says, can reason more plausibly than cooks, they still suffer the same fate as then," namely, "They cannot expect a determining ground for their judgment from proofs, but only from the reflection of the subject on his own state (of pleasure or displeasure), rejecting all precepts and rules" (*Judgment*, §34). This is a reference to a comment in Hume's essay "The Sceptic" (*Essays*, 163), and it is not actually a completely reliable interpretation of Hume's position in "Of the Standard of Taste": there Hume argues that there can be no "precepts or rules" for judgments of taste that would directly entail aesthetic verdicts from the presence of determinate properties in objects, but he also argues that the collective body of judgments of qualified critics over time—a historical canon of works that have withstood the test of time—can provide a model for the development of individual taste, so that the individual appreciator is not dependent on nothing but his own reflection on his feelings of pleasure or displeasure.

But "Of the Standard of Taste" is also more fundamental for the problem and structure of Kant's aesthetic theory in the

Ideas of the Sublime and Beautiful (1759), no doubt in response to Hume's essay, which had appeared at the same time as Burke's first edition (1757), and Alexander Gerard, whose *Essay on Taste* also appeared in 1759. The 1762 *Elements of Criticism* by Hume's older cousin, Henry Home, Lord Kames, also concluded with a chapter on "The Standard of Taste." All of these works were widely known or known of in Germany. Burke's work was influentially reviewed by Moses Mendelssohn as soon as 1758, and Mendelssohn's friend Gotthold Ephraim Lessing began a translation, although it was Christian Garve, later to become significant in Kant's career, who first published a translation of Burke, in 1773, with Kant's own publisher Hartknoch in Riga. Gerard's essay, along with accompanying essays by Voltaire and d'Alembert drawn from the great French *Encyclopédie*, was translated into German in 1766.

Critique of the Power of Judgment than Kant ever explicitly says. Hume had posed the problem to be resolved in his essay as a conflict between two "species of common sense," one starting from the premise that "All sentiment is right," from which "the proverb has justly determined it to be fruitless to dispute concerning tastes," and the other holding that some tastes are sounder than others, so that "Whoever would assert an equality of genius and elegance between OGILBY and MILTON, or BUNYAN and ADDISON, would be thought to defend no less an extravagance, than if he had maintained a mole-hill to be as high as TENERIFFE, or a pond as extensive as the ocean" (*Essays*, 230–31), and had then attempted to steer a way between these two positions by arguing that there are *standards* for judgments of taste in the verdicts of qualified critics but no *principles* for judgments of taste that can specify invariably good-making properties of their objects. Kant takes over this structure and strategy for his own analysis of taste. This is clear at many points in his work, but perhaps clearest in Kant's formulation of the "antinomy of taste" as the conflict between the thesis that "The judgment of taste is not based on concepts, for otherwise it would be possible to dispute about it (decide by means of proofs)" and the antithesis that "The judgment of taste is based on concepts, for otherwise, despite its variety, it would not even be possible to argue about it (to lay claim to the necessary assent of others to this judgment" (*Judgment*, §56, 5: 338–39). This is Kant's restatement of Hume's conflict between two species of common sense, and Kant will also follow a strategy similar to Hume's at least to the extent of preserving something from both thesis and antithesis by finding an underlying commonality, although for Kant this will be the most un-Humean supposition of an a priori but indeterminate concept or principle underlying judgments of taste rather than a historical canon of critically praised works. But the fact that Kant accepts Hume's formulation of the problem of taste while rejecting Hume's solution to it certainly makes it reasonable to consider Kant's aesthetics as a response to Hume, even though the problem of the universal validity of judgments of taste may not ultimately be the most important issue in aesthetics for Kant.[14]

Since Kant adopts Hume's contrast between two species of common sense, it seems fair to say that his strategy in the "Analytic of the Beautiful" of the *Critique of the Power of Judgment*, as in his *Groundwork for the Metaphysics of Morals*, is to begin with an analysis of commonsense assumptions, find something true but also something problematic in them, and then provide the philosophical theory that is necessary to support the sound assumptions of common sense while dispelling its confusions. Kant begins his analysis with the claim that "the satisfaction that determines the judgment of taste is without any interest" (*Judgment*, §2, 5: 204), or is disinterested. By this he means that one's pleasure in a beautiful object is not a recognition that the existence of the object serves any merely physiological purpose, in which case it would be "agreeable" (§3), nor any moral purpose, in which case it would be "good" (§4), but concerns only one's response to the representation of the object: "It is readily seen that to say that [an object] is **beautiful** and to prove that I have taste what matters is what I make of this representation [of it] in myself, not how I depend on the existence of the object" (§2, 5: 205). Kant supports this first step of his analysis not with any theoretical argument, but with an appeal to what he takes to be our ordinary response to an example:

[14] My first work on Kant's aesthetics, *Kant and the Claims of Taste*, focuses largely on the problem of the standard of taste. In *Kant and the Experience of Freedom* (Cambridge: Cambridge University Press, 1993), I focus largely on Kant's treatment of the connections between aesthetics and morality. A number of the essays in my *Values of Beauty* further explore Kant's account of the connections between aesthetics and morality, while several also discuss connections between beauty and nonmoral utility. In "Bridging the Gulf: Kant's Project in the third *Critique*," in *The Blackwell Companion to Kant*, ed. Graham Bird (Oxford: Blackwell Publishing, 2006), 423–40, I also focus on the connections between aesthetics and morality in a way I do not here. Among other work that stresses the connection between Kant's aesthetics and morality, Donald W. Crawford, *Kant's Aesthetic Theory* (Madison: University of Wisconsin Press, 1974), remains important, and Birgit Recki, *Ästhetik der Sitten: Die Affinität von ästhetischem Gefühl und praktischer Vernunft bei Kant* (Frankfurt: Klostermann, 2001), is also valuable.

If someone asks me whether I find the palace that I see before me beautiful, I may well say that I don't like that sort of thing, which is made merely to be gaped at, or, like the Iroquois sachem, that nothing in Paris pleased him better than the cook-shops; in true **Rousseauesque** style I might even vilify the vanity of the great who waste the sweat of the people on such superfluous things. . . . All of this might be conceded to me and approved; but that is not what is at issue here. One only wants to know whether the mere representation of the object is accompanied with satisfaction in me, however indifferent I might be with regard to the existence of the object of this representation (§2, 5: 205)

—or even, one should add, however hostile to its existence I might be.

Kant next claims that the second "definition" (*Erklärung*)[15] of the beautiful as "that which, without concepts, is represented as the object of a universal satisfaction . . . can be deduced from the previous explanation of it as an object of satisfaction without any interest," for "one cannot judge that about which he is aware that the satisfaction is without any interest in his own case in any way except that it must contain a ground of satisfaction for everyone" (*Judgment*, §6, 5: 211). This might seem like a transition from common sense to philosophical theory. Moreover, strictly speaking, this claim is a non sequitur: it does not follow from the fact that my satisfaction in an object is not caused by its satisfaction of either of the two kinds of interest that have been identified in the previous moment that it cannot simply be idiosyncratic in some other way, due perhaps to some personal and arbitrary association that does not fall within the usual limits of the physiologically agreeable or the morally good.[16] It also does not follow from the previously established claim that our pleasure in and therefore judgment of beauty

---

[15] This is actually a broader term than the English "definition," which could also be translated as "explanation," "exposition," "explication," or "declaration"; Kant points this out at *Pure Reason*, A 730/B 758. Perhaps "explication" would actually be the best translation in the present context.

[16] See my *Kant the Claims of Taste*, 2nd ed., 118–19.

must be independent of a concept of the object as agreeable or good that it must be independent of *any* concept whatsoever, as Kant's second "definition" seems to assert. But this is of little matter, because Kant's next steps are, first, once again to anchor the claim that a genuinely beautiful object should please everyone in an appeal to common sense, and then, second, to introduce a philosophical explanation of our pleasure in beauty that will both justify that claim to intersubjective validity and also explain why (and in what sense) that pleasure is independent of concepts.

Kant appeals to ordinary linguistic usage to anchor the claim that judgments of taste claim intersubjective rather than merely personal validity. "With regard to the agreeable," he says, "everyone is content that his judgment, which he grounds on a private feeling, and in which he says of an object that it pleases him, be restricted merely to his own person." Evidence for this is the fact that one "is perfectly happy if, when he says that sparkling wine from the Canaries is agreeable, someone else should improve his expression and remind him that he should say 'It is agreeable **to me**'" (*Judgment*, §7, 5: 212). But we do not accept this restriction when we call something beautiful: "It would be ridiculous if . . . someone who prided himself on his taste thought to justify himself thus: 'This object (the building we are looking at, the clothing someone is wearing, the concert that we hear, the poem that is presented for judgment) is beautiful for me.'" In calling something beautiful, we speak not with an individual but with a "universal voice" (§8, 5: 216); we do not claim "objective universal validity," that is, that every object falling under some particular concept, or in a particular class, must please, but rather "subjectively universal validity," that is, that *this* object should please everyone (5: 215); indeed, we even demand that others should take pleasure in that which we have found to be beautiful (§7, 5: 213). Kant also puts this point by saying there is a "necessity" in a judgment of taste that "can only be called **exemplary**, i.e., a necessity of the assent of all to a judgment that is regarded as an example of a universal rule that one cannot produce" (§19, 5: 237)—a rule that cannot be produced because, as Kant has by that point more fully argued, although in a way we have not yet discussed, the pleasure in a beautiful object is not connected with its subsumption under any determinate concept.

Kant holds that a judgment of beauty is in a certain sense a synthetic a priori judgment rather than an entirely empirical one, and here he is staking out a contrast with Hume and the British tradition. This is initially implicit in his claims that one "does not count on the agreement of others with his judgment of satisfaction because he has frequently found them to be agreeable to his own" (*Judgment*, §7, 5: 213), and that we should not be deterred from demanding that others should agree with our judgments of taste even when, "as experience teaches," this assent "is often enough rejected" in practice (§8, 5: 214). In calling something beautiful, we claim that everyone would take pleasure in it if everyone—I who make the judgment and the others who should agree with it—were in ideal or optimal circumstances to respond to the object, which is not always the case. (Kant stresses that we are often mistaken in our own judgments of taste, thinking that an object has pleased us in a universally valid way when it has pleased us only because of some hidden personal interest; see §8, 5: 216, §19, 5: 237, and §38, 5: 290–91). Thus far, Kant has not said anything that Hume or other British theorists of taste would reject, since they too all recognized the difference between actual and optimal conditions for making judgments of taste. But Kant makes the difference in his approach explicit when he subsequently explains the question that needs to be answered by a "deduction of judgments of taste": "How is a judgment possible which, merely from one's own feeling of pleasure in an object, independent of its concept, judges this pleasure, as attached to the representation of the same object in **every other subject**, *a priori*, i.e., without having to wait for the assent of others?" (§36, 5: 288). Because we cannot derive our pleasure in a beautiful object from any concept that applies to it, he assumes, it can only be "an empirical judgment that I perceive and judge an object is beautiful," and to this extent Kant agrees with Hume; but because under appropriate circumstances I declare that my pleasure is valid for everyone else and demand that they should agree with my judgment, without having to wait for their assent and even in the face of their actual dissent (see also §32, 5: 282), "it is an *a priori* judgment that I find it beautiful, i.e., that I may require that satisfaction of everyone as necessary"—something that Hume never would have said. Put precisely, "it is not the pleasure but the universal validity of this pleasure perceived in the mind as connected with the mere judging of an object that is represented in a judgment of taste as a universal rule for the power of judgment, valid for everyone" (§37, 5: 289).

Hume had argued that judgments of taste are not based on any determinate concepts of their objects and thus cannot be made in accordance with any determinate rules:

> A man may know exactly all the circles and ellipses of the COPERNICAN system, and all the irregular spirals of the PTO-LEMAIC, without perceiving that the former is more beautiful than the latter. EUCLID has fully explained every quality of the circle, but has not, in any proposition, said a word of its beauty. The reason is evident. Beauty is not a quality of the circle. . . . It is only the effect, which that figure produces upon a mind, whose particular fabric or structure renders it susceptible of such sentiments. In vain would you look for it in the circle, or seek it, either by your senses, or by mathematical reasonings, in all the properties of that figure. ("The Sceptic," *Essays*, 165, and *Enquiry II*, Appendix I, 87)

That is why he argues that we can only look to the particular judgments of critics who have formed their taste under optimal circumstances for our standard of taste, not to any rules that would say that certain qualities are necessary and/or sufficient for the beauty of any objects that have them. Kant fully endorses Hume's premise; in fact, as we saw, he alludes to "The Sceptic" when he says that critics, like cooks, cannot defend their judgments by rational arguments from the concepts of their objects (*Judgment*, §34, 5: 285, referring to Hume's *Essays*, 163). But he breaks with Hume when he insists that judgments of taste are a priori rather than merely empirical in the sense that he has specified. He recognizes that this analysis of what is claimed by a judgment of taste "must be grounded in something as an *a priori* principle, even if only a merely subjective principle," and that such a principle "also requires a deduction, by means of which it may be comprehended how an aesthetic judgment could lay claim to necessity" (§36, 5: 288). Kant's success in breaking from Hume's model of taste depends upon his account of this a priori principle and its deduction, so to that we now turn.

Kant attempts to discharge the burden of proof he has taken on in two main steps. The first step is to provide an explanation of our pleasure in beautiful objects that will show that although this pleasure is not based on the subsumption of such objects under any determinate concepts, and therefore is not connected to the satisfaction of any interests that depend upon a particular conceptualization of those objects, it is nevertheless connected to a certain state of our cognitive powers. The second step is to argue that the cognitive powers work the same way in every human being, so that if one person's pleasure is genuinely connected to this special state of his cognitive powers, then anyone else who is in optimal circumstances for the exercise of his cognitive powers should be able to feel the same pleasure.

The first step of this argument is Kant's theory that our pleasure in beautiful objects is due to a free yet harmonious "play" between the cognitive powers of imagination and understanding, where imagination has to be understood in a broad sense as the capacity to present imagery to the mind, thus as including both the capacity for present sensation that Kant ordinarily designates as "sensibility" and the capacity for the recall of past experiences and the anticipation of future ones that was ordinarily meant by "imagination" in the eighteenth century,[17] and where understanding has to be understood in a broad sense as the capacity to find unity and coherence in the manifolds presented to us by imagination, whether through a concept or not.

---

[17] See for example Alexander Gottlieb Baumgarten, *Metaphysik*, trans. Georg Friedrich Meier, 2nd ed., 1783 (Jena, Germany: Dietrich Schleglmann Reprints, 2004), §414. For a broad survey of eighteenth-century conceptions of imagination and their transformation on the way to Romanticism, see James Engell, *The Creative Imagination: Enlightenment to Romanticism* (Cambridge, MA: Harvard University Press, 1981).

Kant states the essence of his theory in the Introduction to the third *Critique* when he writes that,

> If pleasure is connected with the mere apprehension . . . of the form of an object of intuition without a relation of this to a concept for a determinate cognition, then the representation is thereby related not to the object, but solely to the subject, and the pleasure can express nothing but its suitability to the cognitive faculties that are in play in the reflecting power of judgment, insofar as they are in play, and thus merely a subjective formal purposiveness of the object. For that apprehension of forms in the imagination can never take place without the reflecting power of judgment, even if unintentionally, at least comparing them to its faculty for relating intuitions to concepts. Now if in this comparison the imagination . . . is unintentionally brought into accord with the understanding . . . through a given representation and a feeling of pleasure is thereby aroused, then the object must be regarded as purposive for the reflecting power of judgment.
> (*Judgment*, Introduction VII, 5: 189–90)

Kant further characterizes this idea of play between imagination and understanding in the first draft of the Introduction by saying that it is a state "which constitutes the subjective, merely sensitive condition of the objective use of the power of judgment in general (namely the agreement of those two faculties with each other)" (*FI*, Section VIII, 20: 223–24). If we think of the fundamental goal of the use of our cognitive powers as finding unity in the manifold of our experience, and think of the subsumption of objects under concepts as the objective way of attaining this goal, then we may think of the state in which it seems to us that our manifold of experience has been unified in a way that does not depend on the subsumption of its object under any determinate concept as the "subjective, merely sensitive condition" for the satisfaction of the ultimate goal of the use of our cognitive powers.

And this interpretation in turn leads to Kant's explanation for why this peculiar state of mind should lead to a feeling of pleasure. Kant explicitly asserts that the "attainment of every aim is combined with the feeling of pleasure," and also seems to assume the converse, that every feeling of pleasure is connected with the attainment of some aim, but then adds that it is only when the attainment of the aim strikes us as "merely contingent" that the pleasure will be actually felt or "specially noticed" (*Judgment*, Introduction VI, 5: 187–88). A state of mind in which it seems to us as if our fundamental cognitive goal of finding unity in our manifolds of experience has been achieved independently of the subsumption of the object of our experience under any determinate concept will surely strike us as a state in which the satisfaction of our goal is merely contingent, and our pleasure in this state will therefore be "specially noticed." Thus Kant's theory of the free play of our cognitive powers explains how we can be pleased with an object independently of its subsumption under a concept, and indeed entails the requirement of the independence of our pleasure from beauty that was initially merely assumed in Kant's exposition of the analysis of judgments of taste.

It is a matter of common sense (as well as an implication of Kant's theory of knowledge in the first *Critique*) that we are never conscious of an object without any concept altogether, and can never make a judgment about an object without using some concept to pick it out. This is true of aesthetic judgments as well; thus, even the most pedestrian aesthetic judgment, such as "This rose is beautiful," or, if you do not know what kind of flower it is, "This flower is beautiful," employs not only the concept of beauty itself as its predicate but also some perfectly ordinary, at least relatively determinate, concept such as "rose" or "flower" to designate its subject. So how can our pleasure in the object and our judgment that our pleasure is universally valid, and thus our application of the predicate "beautiful" to it, be independent of the subsumption of the object under any determinate concept? The answer to this question can only be that a beautiful object leaves the imagination and understanding room to play beyond what is regulated by the determinate concept or concepts that apply to it, in other words, that a beautiful object is one that gives us a feeling of unity and coherence that goes beyond the satisfaction of the conditions needed to satisfy the determinate concept that is applied to it. A beautiful rose is one that somehow gives us a greater sense of unity than a merely indifferent one, a degree of harmony in its shape or between its shape and color, or whatever, that is more than is needed just to count as a rose.[18]

This interpretation of what Kant means by the harmony of imagination and understanding, in addition to satisfying common sense and Kant's own epistemology, also has the virtue of explaining Kant's immediate expansion of the class of genuine aesthetic judgments beyond the case of simple judgments like "This rose is beautiful," which he designates as "pure" and subsequently "free" judgments of taste. Beyond these judgments, Kant recognizes at least four more classes of aesthetic judgments: judgments of "adherent" beauty, which do involve a concept of the purpose of their object; judgments about the "ideal of beauty," which involve a sense of harmony between the outward form and the invisible moral virtue of a human being; judgments of sublimity, which involve a feeling of harmony between the imagination and ideas of reason rather than understanding; and judgments about the beauty of fine art, which depend upon a feeling of harmony between the form of a work of art and the special kind of content that Kant calls an "aesthetic idea." A discussion of Kant's theory of the sublime would exceed the boundaries of this chapter,[19] but some comments on the other cases will help illustrate the virtues of Kant's theory of the harmony of the faculties as an explanation of our pleasure in beauty.

---

[18] I have defended this interpretation in detail in "The Harmony of the Faculties Revisited," in my *Values of Beauty*, chap. 3. There I respond to a number of alternative interpretations of Kant's concept of the harmony of the faculties, including Hannah Ginsborg, "Lawfulness without a Law: Kant on the Free Play of Imagination and Understanding," *Philosophical Topics* 25 (1997): 37–83; Fred L. Rush Jr., "The Harmony of the Faculties," *Kant-Studien* 92 (2001): 38–61; and Henry E. Allison, *Kant's Theory of Taste: A Reading of the Critique of Aesthetic Judgment* (Cambridge: Cambridge University Press, 2001), especially chaps. 5 and 8.

[19] I have dealt with the sublime in a number of places, including "The Beautiful and the Sublime," chapter 6 of my *Kant and the Experience of Freedom*, and "Kant on the Purity of the Ugly," in *Values of Beauty*, chap. 6.

Kant's distinction between "free" and "adherent" beauty is his own version of Hume's distinction between beauty of appearance and beauty of utility.[20] In Kant's theory, free beauty involves a feeling of pleasure that is not connected to any concept by means of which the object is identified, while adherent beauty is *connected to* but not *determined by* the concept of its purpose that is implicit in the very concept by means of which an object is identified. When we call something an arsenal or a church, a race horse or even a human being, a concept of its purpose or in the case of a human being its moral vocation is implied, and this purpose places a limit on what forms we could possibly find acceptable in such an object—we cannot find an arsenal beautiful if it has light walls with many openings, nor, on Kant's views, is extensive tattooing consistent with the moral imperative always to treat one's body as well as one's personality as an end and not merely as a means (*Judgment*, §16, 5: 230). But not every arsenal or human being that satisfies such constraints inherent in the concept of its purpose is beautiful; a beautiful one must give us a sense of unity or harmony that goes beyond what is necessary for satisfaction of its concept, or perhaps even an unusual sense of harmony between its purpose and its form, which it need not have merely in order to satisfy the concept of its purpose alone. And this suggests that sometimes the free play of imagination can be a play with concepts although not determined by concepts.

Kant exploits this possibility in his brief treatment of the "ideal of beauty" and in his more extensive discussion of the traditional subject matter of aesthetics, the fine arts. An ideal of beauty would be a "highest model" or "archetype" of taste. Nothing in the logic of judgments of taste alone actually re-

[20] Recent discussion of Kant's distinction begins with Eva Schaper, "Free and Dependent Beauty," originally in *Akten des 4. Internationalen Kant-Kongresses*, Teil 1 (Berlin: Walter de Gruyter, 1974), 247–62; reprinted in her *Studies in Kant's Aesthetics* (Edinburgh: Edinburgh University Press, 1979), 78–98. I have discussed the distinction in more detail in two recent articles, "Beauty and Utility in Eighteenth Century Aesthetics," *Eighteenth Century Studies* 35 (2002): 439–53, and "Free and Adherent Beauty: A Modest Proposal," *British Journal of Aesthetics* 42 (October 2002) 357–66, both reprinted in *Values of Beauty*, chaps. 4 and 5.

quires such an ideal; the logic of taste requires ideal agreement about any particular beautiful object, but not any sort of hierarchy among beautiful objects, let alone that there be any one object or kind of object that is maximally beautiful. The requirement of an ideal of beauty comes instead from "reason's indeterminate idea of a maximum" (*Judgment*, §17, 5: 232). Such an ideal arises when a human form is both judged to be beautiful, in a way that itself goes beyond any merely normal, average, or "correct" human form (5: 234–35), and also felt to be in harmony with the "highest purposiveness" of a human being— "goodness of soul, or purity, or strength, or repose, etc."—in a way that cannot be derived from any determinate concept but instead requires both "pure ideas of reason and great imagination" (5: 235). In other words, in judging a human being (or the depiction of one) to represent the ideal of beauty we judge it to have a beauty of form that goes beyond any determinate concept and a harmony between its form and central moral ideas that goes beyond any determinate concept.

Kant's theory of fine art also depends on the possibility of a harmony between the form of an object and concepts, in this case its content, which is not determined by those concepts.[21] Kant analyzes a work of fine art as a product of human intentionality, which must be guided by a concept, but which aims at producing a free play of the imagination and understanding, and which therefore cannot be fully determined by any concept (*Judgment*, §§43–44, 5: 303–6). This is why (successful) fine art must be the product of genius, which is nothing less than a natural gift to produce something exemplary in a way that uses rules (of technique, composition, and so on) but also goes beyond them (§46, 5: 307–8). Kant further assumes that a work of art typically has a content—like everyone else in the eighteenth

---

[21] I have discussed Kant's theory of fine art in "Kant's Conception of Fine Art," *Journal of Aesthetics and Art Criticism* (1994): 175–85, reprinted as chapter 12 of the second edition of my *Kant and the Claims of Taste*. An interesting treatment of Kant's philosophy of art, which, however implausibly, argues that Kant placed more value on artistic than on natural beauty, is Salim Kemal, *Kant and Fine Art: An Essay on Kant and the Philosophy of Fine Art and Culture* (Oxford: Clarendon Press, 1986).

century, Kant did not yet envisage abstract or "nonobjective" art
or see the need for defending the assumption that all fine art is
mimetic—but that its beauty consists precisely in our sense of
a free play between its content and its form. Thus a work of
artistic genius is an "aesthetic idea," a "representation of the
imagination that occasions much thinking without it being possible for any determinate thought, i.e., **concept**, to be adequate
to it, which, consequently, no language fully attains or can make
intelligible" (§49, 5: 313). An aesthetic idea is a conception for
a work that mediates between the rational ideas that are its
theme and the form and material of the work in a way that
cannot be determined by any rule but yet gives us the sense of
harmony we need to find it beautiful. "If we add to a concept a
representation of the imagination that belongs to its presentation, but which by itself stimulates so much thinking that it
can never be grasped in a determinate concept, hence which
aesthetically enlarges the concept itself in an unbounded way,
then in this case the imagination is creative" (5: 315).

Thus we can see how Kant's idea of the free and harmonious
play of imagination and understanding, which initially seems to
explain only a narrow range of aesthetic judgments such as "This
rose is beautiful," can illuminate the broad range of aesthetic
judgments we actually make. But now we must return to the
question of whether this concept can provide the a priori principle of taste that Kant needs to support his insistence against
Hume that judgments of taste make an a priori claim to universal validity even though they are not based on rules. This is the
burden of proof in Kant's "Deduction of Judgments of Taste."

The a priori principle underlying judgments of taste obviously
cannot be what Kant introduced as the general, "transcendental"
principle of reflecting judgment in the Introduction to the third
Critique, namely the principle that the particular empirical laws
of nature must be regarded as if they were part of a system of
laws given by an understanding greater than our own but "for
the sake of our faculty of cognition" (*Judgment*, Introduction IV,
5: 180), because for reasons we have just seen, aesthetic judgments do not depend upon any concepts that classify their objects and thus neither depend upon nor give rise to anything

resembling particular empirical laws. In fact, for his theory of taste Kant has in mind a different a priori principle concerning "our faculty of cognition," the a priori principle that we all have the same cognitive faculties and that they work in the same way, from which it should follow that an object that genuinely induces the free play of imagination and understanding in one optimally situated subject will induce it in any other such subject.

Kant presents the argument for the principle as briefly as possible in the official "Deduction of Judgments of Taste" by saying that since a proper judgment of taste is based only on "the subjective conditions of the use of the power of judgment in general (. . . restricted neither to the particular kind of sense nor to a particular concept of the understanding)," it therefore involves only "that subjective element that one can presuppose in all human beings (as requisite for possible cognitions in general)," or that "In all human beings, the subjective conditions" of the aesthetic power of judgment, "as far as the relation of the cognitive powers therein set into action to a cognition in general is concerned, are the same, which must be true, since otherwise human beings could not communicate their representations and even cognition itself" (*Judgment*, §38, 5: 290). The claim is that for different human beings to be capable of knowledge, they must all have all the faculties necessary for knowledge, *and* that each human being knows this a priori about all other human beings—both of these claims are necessary to make an individual's claim to the agreement of others on the basis of his own feeling something the individual knows to be justified a priori.

It might be objected that one must assume these claims in order for it to be rational to attempt to communicate one's knowledge to others, but that one could still be defeated in all of one's attempts to communicate knowledge to someone who seems to satisfy all imaginable criteria for being human, and thus that one's assumption is ultimately defeasible, thus is not a priori but only empirical knowledge.[22] However, the more

---

[22] To be sure, some contemporary philosophers have accepted something like Kant's claim. Donald Davidson accepted that we can only recognize something as another human being if we assign to it not only the same cognitive powers but also

serious objection to Kant's argument would be that even if we are entitled to assume a priori that everyone has the same cognitive capacities, it still would not follow that they must all work in exactly the same way, and in particular that they must all play in exactly the same way, or be set into play by the very same objects. After all, even people who do exactly the same job at work do not play the same games away from work. It thus seems to be an empirical question whether every normal human being is capable of the free play of imagination and understanding and would experience this state in response to the same objects even under optimal conditions. It thus seems questionable whether Kant has succeeded in replacing the empirical assumptions underlying Hume's expectation of a standard of taste from the collective judgments of qualified critics with an a priori principle accessible to every subject.

Kant tried to address such an objection in a preliminary version of the deduction in the "Analytic of the Beautiful."[23] In response to the question "Whether one has good reason to presuppose a common sense," Kant argues that we must assume not only that "if cognitions are able to be communicated, then the mental state, i.e., the disposition of the cognitive powers for a representation in general, and indeed that proportion which is suitable for making cognition out of a representation . . . must also be capable of being universally communicated," but further that "although this disposition of the cognitive powers has a different proportion depending on the difference of the objects

---

the same fundamental conceptual scheme, thus that we cannot even understand the idea of *alternative* conceptual schemes, in his famous article "On the Very Idea of a Conceptual Scheme" (1974), reprinted in his *Inquiries into Truth and Interpretation* (Oxford: Clarendon Press, 1984), 183–98.

[23] In his treatment of the deduction, Henry Allison denies that Kant's discussion of "common sense" in §21 of the "Analytic of the Beautiful" should be regarded as a preliminary version of the deduction, and maintains instead that it is only an attempt to display the intersubjective validity of the condition of cognition in general, which will only later become a premise of the deduction of judgments of taste (Allison, *Kant's Theory of Taste*, 149–55). This seems to be incompatible with Kant's claim in this section, about to be explicated, that there is a unique proportion between imagination and understanding that can only be determined through *feeling*—the fundamental criterion of the *aesthetic* for Kant.

that are given[, n]evertheless there must be one in which this inner relationship is optimal for the animation of both powers of mind" (*Judgment*, §21, 5: 238). In posing this question, Kant is asking whether there is a shared ability to judge by means of feeling, a *Gemeinsinn* or *sensus communis*, rather than a "common understanding" (*gemeiner Verstand*) in the sense of a shared ability "to judge in accordance with concepts, although commonly only in the form of obscurely represented principles" (§19, 5: 238)—but establishing that we have a common ability to judge by feeling would in turn be necessary to establish the commonsense assumption that we can make shared aesthetic judgments without reliance upon determinate concepts. However, Kant's pseudo-mathematical talk of an "optimal proportion" cannot mask the fact that he offers no further argument to bar the possibility that even if in some general way all human beings have the same cognitive capacities, different people might find that different objects set those faculties into free and harmonious play, even when personal interests in the agreeable, the good, and any other identifiably idiosyncratic association have been set aside. Kant's insistence that the cognitive powers of all humans must be alike both at work and at play seems more a matter of faith than a justifiable a priori principle.[24]

The empiricist premise of Hume's essay on taste could only have been that experience will reveal a high degree of agreement among the judgments of qualified critics, and that the rest of us will find that modeling our tastes on theirs largely optimizes

[24] Kant's deduction has been defended by Karl E. Ameriks, "How to Save Kant's Deduction of Taste," *Journal of Value Inquiry* 16 (1982): 295–302, and "Kant and the Objectivity of Taste," *British Journal of Aesthetics* 23 (1983): 3–17, both reprinted in his *Interpreting Kant's* Critiques (Oxford: Clarendon Press, 2003), as well as by Allison, *Kant's Theory of Taste*, 184–92. Ameriks tries to defend the intersubjective validity of aesthetic judgment by assimilating it to empirical judgment in general, but does not show that we must all make the same empirical judgments under (ideally) similar conditions. Allison argues that our disagreements about particular judgments under *actual* conditions does not undermine the "normativity" of aesthetic judgments in general, but this seems to miss the point of my claim that Kant has not shown that our minds must all work the same way even under *ideal* conditions.

our aesthetic experiences. In spite of his attempt to deduce an a priori principle of taste, Kant does not seem entitled to assume more than this. Does this mean that his entire effort at an aesthetic theory has been in vain? Not at all, because the explanation of our pleasure in beauty to which Kant has been led in his search for an a priori principle yields a far more systematic account of our aesthetic judgments than Hume had to offer. For Hume, there is no obvious connection between the two main species of beauty he recognized, the beauty of species and the beauty of utility, except perhaps the phenomenological claim that they yield the same feeling of pleasure, unlike any other kind of pleasure: he asserts that "the beauty of all visible objects causes a pleasure pretty much the same, tho' it be sometimes deriv'd from the mere *species* and appearance of the objects; sometimes from sympathy, and an idea of their utility," while "On the other hand, a convenient house, and a virtuous character, cause not the same feeling of approbation" (*Treatise*, III.-iii.5, 393). Kant, by contrast, assumes that all pleasures, whether in the agreeable, the beautiful, or the good, feel pretty much the same, although reflection can show them to have very different origins (see *Judgment*, §5, 5: 209–10), but then uses the theory of the free play of imagination and understanding that he first proposes to explain our pleasure in free beauty to show the underlying resemblances between the superficially very different cases of free beauty, adherent beauty, artistic beauty, and more. This by itself is a theoretical gain over Hume.

Further, Kant's theory that aesthetic judgment is not a form of cognition but nevertheless involves the cognitive powers should offer some guidance for aesthetic discourse, that is, for the conversations in which we may try to share our aesthetic judgments with one another or even to justify them to one another even though we have no a priori guarantee that we can succeed in doing so; we can point out how elements of a work seem to cohere with one another or follow from one another or fit together in any of the myriad ways in which components of cognition fit with one another, even though they do not do so literally. The rationality of seeking agreement in judgments of taste may not require an antecedent guarantee of success of the sort that would be provided by an a priori principle, but it is surely supported by the availability of a mode of discourse through which we might reach the desired end.

Kant on the Purpose of Nature

The "Critique of the Teleological Power of Judgment" can be read as Kant's reply to Hume's critique of the traditional argument from design.[25] Kant agrees completely with Hume that the thought that nature has been designed by an intelligent and purposive designer can never amount to theoretical cognition. But where Hume, or at least his apparent spokesman in the *Dialogues concerning Natural Religion*, seemed content to concede that we nevertheless have a natural and ineliminable tendency to believe that nature has such a designer, Kant argues that this thought is an a priori idea of pure reason that can be made more determinate by reflecting judgment and that has heuristic value in the conduct of scientific inquiry as well as moral value for our conduct in general. Kant makes it clear that the "physicotheology" (*Judgment*, §85, 5: 436), which had been so thoroughly discredited although not entirely eliminated from human psychology by Hume, can and should be replaced with an "ethicotheology" (§86, 5: 442), but he also uses the idea of design for a richer philosophy of science than Hume had conceived.

Kant begins his argument with the statement that "the general idea of nature as the sum of the object of the senses" provides "no basis at all" for the specific idea "that things of nature serve one another as means to ends, and that their possibility itself should be adequately intelligible only through this kind of causality" (*Judgment*, §61, 5: 359). He defends this general claim with two sorts of considerations. First, what appears to

---

[25] For an earlier reference to this connection, see Jerry E. Sobel, "Arguing, Accepting, and Preserving Design in Heidegger, Hume, and Kant," in *Essays in Kant's Aesthetics*, ed. Ted Cohen and Paul Guyer (Chicago: University of Chicago Press, 1982), 271–305.

be "objective purposiveness" in the structure of organisms, such as "the structure of a bird, the hollowness of its bones, the placement of its wings for movement and of its tail for steering, etc.," can be taken as evidence of the contingency of the occurrence of such natural forms as easily as it can be taken as "being **necessarily** connected" with "objective purposiveness, as a principle of the possibility of the things of nature" (5: 360); in other words, the very fact that the occurrence of such structures seems contingent relative to the basic "mechanism" of nature, the fundamental laws of motion and force, can just as easily argue against the idea that nature has been designed with an eye to such structures as for that idea. Second, Kant argues that natural forces and processes that turn out to be useful to us and to which we may therefore egocentrically assign "relative purposiveness," as if they had been designed for our benefit, can seem to have very different purposes or none at all if looked at from other points of view. We may think that plants exist to nourish herbivores that are of use to predators and ultimately to us— but we could just as easily think that all of these animals, even including ourselves, really exist only to encourage the growth and spread of the plants (§63, 5: 367–68; §82, 5: 427). Or we may think that ocean currents exist to bring driftwood to the human inhabitants of arctic regions and "great sea animals filled with oil" exist to bring them calories and lamp oil—but as soon as we ask "why human beings have to live" in such inhospitable regions any appearance of intelligent design in nature must quickly dissolve (5: 369).

However, Kant next argues that there are specific things within nature that we inevitably experience as if they were products of design, namely organisms, and that the "internal" purposiveness we must ascribe to such things will in turn lead us to the idea that nature as a whole is a system that is purposive relative to some ultimate end or goal. Kant argues that we must experience organisms as "natural ends" that manifest intelligent design because there are various organic processes in which it seems that the whole of the organism is the cause of its parts as well as its parts being the cause of the whole, and that the only way in which we human beings, whose understanding of causality is ordinarily confined to the idea that the antecedent condition of parts explains the subsequent condition of the whole, can make any sense of this is by thinking of the parts of the organism as if they were the product of an antecedent design of the whole, and thus of a designer of the whole. Kant instances paradigmatic organic processes such as reproduction, in which one individual "generates itself" at least "as far as the species is concerned," growth, in which the whole organism takes up "components that it receives from nature outside of itself" as new parts, and self-preservation, in which parts necessary for the survival of the whole, such as leaves for a tree, are replaced or repaired by the whole organism (*Judgment*, §64, 5: 371–72), as processes we can make sense of only by conceiving of the whole as antecedently designed to produce the parts that can in turn produce or preserve the whole. Kant concludes that,

> Organized beings are thus the only ones in nature which, even if considered in themselves and without a relation to other things, must nevertheless be thought of as possible only as its ends, and which thus first provide objective reality for the concept of an **end** that is not a practical end but an end of **nature**, and thereby provide natural science with a basis for a teleology, i.e., a way of judging its objects in accordance with a particular principle the likes of which one would otherwise be absolutely unjustified in introducing at all . . . (§65, 5: 375–76)

This principle is that "**An organized product of nature is that in which everything is an end and reciprocally a means as well.** Nothing in it is in vain, purposeless, or to be ascribed to a blind mechanism of nature" (§66, 5: 376). The idea of purposive design and thus of an intelligent and purposive designer is one we must bring to our experience of nature in analogy with our own productive capacities (§65, 5: 373–74), and which is thus a priori rather than merely copied from nature, but which we are driven to apply to nature by our specific experience of organisms.

One might well ask what the principle of teleological judgment that Kant has just formulated has to do with his general conception of reflecting judgment. The answer seems to be that

Kant intends this principle to serve as a heuristic to guide our search for mechanical explanations of natural phenomena, and thus ultimately as a help in bringing given particulars that initially seem resistant to scientific explanation into the system of our scientific concepts. To be sure, Kant's thought on this matter is involuted and hard to follow. He begins, as we have seen, with the clear idea that certain specific organic processes and structures defy our ordinary mechanistic model of explanation. But he quickly adds that it would be incoherent for us to explain the features or organisms by "two heterogeneous principles . . . jumbled together," so that once we have been forced to adopt the teleological point of view toward some features of organisms we must take it toward all, and seek the purpose even of parts of organisms such as "skin, hair, and bones" that might readily seem explicable entirely on mechanical principles (*Judgment*, §66, 5: 377). Yet very shortly Kant also insists that the concept of God as an intelligent designer should not be used within natural science, thus that "natural science must not jump over its boundaries in order to bring within itself as an indigenous principle that to whose concept no experience at all can ever be adequate and upon which we are authorized to venture only after the completion of natural science" (§68, 5: 382), thus suggesting that the idea of purposiveness should be used only to alert us to relations among parts of organisms that we might otherwise overlook but which we should then seek to explain along mechanistic lines.

This impression is strengthened as Kant seems to shift his position from insisting that there are specific organic functions we could never succeed in explaining to the more general claim that we cannot explain the origin of life itself in purely mechanical terms—at one point he suggests that the ability to originate motion, which is characteristic of life, is incompatible with the principle of inertia that is characteristic of matter under mechanical laws (§73, 5: 394)—but that apart from this general restriction on the mechanical explanation of life there are no specific a priori limits to the mechanical explanation of organic functions. Indeed, Kant says that "It is of infinite importance to reason that it not allow the mechanism of nature in its productions to drop out of sight and be bypassed in its explanations; for without this no insight into the nature of things can be attained" (§78, 5: 410); and he suggests that, once we have admitted the inexplicable fact of life and possibility of reproduction itself, then perhaps the immense variety of organic species could be entirely explained along mechanical lines, by such means as "the shortening of one part and the elongation of another, by the involution of this part and the evolution of another," allowing "the mind at least a weak ray of hope that something may be accomplished here with the principle of the mechanism of nature, without which there can be no natural science at all" (§80, 5: 418).[26]

The shift in Kant's argument from the claim that there are very specific functions within nature that cannot be explained mechanistically to the idea that we should use the idea of an intelligent design for nature, which we are led to apply to nature by our experience of organisms only for guidance in seeking to expand the scope of our mechanistic explanations, also seems to be confirmed by the course of Kant's argument in the "antinomy" of teleological judgment (*Judgment*, §§69–78). Here Kant begins by suggesting that the thesis that "All generation of material things is possible in accordance with merely mechanical laws" and the teleological antithesis that "Some generation of such things is not possible in accordance with merely mechanical laws" would be in outright contradiction unless they are interpreted as merely regulative principles (§70, 5: 387). The idea seems to be that if both of these principles are merely regulative then the full scope of neither is fully determinate, so no truly

[26] I have discussed Kant's several arguments for our necessarily teleological (although nonconstitutive) conception of organisms in "Organisms and the Unity of Science," in *Kant and the Sciences*, ed. Eric Watkins (Oxford: Oxford University Press), 259–81; reprinted in my *Kant's System of Nature and Freedom* (Oxford: Oxford University Press, 2005). In the Watkins volume, see also Hannah Ginsborg, "Kant on Understanding Organisms as Natural Purposes," 231–58. Another important work on Kant's philosophy of biology is Peter McLaughlin, *Kant's Critique of Teleology in Biological Explanation: Antinomy and Teleology* (Lewiston, NY: Edwin Mellen Press, 1990). The most detailed study of Kant's philosophy of biology in recent literature is Reinhard Löw, *Philosophie des Lebendigen: Der Begriff des Organischen bei Kant, sein Grund und seine Aktualität* (Frankfurt: Suhrkamp Verlag, 1980).

universal principle of mechanism will be violated if we come across something in nature that cannot be explained mechanistically. However, Kant then says that this is a merely "preparatory" resolution of the antinomy (§71, 5: 388), and the real resolution of the antinomy seems to be the two-leveled, transcendental idealist solution that we must conceive of the designer of nature as existing outside of the appearances of nature and as accomplishing his purposes through the uniformly mechanistic laws of nature (§73, 5: 395).[27] Kant's ultimate position thus seems to be that,

> Since it is still at least possible to consider the material world as a mere appearance, and to conceive of something as a thing in itself (which is not an appearance) as substratum, and to correlate with this a corresponding intellectual intuition (even if is not ours), there would then be a supersensible real ground for nature, although it would be unknowable for us, to which we ourselves belong, and in which that which is necessary in it as object of the senses can be considered in accordance with mechanical laws, while the agreement and unity of the particular laws and corresponding forms, which in regard to the mechanical laws we must judge as contingent, can at the same time be considered in it, as object of reason (indeed the whole of nature as a system) in accordance with teleological laws, and the material world would thus be judged in accordance with two kinds of principles, without the mechanical mode of explanation being excluded by the other, as if they contradicted each other. (§78, 5: 409)

Instead of the mechanical and teleological principles each having a potentially limited sphere, on this account each would have a potentially unlimited sphere of application: everything in nature could potentially receive a mechanical explanation, while at the same time everything in nature could also potentially turn out to be purposive.

[27] I have defended this interpretation in more detail in "Purpose in Nature: What Is Living and What Is Dead in Kant's Teleology," in my *Kant's System of Nature and Freedom*.

What does Kant think the value of such a twofold view of nature is? One point is already clear: the idea that everything in nature has a purpose that is to be achieved through mechanical laws can both spur us and guide us in the search for the mechanical means by which that purpose is achieved. The other point is that we must seek to comprehend, in terms accessible to us, what the purpose of nature could possibly be, and to guide our conduct in general and not just our conduct of scientific inquiry in light of this conception of the goal of nature.

To understand this aspect of Kant's teleology, we must go back and retrace a step that was alluded to in the last quotation but has not yet been explained.[28] As we have seen, Kant has begun his train of thought with the idea that there are certain functions of organisms that lead us to think of them as if they have been designed. He has then added the idea that if we see some aspects of organisms as purposive, our predilection for unitary rather than heterogeneous models for explanation will lead us to the thought that every aspect of an organism must be purposive. But he applies this principle a second time when he proposes that once we have been led to think of some things in nature as if they were the product of purposive design, then it will be natural for us to think of the whole of nature as if it were a system designed in behalf of some end:

> It is therefore only matter insofar as it is organized that necessarily carried with it the concept of itself as a natural end, since its specific form is at the same time a product of nature. However, this concept necessarily leads to the idea of the whole of nature as a system in accordance with the rules of end, to which idea all of the mechanism of nature in accordance with principles of reason must now be subordinated (at least in order to test natural appearances by this idea) . . . by means of the example that nature gives in its organic prod-

---

[28] I have analyzed the following argument in more detail in "Purpose in Nature" as well as "From Nature to Morality: Kant's New Argument in the 'Critique of Teleological Judgment,'" in *Architektonik und System in der Philosophie Kants*, ed. Hans Friedrich Fulda and Jürgen Stolzenberg (Hamburg: Felix Meiner Verlag, 2001), 375–404; also reprinted in my *Kant's System of Nature and Freedom*.

ucts, one is justified, indeed called upon to expect nothing in nature and its laws but what is purposive in the whole. (*Judgment*, §67, 5: 378–79)

Indeed, once we have been led by our experience of organisms as purposive systems to look at the whole of nature as a purposive system, it will also become natural for us to look upon "even beauty in nature . . . as an objective purposiveness of nature in its entirety, as a system of which the human being is a member" (5: 380), even though this was not part of our aesthetic experience as originally analyzed.

Kant does not say what it is that "necessarily" leads us from the idea of organisms as purposive systems to the idea of nature as a whole as a purposive system, but it would seem to be the same rational idea of unitary explanation that he had appealed to in extending the teleological point of view from some functions of organisms to all of their parts. The next great step in Kant's argument is to infer, perhaps in analogy with our conception of our own rationality, that if the whole of nature is a product of intelligent design then there must be some point or goal to the whole of nature, and to commence a search for what that goal might be.

As we saw earlier, it is natural enough for us egocentrically to suppose that we are the ultimate point of nature. But we also saw that such a thought, at least in isolation, is completely arbitrary. Moreover, if we assume that it is our happiness as such that is the goal of nature, we are in for a big disappointment:

It is so far from being the case that nature has made the human being its special favorite and favored him with beneficence above all other animals, that it has rather spared him just as little as any other animal from its destructive effects, whether of pestilence, hunger, danger of flood, attacks by other animals great and small, etc.; even more, the conflict in the **natural predisposition** of the human being, reduces himself and others of his own species, by means of plagues that he invents for himself, such as the oppression of domination, the barbarism of war, etc., to such need, and he works so hard for the destruction of his own species, that even if the most beneficent nature outside of us had made the happiness of our species its end, that end would not be attained in a system of nature upon the earth, because the nature inside of us is not receptive to that. (*Judgment*, §83, 5: 430)

However, Kant supposes that we can conceive of a goal that is not so obviously at odds with the actual tendency of our own nature and also has more than the merely conditional value of happiness, namely the unconditional value of morality itself, or of the human being as a moral value. Indeed, this is the only thing we can conceive to have unconditional value, and thus to be a proper end for the system of nature:

Now of the human being . . . as a moral being, it cannot be further asked . . . why (*quem in finem*) it exists. His existence contains the highest end itself, to which, as far as he is capable, he can subject the whole of nature . . . only in the human being, although in him only as a subject of morality, is unconditional legislation with regard to ends to be found, which therefore makes him alone capable of being a final end, to which the whole of nature is teleologically subordinated. (§84, 5: 436)

Forced by our experience of organisms to think of the whole of nature as if it were purposive and by the character of our reason to think of a purpose for the whole of nature, the only thing we can conceive of as such an end is our own morality, our "supersensible faculty (freedom) and even the law of the causality together with the object that it can set for itself as the highest end (the highest good in the world)" (§84, 5: 436).

Here, however, one will surely ask how Kant, who thinks that the freedom of the will can exist only in a noumenal realm, could conceive of human morality, which must be an expression of human freedom, and the highest good, which is human happiness achieved through human virtue and thus through human freedom,[29] as itself a product of nature, the phenomenal realm

---

[29] See especially *Critique of Pure Reason*, A 808–9/B 836–37, and "Idea for a Universal History from a Cosmopolitan Point of View," Third Thesis, 8: 19–20.

of deterministic law that is the very antithesis of freedom? This question must be answered in two steps. First, Kant does not see the freedom of the human will as an end that can be directly achieved within nature; more precisely, it is "the culture of training (discipline) . . . the liberation of the will from the despotism of desires" (*Judgment*, §83, 5: 432), that he thinks could be achieved within nature by entirely natural mechanisms, and this is more like a natural "condition of aptitude" for the exercise of genuine virtue than virtue itself—even once we have achieved such discipline, by natural means, we must still make the free choice to use it for the sake of morality rather than contrary to it. Second, although Kant cannot conceive of human freedom and morality properly speaking as something that can be realized entirely within nature, he can see the universal happiness, not of the individual but of the species, that is to be included in the highest good, as the object and the product of our moral use of our freedom, as something that can and indeed must be realized within nature.[30] So even though human happiness does not initially appear to be any special aim of nature, it can be seen as the final end of human morality to be realized within nature.

We must now take stock of Kant's teleology as briefly as we have expounded it. The most obvious internal question one might ask is how Kant's account of teleology and its principle comports with his original account of reflecting judgment and its transcendental principle. Initially, there seems to be a significant disanalogy, because Kant's original principle postulated that nature can ground a system of laws (*Judgment*, Introduction IV, 5: 180), while Kant's account of our transition from the experience of organisms to a conception of nature as a whole as a purposive system seems to concern objects in nature rather than laws. But as we saw in our discussion of the antinomy of teleological judgment, Kant's aim is to show how the mechanical laws of phenomenal nature can be reconciled with the teleological law that nature must have a purpose, so that those two

---

[30] See especially "On the common saying: That might be correct in theory but it is of no use in practice," Section I, 8: 279–80.

forms of law can comprise a single system. So if Kant's initial principle were modified to state that we must be able to consider particular empirical and moral laws as if they comprise a single system of laws given for the sake not just of our faculty of cognition but of our powers of mind as a whole, then we could see a single principle of reflecting judgment at work. And Kant's idea that through teleological judgment we seek to find the moral purpose of nature can also be reconciled with his initial account of reflecting judgment: for while the conception of the moral end of nature must be regarded as given through pure reason and as by no means completely unknown, what we actually seek to do through teleological judgment is to find a way to apply that idea of reason to nature as it is actually given to us, just as in the initial case of reflecting judgment we are actually given the pure concepts of the understanding but need to find the intermediate concepts of natural laws by which those pure concepts can be applied to nature as it is given to us. In these ways Kant's account of teleological judgment is more readily fit into his general model of reflecting judgment than is his account of aesthetic judgment.

The second question we must ask is how does Kant's teleology fare as a response to Hume's critique of teleology in the *Dialogues concerning Natural Religion*? Hume held the argument from design in the universe to a benevolent designer to be worthless, because we have neither adequate evidence of any benevolent design within the natural and human world that we encounter nor a justifiable principle to infer from whatever design we do observe to a unique designer outside of our experience. Yet he seems to have conceded that the belief in a designer is natural and that it can even be put to good use in our conduct of inquiry—even Hume was not so prescient as to have been a post-Darwinian. Kant goes beyond Hume in detailing what in our experience of nature makes the thought of design inevitable for us, namely, our experience of organisms, and also has a somewhat more fully developed idea of how the thought of design might work as a heuristic for the discovery of mechanical laws of nature.

The main difference between the two philosophers, however, concerns the moral value of the idea of nature as a purposive system. Hume makes no allusion to such an idea, and it would have been out of character for him to do so for two reasons. First, he recognizes no moral good that cannot be subsumed under the natural goal of happiness (although, as we noted, he does not believe that all natural goods are commensurable or aggregable under a single conception of happiness), and thus would not have any use for the idea of a designer of nature who might have a nonnatural goal, of moral perfection rather than happiness, in mind for us. Second, Hume never suggests that we need any sort of assurance that our moral practices are efficacious in attaining their goals in order for it to be rational for us to strive to be moral; on the contrary, for example in his famous account of our sense of justice, he argues that we come to attach moral sentiments to practices we have found to be efficacious in increasing our happiness, not that we have an antecedent conception of the morally good to which we must then attach efficacy through the thought of a benevolent designer of nature (see *Treatise*, III.ii.2). Kant, by contrast, holds that we have a moral goal that is set for us by our pure practical reason, that this moral goal requires that we strive for the happiness of all as part of its object, although not its motive, and that we must postulate, also as an act of pure practical reason, that the laws of nature have the same author as the laws of reason in order to ground the assumption of the realizability of this object of morality, an assumption that is necessary in order to make our moral efforts reasonable; he then holds that as sensible as well as intellectual creatures, we human beings need some sensible confirmation or at least suggestion of our pure rational goal and our postulate of pure practical reason, and that our experience of purposiveness in nature, beginning with our experience of organisms, plays this role for us. On these issues about the fundamental source of our moral principles and the conditions of the rationality of acting upon them, unlike the empirical aspects of motivation we examined in chapter 4, the distance between Hume and Kant is very great, and there would be no way to compare the merits of their responses to traditional teleology without comparing the merits of their moral theories as a whole. That I will not attempt to do here. Perhaps I can just suggest that it would be welcome if we could find a way to retain Kant's normative moral philosophy, that is, his view that human freedom is unconditionally valuable and that adherence to the categorical imperative is the way to preserve and promote that value, without taking on all of the burden of his reconstruction of teleology as well as of his metaphysics of the will.

Finally, stepping beyond the historical comparison that has been central to this book, we can ask whether at this moment in our intellectual history we can still make any use of Kant's teleology considered merely as regulative ideal. Kant certainly seems to capture the systematic ambitions of practicing scientists: the twentieth-century revolutions in chemistry and genetics are clear cases of extending the scope of a unitary system of laws, and the continued search for a way to unify the four most fundamental kinds of physical force is completely within the Kantian spirit. At the same time, the Darwinian-Mendelian explanation of inheritance together with its subsequent explanation by the behavior of DNA undermines any claim that we cannot understand organic processes in mechanical terms. The physical generation of mutations combined with their selection through reproductive success outlines precisely the sort of mechanical model of the kinds of processes that Kant seems to have thought must forever remain beyond the bounds of human comprehension. Further, Kant's idea that mechanical explanation, even if maximally extensive, must be completely consistent with the principle of purposiveness now seems hopeless: whatever disagreements there may be among contemporary Darwinians, surely they all agree that not every trait that survives natural selection is purposive in the sense of being advantageous to the reproductive success of the organism, but that traits may survive as long as they are not *dis*advantageous in any competition for an ecological niche that may actually exist, and may do so particularly if they are mechanically linked to some other trait that is advantageous.

So Kant's ideal that natural science must ultimately yield a unified set of laws certainly continues to drive the practice of it. It is, by contrast, unlikely that many will be convinced that we must conceive of nature as morally purposive unless they are already starting from a theological point of view, precisely what Kant was attempting to avoid. Nevertheless, all but those who do hold a nonnatural conception of human happiness or salvation will presumably agree with Kant that both our virtue and our happiness must be perfected within nature, not someplace else, and here Kant's teleological view of nature suggests some considerations of enduring value. One lesson we can take from Kant's teleology is that it is only our own moral ends that might give us anything like a right to use the rest of nature as means, not our mere whims and lusts. Thus we might infer that it is morally permissible or even mandatory to use and destroy other animals to test medicines that may significantly alleviate human suffering, but impermissible to do so in order to test the efficacy or even the safety of cosmetics that will merely enhance our appearance. Second, the idea that nature is a system suggests that in any of our interventions in nature as we find it, even if undertaken for the most morally acceptable or even obligatory of reasons, our actions will have consequences far beyond our immediate concerns, and we must always attempt to weigh the remote and long-term ecological consequences of our actions as well as their current value. Here is a point where Kant's insistence upon the limits of the human powers of cognition seems entirely appropriate, and where we must limit our confidence in the rectitude of our goals with modesty in our claims to understand both the efficacy and the consequences of our means.

Bibliography

Allison, Henry E. *Idealism and Freedom: Essays on Kant's Theoretical Philosophy.* Cambridge: Cambridge University Press, 1996.

———. *Kant's Theory of Freedom.* Cambridge: Cambridge University Press, 1990.

———. *Kant's Theory of Taste: A Reading of the* Critique of Aesthetic Judgment. Cambridge: Cambridge University Press, 2001.

———. *Kant's Transcendental Idealism: An Interpretation and Defense.* New Haven, CT: Yale University Press, 1983; rev. ed., 2004.

Ameriks, Karl. "How to Save Kant's Deduction of Taste." *Journal of Value Inquiry* 16 (1982): 295–302; reprinted in his *Interpreting Kant's* Critiques, 285–306.

———. *Interpreting Kant's* Critiques. Oxford: Clarendon Press, 2003.

———. *Kant and the Fate of Autonomy: Problems in the Appropriation of the Critical Philosophy.* Cambridge: Cambridge University Press, 2000.

———. *Kant and the Historical Turn.* Oxford: Clarendon Press, 2006.

———. "Kant and the Objectivity of Taste." *British Journal of Aesthetics* 23 (1983): 3–17; joined to "How to Save Kant's Deduction of Taste" in *Interpreting Kant's* Critiques, 285–306.

———. "Kant's Deduction of Freedom and Morality." *Journal of the History of Philosophy* 19 (1981): 53–79; revised as chapter VI of Ameriks, *Kant's Theory of Mind,* 189–233; new ed., Oxford: Clarendon Press, 2000.

———. "Kant's Transcendental Deduction as a Regressive Argument." *Kant-Studien* 69 (1978): 273–87; reprinted in his *Interpreting Kant's* Critiques, 51–66.

Aune, Bruce. *Kant's Theory of Morals.* Princeton, NJ: Princeton University Press, 1979.

Baumgarten, Alexander Gottlieb. *Metaphysik.* Translated by Georg Friedrich Meier. 2nd ed., 1783. Jena, Germany: Dietrich Schleglmann Reprints, 2004.

Beattie, James. *Essays on the Nature and Immutability of Truth, On Poetry and Music,* etc. Edinburgh: William Creech, 1776.

Beck, Lewis White. *A Commentary to Kant's Critique of Practical Reason*. Chicago: University of Chicago Press, 1960.

———. *Early German Philosophy: Kant and His Predecessors*. Cambridge, MA: Harvard University Press, 1969

———. *Essays on Kant and Hume*. New Haven, CT: Yale University Press, 1978.

Bennett, Jonathan. *Kant's Analytic*. Cambridge: Cambridge University Press, 1966.

———. *Kant's Dialectic*. Cambridge: Cambridge University Press, 1974.

Bird, Graham. "The Neglected Alternative: Trendelenburg, Fischer, and Kant." In *A Companion to Kant*, edited by Graham Bird, 486–99. Oxford and Malden: Blackwell, 2006.

Bittner, Rüdiger, and Konrad Cramer, eds. *Materialen zu Kants "Kritik der praktischen Vernunft."* Frankfurt: Suhrkamp, 1975.

Brown, Charlotte. "Is Hume an Internalist?" *Journal of the History of Philosophy* 26 (1988): 69–87.

Crawford, Donald W. *Kant's Aesthetic Theory*. Madison: University of Wisconsin Press, 1974.

Davidson, Donald. "On the Very Idea of a Conceptual Scheme." *Proceedings and Addresses of the American Philosophical Association* 47 (1974); reprinted in his *Inquiries into Truth and Interpretation*, 183–98. Oxford: Clarendon Press, 1984.

Dickerson, A. B. *Kant on Representation and Objectivity*. Cambridge: Cambridge University Press, 2004.

Eberhard, Johann August. *Vorbereitung zur natürlichen Theologie*. Halle, Germany: Im Waisenhause, 1781; reprinted in the *Akademie* edition, 18: 491–606.

Engell, James. *The Creative Imagination: Enlightenment to Romanticism*. Cambridge, MA: Harvard University Press, 1981.

Floyd, Juliet. "The Fact of Judgment: The Kantian Response to the Humean Condition." In *From Kant to Davidson: Philosophy and the Idea of the Transcendental*, edited by Jeff Malpas, 22–47. London: Routledge, 2003.

———. "Heautonomy: Kant on Reflective Judgment and Systematicity." In *Kant's Ästhetikk—Kant's Aesthetics—L'esthétique de Kant*, edited by Herman Parret, 192–218. Berlin: Walter de Gruyter, 1998.

Fogelin, Robert J. *Hume's Skepticism in the Treatise of Human Nature*. London: Routledge and Kegan Paul, 1985.

Forster, Michael N. *Hegel's Idea of a Phenomenology of Spirit*. Chicago: University of Chicago Press, 1998.

Friedman, Michael. "Causal Laws and the Foundations of Natural Science." In *The Cambridge Companion to Kant*, edited by Paul Guyer, 161–99. Cambridge: Cambridge University Press, 1992.

———. *The Dynamics of Reason*. Stanford, CA: CSLI Publications, 2001.

———. *Kant and the Exact Sciences*. Cambridge, MA: Harvard University Press, 1992.

Garrett, Don. "Hume's Self-Doubts about Personal Identity." *Philosophical Review* 90 (1981): 337–58.

Gawlick, Günter, and Lothar Kreimendahl. *Hume in der deutschen Aufklärung: Umrisse einer Rezeptionsgeschichte*. Stuttgart: Fromann Holzboog, 1987.

Ginsborg, Hannah. "Kant on Understanding Organisms as Natural Purposes." In *Kant and the Sciences*, edited by Eric Watkins, 231–58. Oxford: Oxford University Press, 2001.

———. "Lawfulness without a Law: Kant on the Free Play of Imagination and Understanding." *Philosophical Topics* 25 (1997): 37–83.

Grier, Michelle. *Kant's Doctrine of Transcendental Illusion*. Cambridge: Cambridge University Press, 2001.

Guyer, Paul. "Bridging the Gulf: Kant's Project in the Third *Critique*." In *The Blackwell Companion to Kant*, edited by Graham Bird, 423–40. Oxford: Blackwell, 2006.

———. "The Derivation of the Categorical Imperative: Kant's Correction for a Fatal Flaw." *Harvard Review of Philosophy* 10 (2002): 64–80.

———. *Kant*. London and New York: Routledge, 2006.

———. *Kant and the Claims of Knowledge*. Cambridge: Cambridge University Press, 1987.

———. *Kant and the Claims of Taste*. Cambridge, MA: Harvard University Press, 1979; rev. ed., Cambridge: Cambridge University Press, 1997.

———. *Kant and the Experience of Freedom*. Cambridge: Cambridge University Press, 1993.

———. "Kant on Apperception and *A Priori* Synthesis." *American Philosophical Quarterly* 17 (1980): 205–12.

———. *Kant on Freedom, Law, and Happiness*. Cambridge: Cambridge University Press, 2000.

———. *Kant's Groundwork for the Metaphysics of Morals: A Reader's Guide*. London: Continuum Books, 2007.

———. "Kant's Intentions in the Refutation of Idealism." *The Philosophical Review* 92 (1983): 329–83; reprinted in *Immanuel Kant*, edited by Heiner F. Klemme and Manfred Kuehn, 1: 277–332. Dartmouth, UK: Ashgate, 1999.

———. "Kant's Principles of Reflecting Judgment." In *Kant's Critique of the Power of Judgment: Critical Essays*, edited by Paul Guyer, 1–61. Lanham, MD: Rowman and Littlefield, 2003.

———. *Kant's System of Nature and Freedom: Selected Essays*. Oxford: Clarendon Press, 2005.

———. "The Postulates of Empirical Thinking in General and the Refutation of Idealism." In *Kant: Kritik der reinen Vernunft*, edited by Georg Mohr and Marcus Willaschek, 297–324. Berlin: Akademie-Verlag, 1998.

———. "Psychology and the Transcendental Deduction." In *Kant's Transcendental Deductions: The Three "Critiques" and the "Opus Postumum,"* edited by Eckart Förster, 47–68. Stanford, CA: Stanford University Press, 1989.

———. "Space, Time, and the Categories: Kant's Project in the Transcendental Deduction." In *Idealismus als Theorie der Repräsentation?* edited by Ralph Schumacher, 313–38. Paderborn, Germany: Mentis, 2001.

———. "Transcendental Idealism and the Limits of Knowledge: Kant's Alternative to Locke's Physiology." In *Kant and the Early Moderns*, edited by Daniel Garber and Béatrice Longuenesse. Princeton: Princeton University Press, forthcoming.

———. *Values of Beauty: Historical Essays in Aesthetics*. Cambridge: Cambridge University Press, 2005.

Hanna, Robert. *Kant and the Foundations of Analytic Philosophy*. Oxford: Oxford University Press, 2001.

Hatfield, Gary. "The *Prolegomena* and the *Critiques of Pure Reason*." In *Kant und die Berliner Aufklärung: Akten des IX. Internationalen Kant-Kongresses*, edited by Volker Gerhardt, Rolf-Peter Horstmann, and Ralph Schumacher, 1: 185–208. Berlin: Walter de Gruyter, 2001.

Henrich, Dieter. "Kants Deduktion des Sittengesetzes." In *Denken im Schatten des Nihilismus*, edited by Alexander Schwan, 55–112. Darmstadt, Germany: Wissenschaftliches Buchgesellschaft, 1975; translated in *Kant's Groundwork of the Metaphysics of Morals: Critical Essays*, edited by Paul Guyer, 303–41. Lanham, MD: Rowman and Littlefield, 1998.

Herman, Barbara. "On the Value of Acting from the Motive of Duty." *Philosophical Review* 90 (1981): 359–82; reprinted in her *The Practice of Moral Judgment*, 1–22. Cambridge, MA: Harvard University Press, 1993.

Hill, Thomas E., Jr., "The Rationality of Moral Conduct." *Pacific Philosophical Quarterly* 66 (1985): 3–23; reprinted in his *Dignity and Practical Reason in Kant's Moral Theory*, 97–122. Ithaca, NY: Cornell University Press, 1992.

Höffe, Ottfried. *Kants Kritik der reinen Vernunft: Die Grundlegung der modernen Philosophie*. Munich: C. H. Beck, 2003.

Hutcheson, Francis. *An Essay on the Nature and Conduct of the Passions, with Illustrations on the Moral Sense*. Edited by Aaron Garrett. Indianapolis: Liberty Fund, 2002.

Kemal, Salim. *Kant and Fine Art: An Essay on Kant and the Philosophy of Fine Art and Culture*. Oxford: Clarendon Press, 1986.

Kerstein, Samuel J. "Deriving the Formula of Universal Law." In *A Companion to Kant*, edited by Graham Bird, 308–21. Oxford and Malden: Blackwell, 2006.

Kitcher, Philip. "Projecting the Order of Nature." In *Kant's Philosophy of Physical Science*, edited by Robert E. Butts, 201–35. Dordrecht, the Netherlands: D. Reidel, 1986; reprinted in *Kant's Critique of Pure Reason: Critical Essays*, edited by Patricia Kitcher, 219–38. Lanham, MD: Rowman and Littlefield, 1998.

Kivy, Peter. "Hume's Standard of Taste: Breaking the Circle." *British Journal of Aesthetics* 7 (1967): 57–66.

Klemme, Heiner F. *Kants Philosophie des Subjekts: Systematische und entwicklungsgeschichtliche Untersuchungen zum Verhältnis von Selbstbewußtsein und Selbsterkenntnis*. Kant-Forschungen, Band 7. Hamburg: Felix Meiner Verlag, 1996.

Korsgaard, Christine M. "Kant's Formula of Humanity." *Kant-Studien* 77 (1986): 183–202; reprinted in her *Creating the Kingdom of Ends*, 106–32. Cambridge: Cambridge University Press, 1996.

Kreimendahl, Lothar. *Kant—Der Durchbruch von 1769*. Cologne: Jürgen Dinter, 1990.

Kuehn, Manfred. "Kant's Conception of Hume's Problem." *Journal of the History of Philosophy* 21 (1983): 175–93.

———. *Scottish Common Sense in Germany, 1768–1800: A Contribution to the History of Critical Philosophy*. Kingston, ON: McGill-Queen's University Press, 1987.

Langton, Rae. *Kantian Humility: Our Ignorance of Things in Themselves*. Oxford: Clarendon Press, 1998.

Locke, John. *An Essay concerning Human Understanding*. Edited by P. H. Nidditch. Oxford: Clarendon Press, 1975.

Longuenesse, Béatrice. *Kant and the Capacity to Judge*. Translated by Charles T. Wolfe. Princeton, NJ: Princeton University Press, 1998.

Loparic, Zeljko. *A Semântica Transcendental de Kant.* Campinas, Brazil: UNICAMP Centro de Lógica, Epistemologia e História da Ciência, 2002.

Lovejoy, Arthur. "On Kant's Reply to Hume." *Archiv für Geschichte der Philosophie* (1906): 380–407; reprinted in *Kant: Disputed Questions,* edited by Moltke S. Gram, 284–308. Chicago: Quadrangle Books, 1967.

Löw, Reinhard. *Philosophie des Lebendigen: Der Begriff des Organischen bei Kant, sein Grund und seine Aktualität.* Frankfurt: Suhrkamp Verlag, 1980.

McLaughlin, Peter. *Kant's Critique of Teleology in Biological Explanation: Antinomy and Teleology.* Lewiston, NY: Edwin Mellen Press, 1990.

Melnick, Arthur. *Kant's Analogies of Experience.* Chicago: University of Chicago Press, 1973.

Milgram, Elijah. "Was Hume a Humean?" *Hume Studies* 21 (1995): 75–93.

Osborne, Harold. "Hume's Standard and the Diversity of Taste." *British Journal of Aesthetics* 7 (1967): 50–56.

Paley, William. *Natural Theology, or Evidence of the Existence and Attributes of the Deity, Collected from the Appearances of Nature.* Edited by Matthew W. Eddy and David Knight. Oxford: Oxford University Press, 2006.

Paton, Herbert James. *Kant's Metaphysic of Experience.* 2 vols. London: George Allen and Unwin, 1936.

Radcliffe, Elizabeth S. "How Does the Humean Sense of Duty Motivate?" *Journal of the History of Philosophy* 34 (1996): 383–407.

———. "Kantian Tunes on a Humean Instrument: Why Hume Is Not *Really* a Skeptic about Practical Reasoning." *Canadian Journal of Philosophy* 27 (1997): 247–70.

Rawls, John. *Lectures on the History of Moral Philosophy.* Edited by Barbara Herman. Cambridge, MA: Harvard University Press, 2000.

Recki, Birgit. *Ästhetik der Sitten: Die Affinität von ästhetischem Gefühl und praktischer Vernunft bei Kant.* Frankfurt: Klostermann, 2001.

Rush, Fred L., Jr. "The Harmony of the Faculties." *Kant-Studien* 92 (2001): 38–61.

Sassen, Brigitte. *Kant's Early Critics: The Empiricist Critique of the Theoretical Philosophy.* Cambridge: Cambridge University Press, 2000.

Schaper, Eva. "Free and Dependent Beauty." In *Akten des 4. Internationalen Kant-Kongresses,* Teil 1, 247–62. Berlin: Walter de

Gruyter, 1974; reprinted in her *Studies in Kant's Aesthetics*, 78–98. Edinburgh: Edinburgh University Press, 1979.

Sellars, Wilfrid. "Philosophy and the Scientific Image of Man." In *Frontiers of Science and Philosophy*, edited by Robert Colodny. Pittsburgh: University of Pittsburgh Press, 1962; reprinted in his *Science, Perception, and Reality*, 1–40. London: Routledge and Kegan Paul, 1963.

Sidgwick, Henry. *The Methods of Ethics*. 7th ed. London: Macmillan, 1907.

Smith, Norman Kemp. *A Commentary to Kant's Critique of Pure Reason*. 2nd ed. London: Macmillan, 1923.

———. *The Philosophy of David Hume*. London: Macmillan, 1941.

Sobel, Jerry E. "Arguing, Accepting, and Preserving Design in Heidegger, Hume, and Kant." In *Essays in Kant's Aesthetics*, edited by Ted Cohen and Paul Guyer, 271–305. Chicago: University of Chicago Press, 1982.

Stern, Robert. "Metaphysical Dogmatism, Humean Scepticism, Kantian Criticism." *Kantian Review* 11 (2006): 102–16.

Strawson, P. F. *The Bounds of Sense: An Essay on Kant's Critique of Pure Reason*. London: Methuen, 1966.

Stroud, Barry. *Hume*. London: Routledge and Kegan Paul, 1977.

Townsend, Dabney. *Hume's Aesthetic Theory: Taste and Sentiment*. London and New York: Routledge, 2001.

Vaihinger, Hans. *Commentar zur Kants Kritik der reinen Vernunft*. 2 vols. Stuttgart: Union Deutsche Verlagsgesellschaft, 1884–92.

Van Cleve, James. *Problems from Kant*. New York: Oxford University Press, 1999.

Vogel, Jonathan. "The Problem of Self-Knowledge in Kant's 'Refutation of Idealism': Two Recent Views." *Philosophy and Phenomenological Research* 53 (1993): 875–87.

von der Lühe, Astrid. *David Humes ästhetische Kritik*. Hamburg: Felix Meiner, 1996.

Warda, Arthur. *Immanuel Kants Bücher*. Berlin: Breslauer, 1922.

Watkins, Eric. *Kant and the Metaphysics of Causality*. Cambridge: Cambridge University Press, 2005.

———. "Kant's Transcendental Idealism and the Categories." *History of Philosophy Quarterly* 19 (2002): 191–215.

Waxman, Wayne. *Kant and the Empiricists: Understanding Understanding*. New York: Oxford University Press, 2005.

Wolff, Robert Paul. "Kant's Debt to Hume via Beattie." *Journal of the History of Ideas* 21 (1960): 117–23.

Wolff, Robert Paul. *Kant's Theory of Mental Activity: A Commentary on the Transcendental Analytic of the* Critique of Pure Reason. Cambridge, MA: Harvard University Press, 1963.

Wood, Allen W. *Kant's Ethical Thought.* Cambridge: Cambridge University Press, 1999.

Zammito, John. *The Genesis of Kant's* Critique of Judgment. Chicago: University of Chicago Press, 1992.

Index